Triumph Spitfire, GT6 Vitesse & Herald

Restoration Manual

Lindsay Porter & Peter Williams

This manual, originally written in the 1980s on how to restore the Triumph Herald and Spitfire family of cars has always been well regarded but suffered from graphics that were pretty ropey, even for Haynes Publishing in the '80s. Indeed, I well remember the Haynes Sales Director of the day telling me that, when customers complained that the paper being used for Haynes manuals was so poor you could see the print on the other side, he replied, "What a time saver! You can read both sides without having to turn the page!"

Seriously though, it made some of their stuff hard to follow – and this manual was no exception. So, when I decided to put it back into print, the decision was made to digitally rescan every one of the original photographs – all 900+ of them! - and present them anew.

It's been a painstaking exercise and you still can't get away from the snap-shot quality of some of the photographs that were taken at the time. But at least you can now see what's in each photo and, thanks to modern print-on-demand techniques, the paper is excellent. And I'm sorry. You really can't read both sides of the page at once ;).

Lindsay Porter, April, 2019

First published by G. T. Foulis & Co as
Triumph Spitfire, GT6, Vitesse & Herald
Guide to Purchase & DIY Restoration in 1988
Reprinted 1988, 1992, 1995 and 1997
Reprinted by Haynes Publishing 2002
Second Edition as Triumph Spitfire, GT6,
Herald & Vitesse Restoration Manual,
Porter Publishing 2019

A catalogue record for this book is available
from the British Library

ISBN 978-1-899238-39-2

Library of Congress catalog card
number 88-81067
Published by: Porter Publishing Ltd
Postal Address: BM Porter Publishing,
London, WC1N 3XX
email: contact@porterpublishing.com

Some countries or jurisdictions have strict laws
regarding modifications to a vehicle. You are
advised to check with the appropriate body or
authority whether any proposed modification
complies fully with the law. The author and
publishers accept no liability in this regard.
While every effort is taken to ensure the
accuracy of the information given in this book,
no liability can be accepted by the authors or
publishers for any loss, damage or injury caused
by errors in, or omissions from the information
given.

Credit and thanks go to 'pyntofmyld' for the use,
under Creative Commons Licence, of the Flickr
image of the Triumph Vitesse on the cover of this
book.

Credit and thanks for permission to use, under
Creative Commons Licence, the following images.
WIKIPEDIA: 1962_Triumph_Herald_948cc_Conv:
Joshuablick; 1970 Triumph Herald 13-60 (1296cc):
Chris Sampson; Atlas_van_with_side_windows_
first_registered_September_1959_948cc:
Charles01; Courier van tormentor4555;
Triumph_Herald_1250 Bryn Pinzgauer, uploaded
by Oxyman; Triumph_Herald_948cc_Coupe and
Triumph_Vitesse_Mint_Green: Oxyman. FLICKR:
Triumph_Herald_1200_Estate_car: Joost J. Bakker.

Special thanks to Karl Fasulo of
KGF Classic Cars for his typically generous
permission to use a number of his excellent
photographs on the cover and inside this book.
KGF Classic Cars' showrooms can be found at
Fengate, Peterborough, PEI 5TA and at
kgfclassiccars.co.uk

Contents

Also available (on Amazon and elsewehere)...

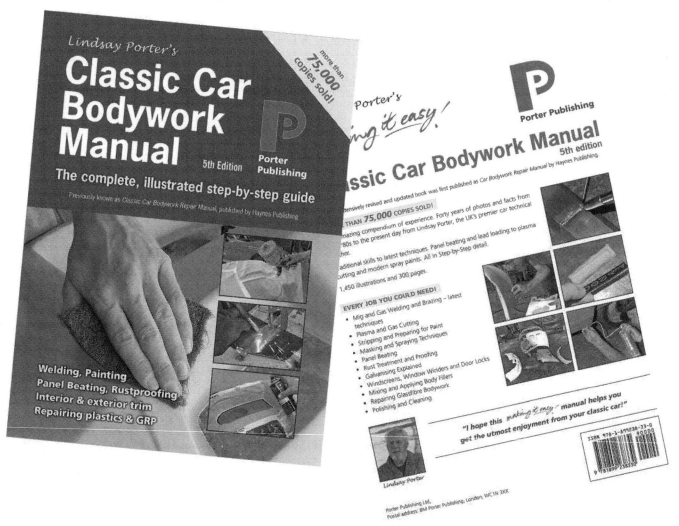

Classic Car Bodywork Manual: The complete, illustrated step-by-step guide

Paperback – 7 Oct 2018

by Mr Lindsay Porter (Author)

> See all formats and editions

Paperback
£17.95 ✓prime

CLASSIC CAR BODYWORK MANUAL by Lindsay Porter MORE THAN 75,000 COPIES SOLD! 1450 illustrations. More than 300 pages - full Letter size 8.5 x 11in (216 x 279mm). B&W photographs. An amazing compendium of experience. Forty years of photos and facts from the '80s to the present day from Lindsay Porter, the UK's premier car technical author. Traditional skills to latest techniques. Panel beating and lead loading to plasma cutting and modern spray paints. All in Step-by-Step detail. EVERY JOB YOU COULD NEED! • Mig and Gas Welding and Brazing – latest techniques • Plasma and Gas Cutting • Stripping and Preparing for Paint • Masking and Spraying Techniques • Panel Beating • Rust Treatment and Proofing • Galvanising Explained • Windscreens, Window Winders and Door Locks • Mixing and Applying Body Fillers • Repairing Glassfibre Bodywork • Polishing and Cleaning. This extensively revised and updated book was first published as Car Bodywork Repair Manual by Haynes Publishing.

4

Foreword

It's not every day that lovers of Triumph Heralds and their stablemates (Vitesses, Spitfires and GT6s) get treated to such a book as this! It has of course been eagerly awaited by Triumph enthusiasts since Lindsay first started the series in 1982.

As an author and regular contributor to several motoring magazines his reputation for detail and clarity is well established. Lindsay is one of those chaps who likes to have a go at anything and is always keen to experiment with new ideas and schemes. Having renovated his cottage and at one time run his car restoration business, he is well placed to identify practical problems and provide clear guidance on how to avoid pitfalls. This book brings together his great wealth of practical experience and his talent for readable, understandable English in harness with the considerable knowledge of 'things Triumph' of Peter Williams. Peter is the highly regarded General Secretary and PRO of the Triumph Sports Six Club. The result is a real d-i-y book which surpasses all others!

Part of the excitement of owning or even wanting to own a "classic", can be in the time spent finding out about the marque. This book is packed with relevant information which all Herald, Vitesse, Spitfire and GT6

John M. Griffiths

enthusiasts will find most rewarding.

It sensibly starts from square one by providing the reader with an informative summary of these Triumphs' origins. But the meat of the book deals with how to go about buying one and how to carry out a full or part restoration. Bodywork, interior, mechanicals, electricals, are all covered in the same clearly written and pictorial style. There's more however – it

also provides practical advice on what tools will be required, where to get extra information and help, how to modify and of course which club to join.

I have owned at least one of all the Herald chassised cars (Specials and Bonds apart) and still have my Vitesse MkII Convertible which I bought as long ago as 1975. I only wish that this book had been available then!

The Herald chassised vehicles are recognised today as one of the most practical and inexpensive cars to own, enjoy and restore. They provide their owner with simple, easily accessible mechanical components. This is one of the main attractions to the d-i-y person, but let's not forget that they are built on a sturdy backbone chassis and all offer a forward hinged bonnet which allows unrivalled access to engine and front suspension. In short, they are the dream of any would-be restorer.

This book will have a major part to play in keeping more of them alive. It removes much of the fear from undertaking a major restoration project and provides the would-be d-i-y person with the confidence to start – "to have a go". In doing so, it will give many hours of enjoyment and self-satisfaction. Follow it carefully and you will avoid much of the sweat and tears that can be encountered. As such this book will prove its worth many times over!

No matter whether you are a first time restorer or an experienced hand, you will benefit from this superb guide.

I would like to wish Lindsay and Peter, on behalf of the Triumph Sports Six Club, every success with this book – it is deserved.

John M. Griffiths

Lindsay Porter, 2019

My goodness it WAS a long time ago that we wrote the first edition of this manual! And what's happened since reminds me of the French proverb, "The more things change, the more they stay the same!"
It's kind of true, too:
• They haven't built any of the cars featured in this manual for many decades now – so the cars haven't changed!
• Most of the techniques used are just the same.
• Best of all, we nutcases who love our classic cars are as daft as ever!

But then some things are different, of course.
Suppliers and manufacturers who were around when the manual was written: some have gone and some remain – see Appendix 8, Clubs and specialists for details.
The main technique that's changed is welding. Very few people use gas welding today – though it DOES have its uses – but MIG has become universal. That's why there's a new, Appendix 10, MIG Welding describing how it's done.

The biggest and most important unchanged aspect of the manual is this: classic Triumph ownership is all about enjoyment. So my sincere wish is that you enjoy your car, enjoy working on it (even the bits that go wrong or give you grief; you can't have one without the other!) and best of all, enjoy spending time communicating with fellow Triumph nutters and remember, next time you meet an MG owner, *"What unites us is greater than what divides us."*

Very best wishes to one and all!

Lindsay Porter

Using this book

The layout of this book has been designed to be both attractive and easy to follow during practical work on your car. However, to obtain maximum benefit from the book, it is important to note the following points:

1) Apart from the introductory pages, this book is split into two parts: chapters 1 to 6 dealing with history, buying and practical procedures; appendices 1 to 7 providing supplementary information. Each chapter/appendix may be sub-divided into sections and even sub-sections. Section headings are in italic type between horizontal lines and sub-section headings are similar, but without horizontal lines.

2) Step-by-step photograph and line drawing captions are an integral part of the text (except those in chapters 1 and 2) – therefore the photographs/drawings and their captions are arranged to "read" in exactly the same way as the normal text. In other words they run down each column and the columns run from left to right of the page.

Each photograph caption carries an alpha-numeric identity, relating it to a specific section. The letters before the caption number are simply the initial letters of key words in the relevant section heading, whilst the caption number shows the position of the particular photograph in the section's picture sequence. Thus photograph/caption 'DR22' is the 22nd photograph in the section headed "Door Repairs".

3) Figures – line illustrations follow consecutively with the photo numbering sequence.

4) All references to the left or right of the vehicle are from the point of view of somebody standing behind the car looking forwards.

5) The bodywork repair chapter of this book deals with problems particular to the Triumph Spitfire, GT6, Herald and Vitesse. In concentrating on these aspects the depth of treatment of body repair techniques in general is necessarily limited. For more detailed information covering all aspects of body repair it is recommended that reference be made to the Haynes 'The Car Bodywork Repair Manual' also by Lindsay Porter.

6) Because this book concentrates upon restoration, regular maintenance procedures and normal mechanical repairs of all the car's components, are beyond its scope. It is therefore strongly recommended that the relevant Haynes *Triumph Herald, Spitfire or Vitesse & GT6 Manual* should be used as a companion volume. (There are 7 different manuals covering most models.)

7) We know it's a boring subject, expecially when you really want to get on with a job – but your safety, through the use of correct workshop procedures, must ALWAYS be your foremost consideration. It is essential that you read, and UNDERSTAND, appendix 1 before undertaking any of the practical tasks detailed in this book and check with the suppliers of equipment and materials so that you have in your possession any health and safety information relating to the work you intend carrying out. Make sure you read it!

8) Before starting any particular job it is important that you read the introduction to the relevant Chapter or Section, taking note of the 'tool box' and 'safety' notes. It is recommended that you read through the section from start to finish before getting into the job.

9) Whilst great care is taken to ensure that the information in this book is as accurate as possible, the authors, editor or publisher cannot accept any liability for loss, damage or injury caused by errors in, or omissions from, the information given.

10) American readers will note that, these being British cars, British terms are used. For instance 'bonnet' = 'hood'; 'wing' = 'fender'; 'sill' = 'body rocker'. See Appendix 9 for a full list of British/US terms.

Introduction
and Acknowledgements

Do the cars that make up the Herald, Vitesse, Spitfire, GT6 range qualify as usable, desirable, restorable classic cars? Make yourself a checklist of the features you may be looking for and see how these cars shape up: Are they popular cars, rising in value? (Yes). Is there a problem getting hold of spares? (No). Are they inexpensive to run? (Yes). Is access good for mechanical repairs? (The best!). Are body repairs straightforward? (Bolt-on panels; chassis beneath; couldn't be better!). In short, whichever model of car you're looking for, the Herald-thru-GT6 range is the ideal owner and restorer's classic car! Even the choice is all you could want: from family motoring, sedate or zippy; open-topped cruising, sports car verve or 6-cylinder power. With almost a million cars having been built in total, you shouldn't have too much trouble getting hold of the car you want, though you may have to search high and low to find one in absolutely pristine condition. Trouble is, people who own pristine examples of these cars often like them so much that they hang on to them. Perhaps the best approach it to take a leaf or two out of this book and restore one of the most restorable of classic cars yourself.

This book was sitting around as an idea at first, then as a growing pile of photographs for quite a while until along came Peter Williams. Peter was known to me as the Triumph Sports Six Club's General Secretary and when I met him at the Birmingham Classic Car Show I asked him if he wanted to write the text for this book. Such is his enthusiasm for all things Triumph that he leapt at the chance. In taking the bulk of the photographs for this book I thought I had grown to know these cars quite well, but I take my hat off to Peter – what he doesn't know about Heralds, Spitfires and their Vitesse/GT6 cousins isn't worth knowing. Just as impressively, Pete knows how to explain himself in a clear and friendly way and also chips in with a good number of his own photographs. I've topped and tailed the text of this book and added a few thoughts of my own, but when you dip or dive into the contents, you won't fail to be impressed by the way Peter has clearly and simply explained every task – and the credit is all his!

John Griffiths, President of the TSCC, has taken such a interest in the development of this book that were it ever to be 'christened', he'd be there as 'godfather'. Many thanks are due to him for his advice and the loan of photographs and brochures for the 'Heritage' section. When I was looking for someone to write the 'Buying' section, John suggested TSCC enthusiast and qualified engineer, Eddie Evans, and I'm sure readers will agree that Eddie has produced a valuable and extremely useful 'Buying' chapter. Many thanks also to Catherine Larner for efficiently organising and producing the 'Contents' listings and to Miranda Horobin for contributing the 'Heritage' chapeter.

Several specialist companies have supplied their advice, expertise and an opportunity to take photographs of processes. They are listed and recommended in 'Clubs and Specialists' but a special word must be given to Classic Car Restorations in the South-West Midlands, where hundreds of photographs were taken of their fine restoration specialists at work. They really do produce some excellent results! Richard Swinfield who had his Spitfire 1500 restored there was most accommodating and the results of the work carried out on the car can be seen in many parts of this book, alongside 'Terry' Johnson's pretty little Herald 1200 convertible. The bodywork repairs and painting were carried out at Classic Car Restorations, while husband Derek carried out the strip-down and fit-up jobs

illustrated himself – an option that some restorers prefer.

Grateful thanks are also due to Sparkford Motor Museum Curator, Mike Penn, for putting in a good 60 hours of work to produce the invaluable information contained in the Appendices on Identification, Production and Paint/trim. What a typically enthusiastic and well-informed Triumph (Vitesse) owner he is!

Thanks are also due from Peter to the host of fellow enthusiasts in the TSSC who answered the many questions raised during the writing of this book. Especial thanks to Bill Sunderland, TSSC Club manager, and *Courier* magazine editor, and to fellow TSSC member and ultimate enthusiast Bernard Robinson.

Thanks also to Michael Williams who demonstrated that you really can learn to MIG weld in an afternoon.

Peter Williams
Northampton

1 Heritage

Beginnings

What sort of images do the slick television adverts of today conjure up? In the wild, open spaces, macho but svelte men and elaborately groomed women, speed over rugged terrains in cars that emerge out of dust clouds as clean as when they left the car sales forecourt. Our cynical minds are aware of the highly sophisticated advertising machine behind all this 1980s launching of new models. Little of it has much in common with 'yer average man' let alone the truths of rallying across deserts or driving anywhere for that matter.

Even in the '50s and '60s a new car's launch was accompanied by the equivalent glossiness of its time. So, for the Triumph Herald to be launched in 1959 following a publicity stunt of almost *Boys Own* heroics was a delightful, schoolboy and madcap entrance into the world: a 10,000 mile journey from Cape Town to London in two months!

This jape could not be described as prototype testing; the car had already been announced, prototypes built and tested, and money invested; a process that had been going on for three years. It definitely 'tested' the car however, (two of them in fact) accompanied by a

support team of three vehicles, a cameraman to add to the publicity and a journalist, Peter Benstead Smith who produced a charming book 'Turn Left at Tangier' as a result of this trip. What a truly pioneering way to launch a car.

But to the beginning. The Triumph Company started making pedal bicycles and then, as those of us who have an additional interest in two motorised wheels will know, went on to producing motorcycles. The car side of things started in 1923 and in 1927 the 'Super Seven' was launched: a small car influenced by the Austin 7 in marketing terms but more expensive. The range extending to include Glorias, Vitesses and Dolomites. Alas finances became rocky and the motorcycle business was sold off.

However this was not sufficient and in 1939 Triumph went bankrupt. After a fallow period of ownership by Thomas Ward Limited, enter Standard Motor Company in 1944. Never the twain had met before in factory, field or furrow, so the seeds of a totally new hybrid were sown.

The story of the Triumph Herald is very much one where company takeovers, mergers, alliances and financial deals with their attendent mysteries were as important as the actual

development of the cars.

The Standard Motor Company started from scratch in 1903 as a car manufacturer in Coventry, with a 'Small Standard' 6hp motor vehicle. Successfully launched, the company started building a new complex outside Coventry at Canley. At the same time as Triumph's Super Seven was announced, Standard announced the 'New Nine', which was actually a car of 9.5 hp. In 1929 the autocratic and egomaniac Captain John Black joined the company as General Manager, from Hillman, and autocratic or not the result was, that in ten years, production output increased from 10,000 to 50,000 cars a year! The range continued to expand but always included the word 'Nine' in its nomenclature. World War II caused a halt in car production, but after it ended, Sir John Black with two personal feathers in his cap; a knighthood (for war efforts) *and* becoming Managing Director of Standard – decided to utilise the Triumph marque in an obsessive attempt to become Britain's number one car manufacturer.

An explanation of the business wheelings and dealings behind all this is necessary. John Black always had his eye open for good deals in attempts to guarantee his own as well as the company's success. However, he

wasn't an easy man to deal with and he wasted a lot of unnecessary energy pursuing those who had, in his eyes, 'got one over on him'. Before the war he made a deal with the equally autocratic William Lyons to supply the mechanical components and engines to power Lyons' very stylish bodied cars which were being marketed as SS and were later to become known as Jaguars. Initially supplying their own make of four-cylinder engines, Standard then invested heavily in the tooling for supplying new six-cylinder engines manufactured to S.S.'s specifications. After the war Standard Motor Company intended to resume car production with only one new model, the Vanguard. Therefore Sir John informed Lyons that they could no longer supply him with the engines and he could have his six-cylinder tooling plant back, for a price of course, but one which was definitely bargain basement. The offer was accepted with alacrity. Lyons was obviously aware of the, what could almost be deemed schizophrenic behaviour of his erstwhile supplier. However Sir John hankered for a sporting image to his company and, in an about turn, tried to persuade Lyons into a partnership. This suggestion refused, he attempted a take over and in a fit of pique threatened to buy Triumph (which Lyons was considering buying) and set up in opposition to S.S. The outcome was that Lyons remained independent and Standard acquired Triumph.

In 1944 Standard had bought up what was left of the Triumph company: basically the name, as the buildings, with the remaining stock of components had been bombed. This was not an expensive acquisition however because the company sold the bomb site to the Morris Group for the same as they had paid for the whole deal!

In the meantime Walter Belgrove who had been Triumph's chief body engineer had been employed by Standard and also played his part in the eventual development of our marque.

So Sir JB set out in direct opposition to Jaguar with the launch, in 1946, of two new models, the Triumph 1800 Roadster and 1800 Town and Country Saloon, based on a cheap-to-build tubular chassis frame but with suspension, engine and running gear from existing Standard Flying 14s. He was not aware however that he didn't have a chance as Jaguar were about to launch their new range of cars powered by twin cam XK engines. Talk about the proverbial non-starter!

So Sir John altered direction, and decided to compete in the export drive of small cars concentrating mainly on the States with an upmarket small car called the Triumph Mayflower, (project 1200T). This idea was unveiled in 1949 but production did not begin until 1950, six years after conception. Again Sir John had been distracted by his 'too many fingers in the pie' syndrome. Another of his 'deals', for instance, had involved the company with Harry Ferguson making tractors.

The car industry in Britain at this time had very little total 'in-house' manufacturing. Individual parts from body to running gear were supplied by specialists sub-contracted to the various car companies who had to take their turn in the inevitable queues that occurred. This method of course had severe disadvantages, as will become increasingly apparent in this particular story.

Because Standard had no body building facilities they contracted with Mulliners to style the 84-inch wheelbase body required for the Mayflower. Then the still independent company of Fisher & Ludlow were to build, in quantity, Vanguard gear boxes and back axles and Standard's own brand of front suspensions, which were later to be built into the 1200T.

After a lot of fiddling around took place the notable innovation of a chassis-less frame was evolved for the 1200T, becoming a crude no-chassis body structure, the first to be used in a Standard-Triumph. Eventually, after limited production, this was abandoned and the decision made that a completely new car would be necessary. So the SC (small car) project was begun in earnest in 1950. The idea was to sell it at a price of £507; the Mayflower being £655 and the four-door Morris Minor (a competitor) being £519. The team working on its development included Harry Webster as chief chassis designer of the company and Ted Grinham, technical director who was, incidentally, not remotely interested in driving or motoring, just in the engineering involved. The Mayflower engine plant was to be converted temporarily to accommodate the building of the new small engine and new permanent advanced transfer-line machinery was ordered, though this wasn't in fact ready until 1955.

The engine size was to match the Austin A40 exactly, but the wheelbase was to be longer by 4.5 inches and therefore the car would weigh more. After the first body had been built with the assistance of Fisher & Ludlow and everyone having thought that all the details had been decided, Sir John then chose a four-speed gear box in preference to the three-speed one already agreed. The Standard 8 was finally launched in 1953 and in an effort to keep costs down it definitely lacked equipment. In fact Sir John dubbed it 'Belsen', a joke in poor taste one would have thought. For example, you couldn't get into the boot from the outside but had to pull the back seats forward. The price was even less than estimated, however, at only £481 *and* with

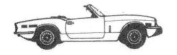

four doors!

The penny pinching ideas were discarded after six months and the Standard 10, with an exterior opening boot and better performance followed. Profits started increasing – £530,631 in 1952 to £1,934,044 in 1955. But the knives were out in the Boardroom and Sir John Black was ousted in 1954 by his fellow directors after another of his unpredictable moods had resulted in the sacking of Ted Grinham. His assistant, Alick Dick, became Managing Director. He did however see the fruition of his desire to manufacture sports cars in the launching of the large and highly successful TR2 in 1952.

Alick Dick gathered around him the basis of the team that ultimately produced the Triumph Herald: the ubiquitous Harry Webster, Ted Grinham, who returned to become his right-hand man, Martin Tustin joined the company and Lord Tedder became Chairman. The company initially stuck to its existing money-spinner however, the Standard 8, though more models were added to the range: The Eight de luxe, Basic Eight, Good Companion, Super Eight and followed by an equivalent expansion to the new 'Family Ten'.

A curious fad became a motoring craze in 1956: the 'two pedal control'. In other words out went the clutch. Standard Triumph's version was called the 'Standrive' and was produced by Newton & Bennett (soon to become a subsidiary of the company). Another overdrive experiment became an option on the 8s and 10s endowing them with seven-speed transmission!

By 1958 the whole of the British Motor Industry was booming but the problems already mentioned of no total 'in house' facilities were making Standard-Triumph's progress increasingly difficult. The internal lack of clearly defined areas of decision making resulted in an arbitrary and ill thought out

decision being made by the non-Board directors to tool up, early in 1958, for a completely new range of 8 and 10 h.p. cars. With Rolls-Royce, Rootes, Jaguar, Rover and Standard Triumph all wanting tooling and body manufacturing facilities there just weren't enough suppliers around. BMC had managed a successful bid for control of Fisher & Ludlow (who had a factory standing empty when Standard's SC contract came to an end). Therefore, when Standard-Triumph went to Fisher & Ludlow naturally they were told, politely to shove off. The new project was shelved and a lot of company time was spent trying to convince other manufacturers to merge with them (Rover in 1954, Rootes and Massey Harris Ferguson in '57 and again Rover in 1959). This added to Alick Dick's constant concern that Standard-Triumph was too small a company to survive any major economic squeeze. In an attempt to consolidate their manufacturing base, Standard-Triumph bid for and acquired a production castings company and Mulliners, as well as fighting off a counter and unwanted takeover bid from Massey Ferguson (remember their tractor involvement?). Sanity returned in 1959 with the undoing of the knot with Massey Ferguson producing a lovely fat pot of gold, twelve-and-a-half million pounds of it in fact. Standard-Triumph started confidently along the road to self-sufficiency. They acquired space for paint and trim facilities, and with some additional merger bids and successes they guaranteed their supplies of front suspension and steering gear, body pressings, sub-assemblies and tooling.

Triumph Herald

But back to the decision of 1956, and its ultimate dream of

producing a car that at 60 m.p.h. achieved a consumption of 60 m.p.g. (Sadly still an unachieved absolute!) The more immediately achievable aim was to produce 3000 cars a week in production. This resulted in the major decision that the car should be based on a separate chassis, meaning that the final assembly would be like putting together bits of a jigsaw. A retrograde step in terms of the progress of car manufacturing thought, the principle was a good one because it meant that you could introduce vans, estate cars, convertibles, coupés or saloons without major design alterations for each model. Obviously it would also be cheaper to tool up. It was known that BMC were working on the Mini, and Ford on the Anglia, so Standard-Triumph were going to have to get a move on if they were going to have a look-in on the British 'small car' market. So there they were, with a concept, and a way of achieving it in theory but . . . the skeleton needed an attractive body and the company didn't have a top stylist! (Walter Belgrove, upset at not being considered capable of the task, retired). Come to that, it didn't have a project name either. Harry Webster, who was by now working on the mechanical design, and perhaps feeling that administration staff seem to do a lot of staring into space, told one of them to compile a list of genuine names beginning with 'Z'. The Zebu you'll be interested to know is a hybrid Tibetan domestic animal, bred from a Yak bull and a common cow! And a Zebu it became. Considering that one of the company's styling ideas being played around with at the time caused Mr. Webster to describe it as a "bath tub on wheels" obviously the mythological hint was very close to the mark!

All good things come to those that wait. And at a tangent the answer came. The company was approached by an

entrepreneur who wanted engine and mechanical supplies for a car which he intended to export. He didn't have any idea of what it would look like, but if Standard-Triumph were interested he could have a prototype built in three months from scratch. With hollow laughter Webster challenged him to do so and promised that the company would pay if he did. He did! The designer was an Italian called Giovanni Michelotti. Standard-Triumph fell on his neck and offered him a freelance contract. However, the malaise didn't seem to want to go away and despite the £10,000 contract to design and construct a prototype Zebu saloon, coupé and estate car shell, nothing seemed forthcoming.

Frustration nearly driving everyone to despair, Harry Webster, at the end of a family touring holiday in Italy, called in on Michelotti to take the Zebu by its horns! After eighteen hours of being closeted together (Webster's family were forgotten and when remembered, found soundly asleep in their car) the problem was solved and on Christmas Eve 1957 a truck rolled into the styling studio in Coventry delivering the first coupé body shell prototype. They all got roaring drunk with triumph!

The ideas, discussions and work went on with renewed heart. Low cost was essential but so was innovation. The chassis design was well ahead of the body engineering. The decisions made so far were: independent front and rear suspension, rack and pinion steering with transverse leaf spring and swing axle geometry at the rear and transverse leaf spring and wishbone layout on the front. This concept was altered by the publicity provoking idea that the vehicle should have a turning circle equal to that of a London taxi. So the front transverse leaf spring would have to go. The progress of the Triumph marque was always hampered by a curious penny pinching approach to the actual development of the vehicles, a hesitancy to spend money where it was needed causing erratic decision making. The car saloon shell was road tested without a front anti-roll bar (a cost saving idea). This had a very unpleasant effect so the roll bar was incorporated. Initially an 803cc engine was to be used, later, wisely, a 948cc unit was installed. The worst result of attempts to keep the costs down was the cheap independent rear suspension chosen for installation. This caused endless problems throughout nearly the whole life span of the Triumph Heralds, Vitesses and Spitfires.

So it went on. In the meantime Michelotti continued to work on engineering the body shells, now to include a convertible, and various permutations of 'bolt-on' body sections. Endurance tests took place in Spain and the serious discussion of what to call the machine continued. This came down to marketing and word association. 'Standard' in everyone's mind seemed to equal solid, safe and middle range. Triumph on the other hand definitely sounds exciting, so Triumph it became. But Triumph what? 'Torch' was the initial thought, the showing of the way, but in the end Alick Dick decided on 'Herald', named after his boat. The public launch was announced for April 1959. Full steam ahead! Assembly of the four major parts was proving a doddle, but the sealing of them to stop the Wuthering Heights-type-noises when being driven, was somewhat of a headache, both for the driver and the factory.

Then suddenly "Let's take two of them and drive from Dakar to the Cape and back!" was heard. The stunned silence as everyone digested this idiotic but apparently serious idea, was long. Protests broke out: No time! Too much to do! Too expensive! (on top of what was proving to be a highly expensive make or break situation) – and perhaps a lone voice of sanity saying, 'You can't take directors and leading members, both technical and administrative, of a company away for six months at such a crucial stage. Anyway what happens if the cars fall to bits? "Come and see our new cars – two small heaps of assorted bits of metal!". But to no avail: the concept was watered down to a certain extent but off they all went Webster, Dick . . . Uncle Tom Cobbly and all.

April 22nd 1959. Finally the Triumph Herald Coupé and Saloon were actually on sale. The final specification included all independent front suspension, with rack and pinion steering; independent rear suspension with swing axle transverse leaf and spring layout, a 948cc 4-cylinder engine with drum brakes front and rear. Unfortunately the price was much more than anticipated, the Saloon at £702 and the Coupé at £731. Also by this time the list of competitors was formidable: and included Ford Anglia, and the BMC Mini, although there were other unique items which the Standard-Triumph publicity machine could spotlight, apart from the unusual jigsaw principle of construction. The car had no grease nipples, an adjustable joint in its steering column both to facilitate the driver position and as a safety measure in the event of a crash (it telescoped): In addition there was the amazing turning circle (though the wear on the tyres was formidable in the event of constant use at full lock), and finally but most impressively the front was a one-piece forward hinged bonnet and wing assembly giving unparalleled access to the engine and front suspension. The Press were extremely kind to the car despite its very suspect road holding, when being driven to its limit, due to the cheap but not satisfactory rear suspension; a

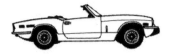

fault known by the technical press, but it didn't prove a major problem in everyday use simply because the car was underpowered. Interestingly, one of the cars the press test drove had been used in the 'Grande Trip' obviously the product was fundamentally sound! It was in fact a satisfactory, small, economic to run car; with very elegant styling and as such it appealed to the public despite the price and competition.

The 'finishing failings' of the Triumph Herald were the main cause for complaint; the rush to meet the launch date and the bitty manufacturing of the jigsaw principle had left little time to iron out the finishing problems. One press man drove with the roof lining sitting on top of his head when at speed! He still gave the car a kind report. The sealing of the bolted together parts still left much to be desired. Unfortunately these niggles were to prove the cars downfall in terms of sale, despite continuous and concentrated efforts to sort them out.

The massive building programme continued and an ironic purchase of the old Fisher & Ludlow factory at Tile Hill took place. The company name Standard-Triumph was used with different variations according to its particular field of activity. Standard-Triumph International was the sales operation set up in 1958, and when the split came with Massey-Harris Ferguson in 1959 the company's car and bus section was called Standard Motor Company Limited, with the tractor shell company called Standard Tractor Co. Ltd. The main company was Standard-Triumph International Limited (from September 1959).

The capital expenditure by this time was £2 million and despite optimism and the introduction of the 'Twin carb' Saloon, with a 45 b.h.p. engine and a Convertible, sales went from bad to worse. Saloons were the best seller of the two

equalling 22,404 in 1959 as opposed to 4,227 Coupés. The Convertible was popular however and could probably have saved the company if things hadn't got quite so out of hand as far as finances were concerned. This linked with a collapse in the British car market and a rapid contraction in exports to the United States and a fatefully over optimistic production of the successor to the TR2 and 3, the TR3A. The fact was that there never seemed time to concentrate on ironing out the small problems. A fact that underlined Alick Dick's worries about the company being too small. The increasing reputation for poor quality was very damaging and the Triumph Herald became 'known' as a car that fell apart and was expensive to purchase. Though the finish of the Convertible had been greatly improved its sales suffered badly from repute and the company staggered from £6 million in the black to £4 million in the red in 1960! Only a year after the optimistic and enthusiastic launch!

A fairy godmother stepped in at this point – Leyland made a bid for the company, and it was accepted. While all the paperwork went on that attends these happenings the company made a foolish attempt to improve sales by producing the 'Herald S,' a totally stripped down to basics model for sale at £664. Signs that the company were positively coping with the finishing problems actually made this a better finished car than the first Heralds! But it was not at all successful, and the concept was never tried again.

This bid though, politely called a merger, was technically a takeover, finalised in early 1961. Leyland were now in control of a company with four makes of car in production, all of which were ailing. The ageing Pennant, an apparently unsaleable six-cylinder Vanguard, the overstocked and not selling TR3A and the

intended saviour, the Triumph Herald being killed by a now not totally justified reputation of poor quality. Leyland must fundamentally have believed in the Herald however and Harry Webster knew that more power was needed and had indeed been working on the project, known as the 1200, from the moment the Triumph Herald was produced. But it was going to be difficult to expand on the existing cylinder block, and it was out of the question financially to design and produce a completely new engine.

This didn't stop him thinking about it though, and he came up trumps by suggesting the principle of désaxé. In other words, unbalancing the existing cylinder head without altering the induction or exhaust arrangements. Obviously it would require a lot of experimental boring and honing but they managed it, and surprisingly cheaply as well – always a satisfactory solution. The initial idea of supplying a twin-carb tune for the Herald was put into cold storage to be used later on the Spitfire. So the 1147 cc engine came into being considerably more torquey and powerful than they had expected. The obvious advantage of this désaxé was that the engine could be dropped into the existing Herald engine space, thereby making it possible to produce the car with the minimum of outlay.

One point not to lose sight of is that despite all the financial upheavals and changes in the Board the continued expansion of the marque was always being planned and worked on almost in the face of apparent disaster. Production having been agreed, the first Herald 1200 appeared on the market in early 1961. There were minimal differences of appearance on the outside: a new badge stating that it was the Herald 1200 and a metal strip around the windscreen, but there were important changes inside apart from the engine! These

were applauded by the press and obviously the buying public as well, and despite severely curtailing production at the end of the year for economic reasons, the company seemed to be reversing its financial straits.

There was a brief internal experiment with a four-door version, and though Britain never saw it, it was sold to Standard Motor Products of India where it went into production as the Standard Gazel. There it sold steadily but it was never re-imported.

The Herald 1200 Estate went on sale in the spring of 1961 and was followed by a mildly re-styled Coupé with a ridged rear quarter 'light' which contributed much to the stability of that section of the body; but Coupés were never the easiest of Triumph versions to sell and these died a death in 1964. The 12/50 Herald, developed to fill the gap between the 1200 and the Vitesse 1600, had the distinction of a folding back sunshine roof as a piece of standard equipment and was the first as such to be fitted in a British car for some years. But the Herald 1200 saloons, convertibles, and estates survived until 1967 when the 13/60 was launched followed by various derivatives.

Vitesse

As we now realise, away from the business wheelings and dealings, the continuous activity on the 'shop floor' – the actual creating of ideas for engines, bodyshells, and prototypes – carried on. Without Harry Webster primarily, the Herald might very well have never come into being let alone expanded, the way it did, to include such exciting offshoots as the Vitesse and Spitfire. He and George Turnball did eventually get elected to the Board in 1962, and this after

Leyland had thrown a wobbly and totally ousted the Standard-Triumph Board in late 1961, and replaced it with Leyland personnel, with interesting results for the Spitfire, as we shall see. However, back to the Zebu project, the rather haphazard approach to forward planning seems to have been one of the company's major stumbling blocks; it always seemed to result in delays, often considerable, in the launching of new models. The Zebu was first mooted in 1957 as a 6-cylinder derivative of the then existing SC project and future Herald 4-cylinder unit. They even announced who would have the contracts for the bodyshells. Styling gave endless problems, as usual, and mechanical problems were cropping up with the advanced chassis layout. So they stuffed the 6-cylinder engine into a Vignale Vanguard to keep the sales staff happy. Harry Webster meanwhile decided that he personally wanted a faster vehicle for the newly opened M1, in 1959, and happening to have a spare Herald Coupé hanging around in the workshop. He and his ever supportive work force, dumped another spare item, a 2-litre 6-cylinder engine into its innards. You couldn't use first gear; it was too torquey, but it suited his needs. He even lent it to the sales force who were definitely *not* interested in a 6-cylinder Herald derivative. They, grudgingly, liked it and as the Zebu got more and more problematic they helped press for the Webster, Tustin and Turnball car code named 'Atom'. This vehicle, in the meantime, had acquired a 'Star' chassis and was nicknamed the "Kenilworth Dragster", after the resident of that town, Harry Webster. The management in March 1961, casting around for a Zebu alternative gave formal approval to building a mock-up of a 6-cylinder, four-doored Herald based on the 'Star' chassis layout, only to discover that the

'Atom' already existed! Then the problems of revising the chassis structure to take the engine had to be sorted out. This time, surprisingly, styling was a simple exercise. Michelotti restyled the front into a distinctive slanting V shape, with four headlamps instead of two. This was highlighted by using duo-tone paintwork with the contrasting colour surrounding the headlamps and grille and flowing back along the sides of the body, like rigid streamers. The back end was left alone except for a chrome plated canopy over the numberplate, but the new extruded, anodized bumper bars, front and rear, proved excellent press copy at the launch. This launch, originally to be at the 1961 Earls Court Motor Show in October, did not actually take place until May 1962. The car was finally named the Vitesse, harking back to a very early Triumph Motor Company success: the 1930 series of sports saloons. The Vitesse was the first new 'small six' from a British company for years and the press response was good. The immediate problem was the high octane rating. Unfortunately, competition appeared in the form of the Ford Cortina GT and this had a higher top speed and gained a very impressive competitions record that unfortunately the Vitesse could not emulate. In fact as far as competitions were concerned, it was a non-starter. The launching of the Triumph 2000 (in late 1963) activated Webster into experimenting with the carburettors and manifolds on the Vitesse. He worked out that at the cost of extra £1.00 a car, he could produce a Mark 2 Vitesse, with additional 13/14 b.h.p. Oddly, however, when the Mark 2 was unveiled in 1965, though they advertised the newly styled facia and panel display, the increase in b.h.p. was an unsung asset. The car was in production for over four years, however, though its original launch partner,

the GT6 is by far the better known companion.

Triumph Spitfire

Myth goes that when the Standard Motor Company decided, in the 1940s, to add a sports car to their range, they looked around the factory floor and picked up bits of discarded components from various sources. The outcome, a TR2, emerged from a witches brew of Triumph Mayflower, a modified tractor engine and a Standard Flying Nine chassis and presumably set the standard of car evolvement for the rest of the company's future! The success of this car and marque is another story, but it did spawn the idea that there should be a complimentary small sports car. The idea was first considered in 1956. The problems of finance and lack of assembly space yet again held the idea up but Michelotti was asked, after production of the Triumph Herald started, to produce a shortened chassis version of the Herald as a sport car prototype. It was a lovely looking beastie, but alas there was no finance available for the project. Fortunately the BMC merger gave new life to the wee thing as they saw that it had definite sale possibilities. Alterations were made to the original design in a small way, such as the increase of the door depth to allow for wind-down windows, thereby in fact making it the first small sports car in Britain to be so equipped and knocking spots off its obvious competitors, the Midget and Sprite in terms of comfort levels. The period of development was extremely short, when one compares it to the other products of Standard Triumph, a mere eighteen months from the go-ahead to production. The original naming of the car has always caused speculation:

Spitfire 4. The Spitfire part is obvious; it honours the famous plane of World War II, but the 4 made everyone positive that there was going to be a follow up version; ie. a Spitfire 6. In fact the company had no intention of following up with a six. They, as they had been wont to do, were looking backwards and acknowledging historically the Standard 8's 4-cylinder engine. Despite our hindsight acceptance of the name 'Spitfire', Harry Webster had in fact wanted to keep its code name and call it Triumph 'Bomb'. One wonders, working along those lines, whether the Triumph Zebu would have achieved the same success as the Triumph Herald. However ours is not to speculate. Webster did in fact get his way with the Triumph 'Stag', yet again another story. Ironically the Vitesse was marketed in America under the title Sports 6 – which underlines even further the company's obvious lack of interest in a Spitfire 6. Many other facets of the Triumph Herald were integral to the Spitfire; the body, though welded steel this time, was bolted onto a separate chassis frame. This frame was in fact different in that the outriggers involved in the support of the Herald Saloon body had gone. Retained were the all independent suspension and the "impactscopic" steering column, as well as the unique front hinging of the complete bonnet giving its more than satisfactory access to the engine and front suspension. These have since been much blessed by the DIY-ers amongst us, and no doubt the mechanics of the day. The engine was a modified 1200. It 'out circled' the Heralds with its rack and pinion steering creating a twenty four foot turning circle! With a completely detachable hood and definitely only two seats it was an uncompromising, visually extremely satisfactory upper-end inexpensive small sports car. The Mark II, in 1965, came with a detachable hardtop. Later, in

conjunction with the introduction of the Triumph 1300, the Spitfire Mark 3 was re-engined as a 1296cc.

In the meantime the GT6 had been launched and the Mark IV Spitfire's designers had finally accepted the endless criticism of the marque's rear suspension and had a revised 'swing spring' fitted on the rear axle.

The Spitfire 1500 naturally had a 1493 cc engine combined with a widening of the rear track (introduced on the late Mk IVs) which meant additional better handling. By this time, the gearbox had been replaced with a single rail box and overdrive was available in J-type rather than the earlier D-type form.

GT6

The GT6 was not a planned addition to the range; it sneaked up from behind so to speak. Standard-Triumph really did not have the production space to seriously consider expanding; so despite the hints and speculation from outsiders they firmly ignored the possibility of a "Spitfire-6". They did, however, consider ways of keeping the Spitfire in the forefront of its particular market and Michellotti was asked to design a fastback body for it. His resultant design added far too much weight to the car so the idea was shelved. The fastback body was in fact fitted onto a Spitfire chassis in Turin, christened the Spitfire GT, and driven home where it joined the small band of experimental one-offs used by a few members of the company. The pleasure the car gave to those that drove it worked an insidious magic and the Spitfire GT project became official policy in 1964. The decision to turn it into a six-cylinder car was the result of progress with the up-grading of the Vitesse to a 1998 cc. It was a bit of a squeeze getting the

1998cc six-cylinder engine into the Spitfire's engine bay, but by dint of creating a rather complicated cooling system they managed it. The GT6's debut was in 1966, a few months earlier than the Vitesse 2 litre; which, like the true parent it was, paused in the wings to enjoy the accolade!

The car was beautifully finished from inside to out. It was fully carpeted with a walnut veneer facia board and swivelling quarter lights at the front – the fixed quarter-lights used during development had tended to be sucked out at speed – and hinged quarter-lights at the rear. The elegant Italian design with its hatchback and two seats only, was a classy small Grand Touring car, even the rocker box was chrome plated.

The car was well received and though it never achieved the production figures of the Spitfire it sold steadily. The inevitable bug bear of the independent rear suspension raised its head again, though mainly in the technical press. The general public did not seem too concerned and in the States, where the car was very well received, there were no complaints. The rear suspension had in fact been modified for the GT6 and the company was seriously trying to find engineering time to concentrate on the problem. This they eventually managed, and when, in 1968, the GT6 Mk2 took over, it was fitted with an advanced lower-wishbone rear suspension layout; double-jointed shafts located by a spring at the top. The effect on the handling of the GT6 was revolutionary – no more cause for complaint! The Mk2 also acquired a new cylinder head, borrowed from the TR5, (giving potential for the engine to become a 2498 cc, an advantage never utilised), but resulting in an increase of bhp from 95 to 104. Despite the formation of British Leyland, no attempt was made to rationalise the range of sports cars for sale under the new

umbrella – the Spitfire, the MGB, the TR6, Stag, MG Midget, the GT6 and Austin-Healey Sprite – all continued to share the market. The real cloud on the horizon was in fact, the increase of legislation, in the United States, on safety and exhaust emission. Taking these facts into account, the intended full re-styling of the GT6 was modified (as with the Spitfire). Internal facelifting of the seats, steering wheel and badging took place prior to the official launch of the GT6 Mk 3 in 1970. In line with the Spitfire Mk IV, the tail was 'chopped-off' and the bonnet flattened out. The rear roof line of the GT6 was altered and petrol cap and door handles ceased to protrude creating a more svelte look. Optimism was high in the sales department but in reality the bell was tolling. The safety legislation meant a considerable increase in weight – the exhaust emission regulations badly effected the power of the six-cylinder engine and sales dropped . . . and dropped. No official death certificate was released but on the thirtieth of November 1973 the last two GT6s produced, quietly left the factory.

Competition achievements

The competitions department of Standard-Triumph was an active and busy place in 1959, its achievements with the TR3A were considerable and soon to reach dizzier heights. Rallying was an international motoring pastime and smaller cars had surprising successes. So, naturally, the Heralds had to be entered into the field. Handicapped by their under-powered 948 cc engine, the advantage of their turning circle seemed of little value. The cars used by the works were Herald Coupes and in 1959 at the Alpine Rally, the solitary

Herald was the ninth of nine cars to complete the course without time faults. Definitely creditable! The real coup was the Tulip rally of 1961. A complicated system of handicapping meant that if only one of the two Heralds in the rally, (one a works entry, the other a private), actually clocked in at the end of the race they *could* gain an outright win! After battling all the way, the works entry simply drove across the line leaving the private to clock in. It worked! Much to everyone's amazement a Triumph Herald gained an outright victory (on a technicality) ahead of a Porsche! The works bowed the Triumph Herald out of the scene.

In 1961 the competitions department closed down; Leyland had taken over and finances were dire. With the arrival of the Vitesse and Spitfire, enthusiasm was renewed and Harry Webster persuaded the company to try again. This time a works Vitesse saloon was entered in the RAC Rally of 1962, driven by Vic Elford. It proved that the car had potential and a team of Vitesses were earmarked for rallying, starting with the Monte Carlo rally in 1963. Yet again credit was achieved; only eight cars completed without road penalties, and Mr Elford was one of them. However the company decided not to financially support any more Vitesse works entries. Vic Elford persuaded them to allow him to try twice more (he actually bearded Sir Donald Stokes about it the second time); but despite excellent placings initially disaster struck. In the Isle of Man the differential failed and in Yugoslavia the car burst into flames!

Harry Webster, motor racing enthusiast, once more persuaded the Board, this time to invest heavily in the development of the Spitfires and Triumph 2000s as competition cars. To compete, the Spitfire would have to go faster: so six months was spent by the engineers, who produced the 70X engine. At this point the Spitfire

GT prototype arrived back from Turin and its fast back was seen to be the perfect shape for the racing Spitfires. John Lloyd, who led the Dakar expedition, was the motivator behind the assaults on the Le Mans with these specially built units. Built from scratch with special bonnets and headlamps, light alloy panels and the new engine installed, three were entered into the 1964 race. Two crashed, wrecking the cars but not the drivers, fortunately. Though the driver of the second car had in fact almost been gassed by exhaust fumes inside the car! More development work took place with emphasis on losing some of the car's weight. The cars for the 1965 Le Mans had lightened frames causing a loss in handling precision. Much to the team's horror four cars were accepted for entry in the race. The lighter frame considerably improved the speeds achieved, though no 'official' victories were credited. The works withdrew from racing after this, though several private owners and ex-team members were loaned the cars to race on their own. Harry Webster and John Lloyd remained keen to promote the Spitfire in races and seriously considered entering a special prototype GT6 in the 1966 Le Mans. This time, however, the competitions programme was being severely curtailed, finances again, so the racing story in Britain came to an end.

In America the tale was one of outright success and between 1968 and 1980 there was always a Spitfire in a prominent race position. So proud were they of the marque's achievements, that every Spitfire since the mid 1970s has a badge on the dashboard, stating that the Triumph Spitfire is an 'SCCA National Champion'. The Vitesse, as we know gained no contemporary competition credibility, and in fact, was only entered twice under the official 'works entry' tag.

But we can still enjoy the Triumph Herald, Vitesse, Spitfire and GT6, because despite the company's problems they produced enough of these wonderful cars for us still to use.

Photo attributes are shown, where relevant, at the end of each caption in brackets.

H1. The Herald 948 Coupé, demonstrating the production flexibility of bolt-together construction techniques.

H2. The 12/50 Herald saloon, with fashionable folding fabric sunroof.

H3.   Excellent load-carrying capacity combined with the famous Herald turning circle made the Estate a favourite with traders. (Flickr: Joost_J._Bakker) And let's not forget the Courier van delivering butter in the early '60s!

H4.   12/50 Herald with more austere paint finish. It's amazing how much difference the side-strip made! (Contemporary advert)

H5.   Growing up and, visually, cleaned up. 13/60 Herald with the ''oriental'' grille/bonnet arrangement. (Wikipedia: Chris Sampson)

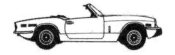

H6.   The nowadays rather rare 948 Herald Convertible. The "chicness" exuded by the car at the time has since been rediscovered; there was a time when all Heralds were poorly regarded.

H7.   Backbone of the Herald suitably modified, became the basis for the Spitfire 4. This is a factory prepared Spitfire "show" chassis.

H8.   Two extra headlights, two extra cylinders: the Vitesse 6 was quite a potent car.
It was first introduced as a 1600, then uprated to 2 litres.
This rather down-at-heel 1967 Cactus Green Vitesse convertible Mk 1 has mock-alloy wheel trims from the Mk2 instead of the Mk1's hubcaps. (Wikipedia: Oxyman)

H9. The heart of the Vitesse was its lusty 6-cylinder engine. This is the GT6's version.

H10. Fitted to a "closed" Spitfire, this engine transformed the little sportscar into the Triumph GT6.

H11. A Standard-Triumph publicity shot of the famous GT6/Vitesse 2-litre engine and gearbox.

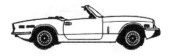

H12.   A restored GT6, featured in some of the pages of this book, with its proud owner Dr. Dennis Cruse.

H13.   Triumphs in competition: January 1965, **Rallye Automobile Monte Carlo**, Simo Lampinen - one of the first of the "Flying Finns" - with Triumph Spitfire 4 in full rally garb.

H14.   John Griffiths, President of the TSSC at the Weston Super Mare Sprint in his very competitive Vitesse MkII Convertible.

HOW TOUGH CAN A CAR TEST BE?

Toughest test for a car is self-drive hire. So says Mr. Venner-Pack, Sales Director of Moons Motors, Ltd. Triumph Heralds with the Moons fleet have averaged 20,000 miles in a season on everything from Autobahns to mountain tracks, handled by all types of drivers. Another success for the Triumph Herald.

TRIUMPH HERALD

The new experience in motoring!

STANDARD TRIUMPH

STANDARD-TRIUMPH GROUP · COVENTRY   LONDON SHOWROOMS · BERKELEY SQUARE

H15. Triumph advertising was considered trend-setting in its day, especially for the Herald which was presented as being the ultimate in motoring chic, not to say élan!

Even after two years, there's no other car in its class!

TRIUMPH herald | the car that's got everything!

STANDARD TRIUMPH AUSTRALIA PTY. LTD. A Member Company of the Australian Motor Industries Ltd. Group - Australia's own Australian Motor Company.

Make this your year of Triumph

Triumph Herald 1200 The car with the 25-ft turning circle. Saloon, estate or convertible versions.

Triumph TR4 Top speed 110 mph. The sports car that separates the men from the boys.

Triumph Vitesse The cheapest 6-cylinder car made in Britain. Saloon, skylight or convertible versions.

Triumph Herald 12/50 Disc brakes and a skylight roof come as part of the deal.

Triumph Spitfire Fast. Potent. Comfortable. Europe's most accomplished light sports car. £642.

See the Triumphs on Stand 115

STANDARD TRIUMPH   *A member of the Leyland Motor Corporation*

Sports Car Club of America drivers call it a champion.
(Typical American understatement.)

In the SCCA National Championships last year, the Mark III Spitfire took first, second and third in its class.

Champion indeed! That's what the English would call a bit of all right.

But we didn't rest on our laurels. We radically reworked the 1970 champion to make it work even better for 1971. On our new Mark IV, we strengthened the engine bearings, designed a new close ratio all-synchro gearbox and modified the suspension for improved balance and road holding.

And while we were doing things for the inside, Ferrari body designer Michelotti did a lot for the outside.

As far as we can tell, the car is now—to use an American term—'A-OK' by anybody's standards. You try it at your Triumph dealer. The new improved champion for 1971.

Triumph Spitfire

For the name of your nearest Triumph dealer, call 800-631-1971 toll free. In New Jersey, call 800-962-2803. British Leyland Motors, Inc., Leonia, N.J. 07605.

H16. According to Canley Classics, the registration ADU 7B has for the past 30 odd years been attached to another ex-works car (or car built up from 'works' parts) that is still in the UK.

H17. The Triumph Courier Van. Though an excellent workhorse, the Courier was expensive when compared against its rivals and hence was only produced during a three year period. (Wikipedia: tormentor4555)

H18. Also part of the overall Heritage was the Standard Atlas Van which featured a Herald engine. Built from around 1959 to 1962, the Atlas preceded the Courier Van. Sales were very poor. It must have been a rare beast indeed in the USA!

H19. As different as any two cars might be but sharing Herald ancestry are the works rally Spitfire and the unique amphibious Amphicar. The connection with the Spitfire is obvious. Less so is the fact that the German built Amphicar uses a rear-mounted Herald 1200 engine.

H20. A totally different family of production cars using many Herald and Vitesse chassis and mechanical components in their manufacture (plus Spitfire engines in the 4-cylinder GT models) are the 4- and 6-cylinder Bond Equipes. This shot shows a selection of Bond Equipe GT4S Saloons and GT 2-litre Saloon and Convertible models. The original 4-cylinder model, the Bond Equipe GT, featured more angular 2+2 Coupé lines as compared with the later GT4S with single, rather than twin headlamps.

H21. Herald family based specials using various combinations of mechanical components were once quite popular including early Spartans.. (Spartan Cars is believed to have operated from 1973 to 1995.)

Footnote: Triumph kit cars were controversial among enthusiasts at the time but have now become 'collectable' in their own right and most if not all have dedicated owners' clubs supporting them.

H22. *. . . Burlington Arrows . . .*
(Kit production seems to have stopped in around 1992 but from 2008, the plans appear to have been made available again for home constructors.)

H23. *. . . Marlins . . .*
(According to the Marlin Owner's Club, *"The last Triumph based kit was produced in June 1983, and of the 236 all Triumph kits produced approximately 160 are known to have been put on the road."*)

H24. *. . . and Moss's to name and show just a few.*
(The last Moss, Triumph based kit appears to have been produced by Moss in June 1983.)

2 Buying

Brief model summary

The range of cars we consider here is peculiar in that each is so very like the other in terms of design, construction and layout; yet each remains a very different car with its own particular characteristics, qualities and vices. The Herald in its various forms, is very much the reliable, uncomplicated and economical saloon car, as are its derivatives namely, the Courier van, the estate and the convertible. The Spitfire, born of the Herald mechanically, if not style-wise, shares many virtues of the Herald whilst being, in its day a "first time" sports car for many buyers. The Spitfire was never the "complete" sports car, though in contemporary refinements such as having wind-up windows and optional overdrive, it outclassed much of the competition of the day. It was more of a "taster" and if the owner found himself at home with the concept of the traditional sports car, then it often became a stepping stone towards a bigger or more powerful vehicle in the same idiom. Inevitably one such progression for Spitfire owners was the GT6. Here the Spitfire driving position and cockpit surroundings were repeated almost identically, though suspension differences and of course the two-litre six-cylinder engine, meant the GT6 was a totally different car in all other respects, and of course, it was only developed as a fixed head coupe. Had Triumph not been producing the TR series of convertibles at the same time, we may well have seen a convertible GT6, and indeed several cars have since been modified as such by enthusiastic owners.

The Vitesse relates to the Herald in much the same way as the GT6 does to the Spitfire.

The Vitesse and Herald body shells are identical save for front end styling in which the Vitesse was given a distinctive V-shaped bonnet (as indeed was the Herald 13/60) incorporating its unique double headlight layout. Interiors are also similar, though the Vitesse is treated to a higher level of comfort and fittings; but here the Herald similarity ends. Mechanically, the Vitesse shares all with the GT6, and indeed, the Vitesse was very much the source of mechanical components during conception of the GT6.

On the road

All of these four cars qualify as "classics" today, some more so than others, and again certain variants qualify to greater degrees. But with so many variants, the question looms as to which is the most appropriate for the potential buyer. Intended usage has a large part to play. If the car is in every day use, then fuel consumption becomes a parameter where the Heralds and Spitfires score highly with their economical 35 – 40 mpg. The 26 mpg average of the Vitesse 2-litre and generally slightly more from the GT6 however, would pose no problem for the owner who wishes to preserve the car for concours exhibiting or even occasional weekend use. Such usage may however involve long journeys for which all the "closed top" cars are ideally suited, being comfortable, reasonably quiet, and well ventilated. Ventilation and comfort remain a feature of the "soft-top" cars, but whilst hoods are quite watertight, they are otherwise un-refined and driving at motorway speeds with soft-tops erected can be very tiring over a long distance.

The number of passengers to be carried is yet another factor to be considered, and where family size may rule out the two-seater sports cars, the sporting driver can find sanctuary in the four-seater Vitesse. Both the Vitesse and Herald convertibles offer four-seat accommodation, though rear seats cannot be recommended for adults over a long distance due to the reduction in leg room in order to incorporate the hood well. It should be remembered of course,

that some GT6s are fitted with a folding rear seat conversion which is suitable for a small child.

Whilst considering accommodation, thought should be given to stowage space, and as far as cockpit stowage is concerned, all cars are found to be lacking.

The GT6 and Spitfire do offer a couple of cubby holes but this advantage is offset by the somewhat cramped confines of the bodyshell.

Luggage-wise the Herald and Vitesse are excellent, having a large, well shaped and accessible boot.

The Spitfire too has an excellent boot for a small sports car but space within the GT6 is restricted within the hatchback, if only due to the fact that any appreciable amount of luggage restricts rearward vision. Door or wing mirrors are hence a sensible addition.

From the driver's viewpoint, all the vehicles are a pleasure to drive, being responsive to the controls, predictable in their handling and with a good degree of controllability in an emergency. They are at home on country roads and particularly in the town where the famed Herald turning circle (which applies to all of these cars), is of great benefit. Their one common vice is the tendency for the rear wheel camber to alter significantly if the throttle is backed off whilst cornering, with consequent loss of rear tyre adhesion. However, the driver soon learns the technique of powering the car out of bends and enjoys the "art" of cornering with a transverse rear road spring. Nevertheless, the problem was eliminated on later models in that the Mk IV 1300 and 1500 Spitfires and later GT6 Mk 3s were given a pivoting rear spring, and the Mk 2 Vitesse and Mk 2 and early Mk 3 GT6 had the more sophisticated lower wishbone system with a flexible joint in the axle shafts, in a similar fashion to the Formula

One Style.

Both systems work satisfactorily, the latter (generally known as Mk 2 suspension) is probably the better type as regards handling but is more complicated and hence less easy to work on. It is probably fair to say that this is the only aspect of these cars which is problematic from a maintenance point of view; the remainder of mechanical components being extremely simple to work on and costs also remaining comparitively low.

Engine access is of course probably the best of any mass produced car thanks to the forward lifting front end, and indeed the whole car can be dismantled like the proverbial "Meccano set", including the body. This makes the cars particularly attractive to the would-be restorer. The body shells can comfortably be removed in a day's work, leaving complete access to all parts of the rolling chassis.

Choosing

The Herald

With bodyshells, chassis and other components being so easily interchangeable, it is important to confirm the originality of a potential purchase. Estate car bodies for example are often fitted in place of saloon shells as are convertible rear ends and so on. This is a particular point to watch with the Herald, which has the widest range of variants, one of the earliest of which, is the Courier Van. There are only a handful of these known to remain in existence and though commanding no great value, they are nevertheless a rare and interesting vehicle to own.

The Herald Coupé in 948 and 1200 cc versions is another rare specimen, being a "two plus two" version of the saloon and

quite sought after. The Herald saloon is available in several forms starting with the 1959, 948 cc, the later 1200 and the slightly more powerful 12/50, recognised by its standard equipment sun-roof and slightly different external trim.

The 1296 cc 13/60 model was the last and best of the saloons and adopted a similar bonnet style to the Vitesse though with single 7 inch headlamps and an improved standard of interior trim. The very practical Estate car versions were available in both 1200 and 13/60 forms whilst convertibles can be found in all engine sizes with the 13/60 being the most plentiful and most highly valued.

The Spitfire

The Spitfire 4 (or 'Mk 1') produced between 1962 and 1964 was mechanically similar to the 1200 Herald, but with engine modifications which included a new camshaft and twin SU carburettors to provide 63 bhp. The Mk 2, recognisable by its horizontally slatted grille had its power increased to 67 bhp due to another change of camshaft, and the addition of a four-branch tubular exhaust manifold, but otherwise the Spitfire remained unchanged until the advent of the Mk 3 in December 1966. Distinguishable by its raised front bumper, the Mk 3 car featured a far more powerful 1296 cc engine in line with the Herald's transition to the 13/60.

Power was up to 75 bhp but another great advantage was that the soft-top and frame was now permanently fixed to the body and folded away behind the seats, unlike the earlier cars in which the hood and frame had to be dismantled and stowed in the boot.

The Mk IV version became available in 1970 with a re-styled body featuring a tail end similar to the Triumph Stag and re-shaped front with recessed bumper.

The most notable, and well received mechanical change was at the rear where the unsophisticated rear suspension of earlier models had been improved by introducing a pivoting action at the centre of the rear spring. The level of interior trim was increased and the lines of the soft-top improved.

An all-synchromesh gearbox was introduced but unfortunately engine power suffered due to emission control requirements, leaving the car slower than the Mk 3, with only 63 bhp. February 1973 saw further improvements to the Mk IV by way of better seats, a wooden facia and a widening of the rear track. In December 1974 a Toledo-based 1493 cc engine was introduced, fitted to the "Spitfire 1500", the fastest derivative, with a top speed of 100 mph and a 0 – 60 time of 13.2 secs., though at the expense of fuel consumption which fell from an average 35 mpg to 32 mpg. The Spitfire continued in this form, with slight interior revisions until August 1980 when all production ceased.

All the above variants were available with optional overdrive, wire wheels and works hard-top which reflect higher values today.

With such recent production, parts availability is good for all but the earliest Spitfires.

The Vitesse

The Vitesse was produced in saloon and convertible form through three model stages, namely the Vitesse 6, the Vitesse 2-litre and the Mk 2 Vitesse 2-litre, all models being available with overdrive.

The Vitesse 6 produced in 1962 featured a 1596 cc derivative of the Standard Vanguard engine producing 70 bhp, 90 mph top speed and a 0 – 50 time of 12 seconds, though fuel consumption was relatively poor. Engine spares

pose a problem here and where originality is important, interior trim parts are also scarce, otherwise much is shared with the Heralds of its time and later. Spares are far less a problem for the Vitesse 2-litre, retrospectively known as the Mk 1, and having the effortlessly smooth 1998 cc engine producing 95 bhp through an all-synchro gearbox.

This model was distinguished by a square "2-litre" badge on grille and boot with the styling remaining unchanged until the introduction of the Mk 2 Vitesse in 1968.

Earlier Vitesses, like the Spitfire and Herald had gained a bad reputation for rear end handling and the Mk 2 now cured this with the introduction of lower wishbones at the rear and a flexible rotoflex drive joint in each axle (plus lever arm dampers), which allowed correct wheel camber to be maintained under all conditions, and this became the great attraction of the Mk 2.

The new Vitesse had engine power increased to 104 bhp by employing the Triumph TR5 cylinder head with a new camshaft giving better top end performance but losing some of the smoothness of the Mk 1.

Styling changes to the grille and boot panel and the use of "Rostyle"-like wheel trims set the Mk 2 apart from its predecessor and the interior was revised with recessed switches and more comfortable seats.

Before leaving the Vitesse, it is worth mentioning the Vitesse Estate car which officially was not produced but in fact, a handful were converted by Standard Triumph Service Division as a modification to existing saloons. Many more have been produced by owners swapping the rear body section for that of a Herald Estate and whilst there is nothing against this, the purist would opt for an ST conversion.

A glance at the interior wood cappings below the rear side

windows will tell you if the car is a "home" conversion, as only Standard Triumph produced a one-piece capping. If there is a break in the capping or it is not full length then the car is definitely not an ST conversion. Of course some owners may go to the trouble of making a full length capping, but have a look at the Commission plate on the front bulkhead, which ST will have altered if they have produced the vehicle. Obviously such a car is now valuable and well worth restoring, but the most sought after Vitesse is the Mk 2 convertible which in recent years has held its head ever higher in classic car circles.

The GT6

Having so many features in common with the Spitfire and Vitesse, it is inevitable that the GT6 developed alongside them, at the same time and in the same ways.

The Mk 1 GT6 appeared in 1966 looking outwardly identical to the Mk 2 Spitfire but with a fastback closed body and wide opening tailgate. Still a two-seater, the GT6 had a more refined interior which included a polished wood facia and centre arm test. However, the Spitfire similarity ends there, the mechanical components being those of the Mk 1 Vitesse 2-litre including, unfortunately, the inferior rear suspension which provoked criticism from its launch date, and to this day is responsible for the Mk 1 being rather unfairly considered something of a 'black sheep'. However, the problem was finally dispensed with in the Mk 2 GT6 of 1968 which took advantage of the new rear suspension of the Mk2 Vitesse being mechanically similar though with telescopic rear shock absorbers and sharing the same improved 2-litre engine.

The interior layout remained generally similar but included a revised dashboard with rocker switches and steering wheel,

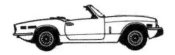

different seats (later reclining) and improved ventilation with face and knee level air ball vents. Externally, the car was given the same front end face lift as the Mk 3 Spitfire. The Mk 2 car is probably the most coveted of the GT6 variants though this is greatly influenced by personal taste, which means many people plump for the later Mk 3 introduced in 1970, with its smoother styling following the pattern of the Mk IV Spitfire body changes.

Beneath the flowing exterior, the chassis and mechanics remained unchanged until in 1972, when, as with the Spitfire, the engine became restricted by exhaust emission regulations bringing power back down to 95 bhp from engine No.KE10,000 onwards. In 1973 the double wishbone rear suspension was replaced by the Mk IV Spitfire pivoting spring system though with different spring rates and at this time tinted glass was introduced together with cloth covered seats with headrests, new instrumentation and servo-assisted brakes.

A particularly desirable option on the GT6 is the factory fitted, fold-back sunroof. Another, overdrive on third and fourth gears is worth searching for, bearing in mind that most overdrive and non-overdrive cars have similar overall top gear ratios due to the non-overdrive having a higher 3.27:1 ratio differential as compared to the overdrive models which generally had a final drive 3.89:1 (optionally 3.27: on the Mk 2).

Where to look

Without doubt, the richest source of cars for sale and also of new and used spares is *The Courier*, the monthly publication of the Triumph Sports Six Club. In its large 'classified' section there are cars ranging from scrap condition

to concours and with a price range to match. For the Herald and Spitfire buyer, the local press should yield a steady supply of cars needing some restoration, and of course, in the UK, the weekly *Exchange and Mart* and local area *Auto-Mart* should be considered for any of the above cars whilst in the United States, *Auto Trader Old Car Book* (published monthly) may be a good source of parts and cars. There are always the car auctions and whilst you may pay less here, you are nevertheless restricted in the time available to examine the car before purchase, and this inevitably introduces a high risk factor.

The Vitesse and GT6 frequently appear in the classified sections of the motoring magazines specialising in the 'classic' and 'sports' cars, along with the convertible Heralds.

Safety

When inspecting a car don't forget safety. NEVER rely on the handbrake to hold a car that is on a slope or up on ramps. Ensure that the wheels are chocked when using jacks or ramps. Use axle stands if you have to inspect the underside of the car. Do not use a naked flame or smoke when inspecting the underside of a car.

Making sure

Before buying any car for restoration, a budget should be thought out and the eventual intended limit of expenditure known. Knowing this limit, together with the asking price of the vehicle, a note should be made of the estimated cost of restoring the car to the standard required. If restoration costs plus purchase price exceed the budget figure then it may be time to reconsider the intended standard

of restoration, review the purchase price or perhaps consider another, lower priced variant. Often a mid-priced car will cost just as much to restore as a tattier looking cheaper car. This is well worth bearing in mind. To form a reasonably accurate picture of the expected restoration costs, it is a good idea to have a friend with you who can write down a list of the defects as you call them out together with a rough estimate of the cost involved for each. In this way you will have a comprehensive record of the state of the car to mull over later, and you can also add up the cost of all the defects to form an idea of the ultimate restoration costs. The list will have further use when you come to plan the actual restoration.

Before going along to see a car, get as much information as possible by telephone – it could save you and the seller a lot of wasted time. On the other hand, it is useul to look at several cars to gain experience of the market before making a choice.

Ideally, you should aim to take with you: overalls, a good torch, a large strong screwdriver for levering and poking at rust, ramps, a trolley jack and a flat board for lying under the car. Allow yourself plenty of time for the visit as you will miss the points if you are rushed or uncomfortable, and don't let the seller's conversation distract you from the job in hand. *Never* crawl under a car supported on a jack. Use axle stands or ramps, and be sure to chock securely the wheels on the ground.

Using the checklist

What follows is a list of points to check, in three stages. The first stage will eliminate the obviously unsuitable cars before you waste any time on them and the second, longer stage will give

you a good general appraisal of the car and enable you to decide whether to proceed with the third stage which is an involved and detailed examination.

Use the notebook as mentioned earlier to record defects and areas requiring some work and jot down the estimated costs involved. Always estimate on the high side and don't be distracted by the car's good points, – look for trouble – there will probably be more than you can see!

The '£' sign symbols will probably give you an idea of how much replacement components (not labour costs) will cost you. A single '£' is meant to be roughly equivalent to the cost of a single tyre; £££ = the cost of a full set of tyres, while ££ suggests that the cost will be somewhere in between.

Stage A: First impressions

1.   Is the exterior presentable? If so is the paintwork original or a respray? If a respray, it could be a quality job or a quick 'blow over' to hide rust. (££ – £££)

2. · Check for body filler and panel beating by sighting along panels looking for ripples, hollows or bumps, especially on door bottoms. Watch for inferior replacement panels which may show twists and mis-shapes, especially on wings. (£££)

3.   Examine chromework for dents and rusting. (£-£££, if available)

4.   Check for mis-alignment of doors and front end. The body may have been removed and re-fitted inaccurately and may need major re-alignment on the chassis.

5.   Ensure that the car is level at each corner – suspension/chassis defects – worn springs. Bounce the car at

each corner by pressing down and allowing it to spring up and back down once. More than one cycle indicates defective shock absorbers. (££ – £££)

6.   Switch on everything electrical and ensure all items function, not forgetting the heater motor. Check indicators, ignition on, with side and brake lights on at the same time. (£ – ££, per item)

7.   Check windscreen for scratches and pitting which would present a problem for night driving. (££)

8.   Check hood where fitted for tears, rotted stitching, fixing studs and clarity of window. Check for broken hood frames and clips. (££)

9.   Check tyres for signs of uneven wear – chassis damage or suspension/steering defects: and for cuts, bulges and general wear. (£ – £££)

10.   Check rubber bumpers on Heralds – difficult to find replacements – and examine the Vitesse aluminium bumpers for damage. (££, if available)

Stage B: Clean hands

Bodywork

1.   Check bonnet for corrosion around wheel arches, beneath bonnet clasps and around front side lights. New bonnets are very expensive and several types are unobtainable, though wings are available for most of the cars. (£££)

2.   Check horizontal bar under grille on Herald/Vitesse. (£)

3.   Check bonnet top for dents, distortion and twisting. (£-£££)

4.   Open bonnet and check for corrosion behind lights and around inner wheel arches. (£-££)

5.   Attempt to rock bonnet whilst open to check condition of hinge bushes. (£)

6.   Look for perforations along bottom of sides of front bulkhead – no repair panels available. (££-£££, if paying someone else)

7.   Examine lower part of A-post for corrosion and at its attachment to door sill. Particularly important on Spitfire. Check sill closing plate at front. (£-££)

8.   Check windscreen side pillars for corrosion on all cars and along front roof lip on the GT6 and early Herald Coupés. Difficult areas to repair, and defective side pillars will probably need to be replaced using those cut from another car. (f for parts; ££-£££ for welding)

9.   On GT6 and Spitfire, examine outer sills and check attachments underneath to floor. Are doors and rear wings correctly aligned with sill panel? If not, replacement sills may have been badly fitted and in the case of the Spitfire permanent body sag may have occured. Steer clear of cars with this problem.

10.   Open door and check along the bottom of the shell, lower parts of the skin and beneath the door handle for corrosion. Doors can be re-skinnned but if the bottom of the shell is corroded, that will need repairing first, (££), or consider purchasing good second-hand doors.

11.   Check for vertical cracks below the quarter-light on Herald/Vitesse door. (£-££)

12.   Do the doors shut correctly and are they set at the right height and flush with the wings when closed? (Probably time required)

13.   Check corrosion in footwells adjacent to the A-post and examine attachment of inner sill to floor pan. (£-£££)

14.   Check seat belt mountings at floor. (£-££)

15.   On Spitfire/GT6 remove carpet from heel board at rear of floor pans and examine for cracks where the rear suspension trailing arm is bolted. (£)

16.   Check rear wings for

corrosion on the front lower area ahead of the rear wheel, and also around the wheel arch. (££)

17. Check inner rear wheel arches and sill ends on Spitfire/GT6 and lower part of wing behind wheel at its attachment to the rear panel and boot floor. (££)

18. Spitfire/GT6, examine rear panel for mis-shape and boot floor and sides for corrosion and crash damage. (££)

19. Check boot lid hinges and rear edge of Spitfire boot lid. (£-££)

Interior

1. Check facia and crash pad for tears, scratches of wood facia, holes cut for extra instruments and badges etc., glued on. (££)

2. Herald/Vitesse carpets are expensive to replace with original quality – pay particular attention to their condition. (££-£££)

3. Check seat, door and headlining fabrics for tears, stains and inground dirt. Are seats secure? Frames may be broken or securing bolts pulled out of the floor. (££-£££)

4. Are instruments, steering wheel etc., standard? (£-£££, if available)

5. Check operation of door locks, window and seat adjusters. (£-££)

6. Examine seat belts which should not be frayed. Ensure buckles lock and test operation of inertia reel seat belts with a sharp tug. They should lock instantly. (££)

7. If sunroof fitted, check for leaks and for ease of operation from the driving seat. (£-££)

Mechanical

1. Check oil and water levels, clutch and brake fluid and fan belt tension. Is there any 'white emulsion' deposited inside the oil filler cap and the rocker box?

2. Start the engine but don't rev it. Listen for initial crankshaft rumble which should only last a couple of seconds until oil light extinguishes. If no rumble, that's fine, but otherwise it is only a problem if pronounced and prolonged. (major overhaul £££). Leave the engine idling while the next checks are made.

3. Depress the clutch pedal and listen for the whirr of a worn release bearing. (£, plus time)

4. Move the gear lever into each position – it should be free and positive. If the lever 'sizzles' with the engine running then this can be cured with a cheap re-bushing kit. (£)

5. Listen to and look at the exhaust for holes. (££)

6. The engine should now be ticking over smoothly without choke. Tappet noise should be minimal. Listen for timing chain rattle. (£)

7. Knocking sounds from the engine suggest worn gudgeon pins. (££) Listen to the alternator/dynamo and distributor bearings. (£-££)

8. Are air filters fitted and are they correct type? Does the oil filter look as if it has been repeatedly renewed in the last few thousand miles? (If not, severe wear = £££)

9. Consider originality of engine parts. (eg Mk 1 GT6 should have chrome rocker cover). (£-££, if available)

10. Release the handbrake and roll the car to ensure brakes are not binding. Pull handbrake on, inefficiency may be lack of adjustment or seized adjusters. (£-££)

11. Check steering wheel and front wheels move accordingly. Attempt to rock steering wheel up and down. Excessive movement means worn column bushes. (£)

Road test

1. Start up and note any slowness or undue noise from the starter motor or grating from the ring gear. (£-££, plus possible engine removal)

2. Move off in reverse. If noisy or jumps out of gear, a complete strip of the gearbox is necessary. (££-£££)

3. Now move off in first, listening for rear end clonks which point to worn rear axle or prop-shaft U/Js (£-££, or on cars with wire wheels, worn or loose fitting splines. (££)

4. Increase speed and play with the gearbox, moving up and down the ratios until you are familiar with it. There should be no baulking and the clutch should be light. Baulking suggests a weak clutch pressure plate. (££) Does the gearbox 'crunch' when you go into any of the (synchromesh) gears? Worn synchromesh suggests a worn out gearbox. Replacement. (£££)

5. Accelerate hard into third gear and listen for bearing noise in the gearbox, then lift of suddenly and note any excessive lifting of the gearlever which shows tired gearbox/overdrive mountings. (£)

6. Try overdrive on third and fourth gears under acceleration and on over-run. Some hesitation to engage is acceptable (especially on earlier D-types), and it may be necessary to ease the throttle when going *into* overdrive. (£-£££, for overhaul)

7. Cruising at around 50 mph, gently tickle the accelerator on and off whilst listening for rear end noises. A regular knocking is likely to be an axle shaft U/J (£), a rumble on over-run is a differential problem (£££) and this can be a weak spot on the 2 litre cars.

8. Still at 50 mph, slip the clutch, build up the revs and re-engage the clutch. It should bite cleanly with no slip. (££ for clutch parts)

9. 'Labour' the car up a steep hill listening for crankshaft bearing noise and pinking. Pinking can be easily cured but it does suggest engine tuning has been neglected and if the

situation has existed for some time, there may be damage to valves, valve seats and even pistons. (££) Slight pinking has to be lived with in the Mk 1 six-cylinder engines as these were designed to operate on the highest octane petrol which is, of course, no longer available. Retard the timing from 13° to 7° BTDC.

10.   Driving along a clear straight road, note any tendency for the car to pull to one side. This could be due to tyre wear problems, but examine the tyres later to see what has caused the abnormal wear. Apply the footbrake with increasing pressure and again note any pulling to one side. This may be a sticking caliper piston or badly adjusted front drums, but it could be a scored or rusted disc – check this later. (££-£££)

11.   Apply the handbrake whilst travelling at around 10 mph (Don't lock the rear wheels) and again check for pulling. Could be worn brakes or seized linkages. (£-££)

12.   Check for propshaft and front wheel vibration at all speeds. The front suspension is a good system and vibration at the steering wheel will almost certainly be caused by lack of wheel balance, a worn steering rack, or wheel bearings (£-££). Propshaft vibration can be difficult to cure, especially on a convertible where it may appear as noise, shuddering or scuttle shake.

13.   Test suspension by braking hard; there should be no appreciable bonnet dip. There should be little roll when cornering under power, except on the softer sprung Heralds. General bangs and rattles from the suspension are cured by re-bushing but seized bushes may cause a dismantling problem at the rear. (£-££ for bushes and/or shock absorbers.)

14.   When driving downhill on the over-run and when accelerating hard, check behind for blue smoke signifying worn rings

and/or valve guides – if excessive, a re-bore may be needed. (££-£££)

15.   Listen for wheel bearing rumble which may well disappear or increase when cornering, depending on which side is the faulty bearing (£-££). Constant rumbling is likely to be differential bearings which are easy to change (£-££). But on the Mk 2 suspension is a more lengthy job.

16.   Mis-firing under acceleration or general poor running when warm on Spitfire 1500s points to faulty carburettor 'wax-stats'. Check heat shield, position of number plate (over radiator grille?) or modify carbs.

17.   Keep an eye on the water temperature gauge throughout the test, especially on the 1500 Spitfire (££, if overheating), and try the heater which may suffer from a faulty water valve. (£)

18.   At the end of the road test the tick-over should be 600 to 800 rpm. If higher, adjust the slow running speed as this may be masking a tuning defect.

19.   Open the bonnet and examine the engine while it is running. Check for oil fumes and oil and water leaks. Fumes from the oil filler cap when removed may be due to a blocked crankcase breather (£), but otherwise points to advanced engine wear. (£££)

20.   Switch off the engine and listen to the radiator and its expansion bottle for signs of boiling up. (£-££)

21.   Check the dipstick for evidence of water in the sump which is probably due to a head gasket fault (£-££) but on later engines, may be the result of a cracked cylinder head. (££-£££)

Boot inspection

1.   Check the existence of spare wheel, jack and handle, hub cap puller and tool pouch. Examine the spare wheel for kerb damage and condition of tyre, (£-££ for replacement, if available)

2.   Check the condition of floor mat on Herald/Vitesse and fibre boards in Spitfire/GT6. (£-££)

3.   See that the boot lid rubber seal is good and that the boot can be locked. (£-££)

4.   If wire wheels are fitted, there should be a mallet for the spinners and also a spanner if hexagon nuts are fitted. (£)

Stage C: Dirty hands

Engine bay

1.   Check wiring for disconnections, damage and repairs. (£-££ for a new loom)

2.   Look around the engine for signs of new gaskets, evidence of recent dismantling or any other work and ask what and why.

3.   Check for oil and water leaks and examine water hoses – check radiator for signs of repair.

4.   Examine engine mountings for oil contamination/tearing. (£)

5.   Note condition of battery and terminals and on Spitfire/GT6. Check for corrosion in battery well. (£-££)

6.   Feel for leaks under carbs and fuel pump and piping. Check throttle spindles for play – may require reconditioned set of carbs. (££-£££)

7.   Have someone turn the steering wheel back and forth whilst you watch for movement in the rubber rack mountings (very early Heralds use solid aluminium mountings). Cheap and easy to replace rubbers as applicable (£). If oil contaminated look for evidence of wear in the crankshaft timing cover seal. (£)

8.   Check brake discs for scoring and rusting, also condition of pads. (££-£££)

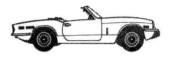

Front underside

With the front end on ramps check the following.

1. Condition of exhaust system and mountings. (££)

2. Oil leakage from bellhousing – crankshaft oil seal failed – major repair job. (££ for parts)

3. Oil leakage from gearbox/overdrive output oil seal. Easily replaced. (£ but time consuming – gearbox removal)

4. Leakage from front shock absorbers. Coil springs should not be sagged. (££)

5. Place a stout screwdriver between the suspension lower wishbone and the trunnion and attempt to lever apart. Movement here will require new inexpensive trunnion bushes or new wishbone arms if bolt holes go oval. Do the same with the shock absorber lower mounting to test for softening of the rubber bush. (£-££)

6. Carefully examine the main chassis members where the suspension is attached, for kinks or cracks which will be the result of severe crash damage. If you find this, the car is best avoided.

7. Move on to the front outriggers, poking with a screwdriver, particularly at the outer ends where they are bolted to the body. Chassis sections can be replaced but body corrosion here is difficult to repair properly. (££-£££)

8. Examine the chassis side rails on the Herald/Vitesse and then the middle outriggers on all cars (£ each for parts). Have a good look and prod over the remainder of the underbody and the central chassis sections, though corrosion on this part of the chassis is very unlikely.

Rear underside

1. With the rear wheels on ramps, continue inspection of the chassis rails and underbody, arriving at the rear outriggers just ahead of the rear wheels on Herald/Vitesse. These are omitted on the Spitfire and GT6 which have a strengthened rear floor heelboard instead. Check shocker mounting "towers" carefully. Check the outriggers/heelboard for corrosion, especially at the attachment of the suspension radius arms and seat belt mounting points.

2. Move inboard to the chassis centre sections and probe carefully for rust on the chassis rearward of this point around the differential mounting area. Any corrosion in the centre sections here is very serious and may be impossible to repair. New chassis are not available, nor are repair sections for this area.

3. Whilst in this area, use the screwdriver to lever the differential in its mountings and to check for movement in axle and propshaft U/Js. The slightest movement between yokes requires a new joint. (£)

4. Complete the inspection of the exhaust system and underbody brake pipes and hoses and handbrake cable. (£-££)

5. On vehicles with Mk 2 suspension, check the Rotoflex joints in the axle shafts. Their rubber segments tend to separate from the metal plates and whilst replacements are not expensive, they do represent a major task. (£-££)

6. The Vitesse and Herald have rear outriggers on the chassis extending from under the boot floor and these should be examined for corrosion together with the underbody where attached. Again, these sections are easily and cheaply replaced. (£ each)

7. Check for oil leaks from the differential pinion seal. (£)

8. Spitfire/GT6 should be carefully checked under the boot and wheel arches for corrosion – the top rear damper mountings on GT6 Mk 2 and early Mk 3 cars are fixed to the inner wheel arches. Rust problems here can be expensive. (££-£££)

9. Condition of lower rear quarters are important on Spitfire/GT6 as it may entail rear panel replacements. (££)

10. Examine rear spring for sag and broken leaves. (££)

11. Test rear trunnions and suspension bushes by levering as for front trunnions. (£)

*To complete the tests, move the car off the ramp and jack the front wheels off the ground. Test for wheel bearing play by rocking each wheel whilst grasping the tyre at 12- and 6-o'clock positions. Owing to the design, a very slight movement in the bearing is acceptable on the front wheel. Don't confuse with trunnion or trunnion bush wear. Remember that no part of you – not even a hand beneath the wheel – should be beneath a car supported only on a jack.

12. If wire wheels are fitted, check the nuts or spinners are really tight and then the splines for play by attempting to rock the wheels back and forward while an assistant holds the brake pedal hard down. Do not confuse movement with a worn trunnion.

To finalise, go over the bodywork once more and make a point of ensuring you have looked at every square inch. Run your hands lightly over panels, since they often pick out undulations and imperfections that the eye may miss. Also have another listen to the engine before making any decisions.

Availability of parts changes constantly as more components are re-manufactured and original supplies become exhausted, although in general, supply of body, mechanical and main trim parts such as seat covering, is getting better all the time. Check! Advertisements and text in the Triumph Sports Six Club's magazine *The Courier* provides details of location, availability and prices of new and used spares; and membership of the owners club is well worthwhile before you purchase your car, as well as afterwards.

By Eddie A Evans, T.Eng, M.B.E.S., M.I.Diag.E. with additional information from Peter Williams.

Buying – Illustrated

The following pictures give an over-view of what to look for when buying. Further pointers regarding originality can be found under 'Production Modifications', while the restoration chapters give a very full view of work that might be required,

BG1.   Have a good look round the body. Both Heralds and Vitesses are prone to rusting around the front wings . . .

BG2.   . . . and tread plates.

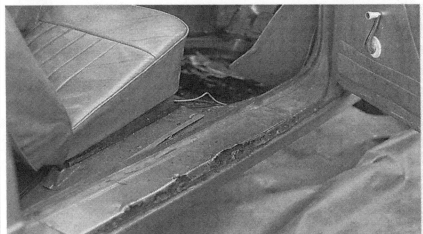

BG3.   Check the doors which often rust from the inside out from the bottom of the door upwards. Maybe just a new skin is required in which case double check the frame itself. A second-hand example may be the answer if the frame has corroded badly.

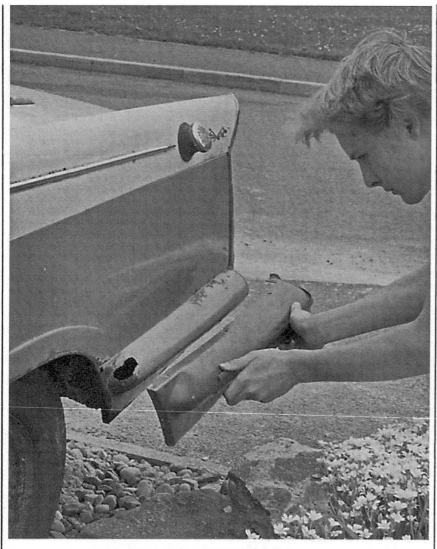

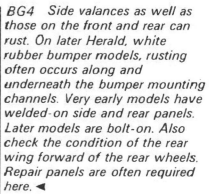

BG4   Side valances as well as those on the front and rear can rust. On later Herald, white rubber bumper models, rusting often occurs along and underneath the bumper mounting channels. Very early models have welded-on side and rear panels. Later models are bolt-on. Also check the condition of the rear wing forward of the rear wheels. Repair panels are often required here. ◄

BG5.▲ Continuing around the back, check for damaged panels including the boot lid return lips and chrome – rather obvious here.

BG6.   A common complaint with earlier GT6s is rot along the lower edge of the roof and rear valance seam.

BG7.▼ Early Coupé roofs especially rust around all the edges.

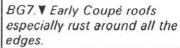

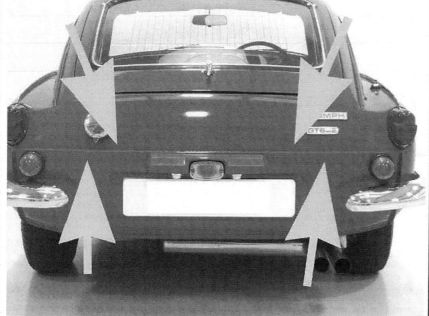

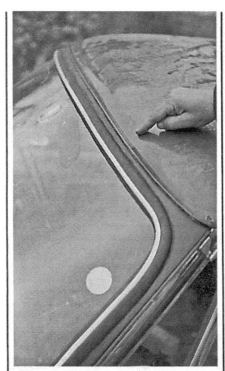

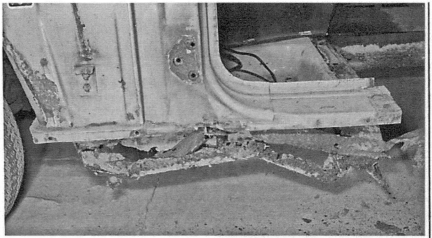

BG10. These side rails look pretty horrific, but repair is quite straight forward and inexpensive if you do the work yourself.

BG8. ▲ GT6s can suffer from roof front edge rot. Damage here may require part replacement or lead loading. Coming down from the roof line, check that the vertical windscreen frame seam is sound, as damp can collect behind the front door glass rubber seal with the usual result.

BG9. Have a good look at the Herald/Vitesse's side rails and outriggers. This check is just as relevant to front outriggers on Spitfires and GT6s. Previous repairs as shown here may have been botched. Replacement is not difficult as long as the main chassis rails are all right. If not, steer clear. ▼

BG11. ▲ Chassis mounting points at the back . . .

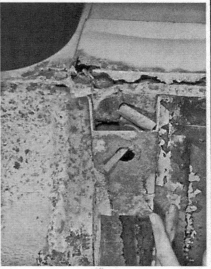

BG12. ▲ . . . and side. Poke hard with an old screwdriver to test the extent of any corrosion.

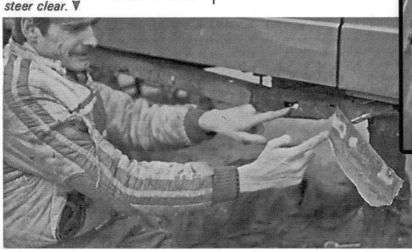

BG13. ▲ On Heralds and Vitesses, check underneath the carpets for thin or holed panels in the footwells and beneath the rear seat space . . .

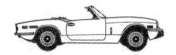

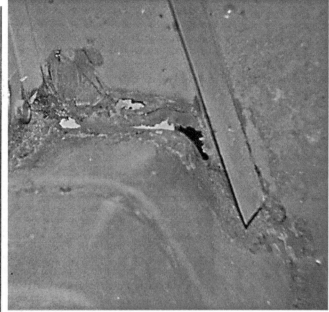

BG14. . . . and around the rear wheel arch.

BG15. Convertible Herald and Vitesse models should be fitted with additional interlocking safety catches on the doors . . . ▶

BG16. . . . and on the B post below the door lock. ◀

BG17. On Spitfires and GT6s again, check around the front corners for rust on the front wings and early single skin and late double skinned valances.

BG18. Late cars may also show some minor impact damage to the black plastic bumper over-riders. These simply unbolt and can be replaced with fibreglass items if desired. ▼

BG19. Continuing rearwards, check out the front wings behind the wheels.

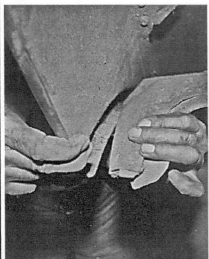

BG20. If there's rot here it may also be the reason for the wing and wheel arch becoming disconnected. ▲

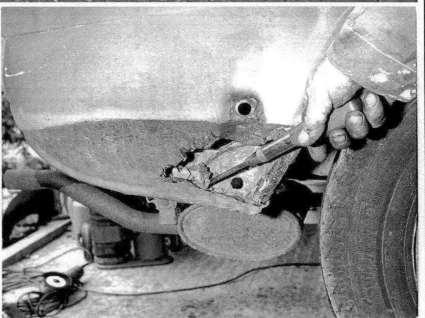

BG21. Rear wings also tend to rot below the bumper line . . . ▲

BG22. . . . and in front of the rear wheels.

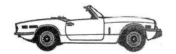 

BG23. The sills on Spitfires and GT6s are vital to the rigidity of the whole body. Sometimes the damage is obvious . . . ▲

BG24. . . . but take a good look at the state of the inner sills under the carpets too. The sill shown here has totally gone and should be replaced. The sill structure is made up of three panels plus end plates. All should be replaced not just the ones you can see. ►

BG25. If you don't replace the lot, this sort of rot could remain lurking behind. ◄

BG26. Unfortunately, rusting around the trailing arm and seat belt mounting points is all too common. Repair these areas first before carrying out sill replacements.

BG27. Pressed steel half floor repair sections are available from specialists mentioned in this book.

BG28. Lift out the spare wheel (check the wheel and tyre are of the same size as fitted on the rest of the car) and give the boot floor a good prod with an old screwdriver.

BG29. Don't forget to lift the bonnet and check the front and top bulkhead regions. Battery boxes are also prone to holing through but can be replaced with new. ▼

BG30. Applicable to all the cars, try to assess the chassis condition around the differential. If damaged here, in principle it is repairable. ▲

BG31. Mechanically, all the cars are much the same. Check for wear in the steering, which should be very direct, and in ball joints and wheel bearings by jacking up and rocking the wheels. This should also show up any wear in the trunnion or trunnion bushes. As with any car, the state of shock absorbers all round can be checked with a bounce test. If the car rebounds more than once, new 'shocks' are in order.

BG32. *Tired front and rear springs should be checked. Note any difference between ride heights on each side of the car.*

BG33. *Different length drive shafts were fitted to early and late swing spring Spitfires (later ones were longer – see Production Modifications), so check your intended purchase hasn't been repaired with one of each.*

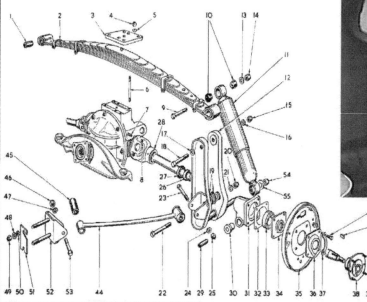

BG35.▲ *Though bodywork is the major concern, a tidy interior is a good selling and buying point. Early Heralds have fibre-board dashes which tend to crack especially around the choke control. Earlier models had a horizontal line of control knobs above the ash tray rather than arranged in an arc as shown here. Still later models were given a metal finger board to stiffen up the knob mounting area. Another difference on very early 948 cars was that the flasher repeater colour is amber rather than green. Also, the main beam warning light was red rather than blue on early Heralds (1200 included).*

BG34. *After a test drive, clonks in the transmission may be due to worn UJs (try reversing then* *going forwards a few times in succession to check this). Alternatively lever inside the UJ yokes to assess wear. (Ensure the car is properly secured by axle stands or ramps, not just by a jack when doing this). On Vitesse 2-litre Mk 2s, GT6 Mk 2 and early Mk 3s, a further cause for transmission irregularities could be worn rotoflex couplings. Replace with the original 'Metalastic' manufactured units if possible. Repro ones tend to wear out very quickly.*

BG36. Later Heralds and Vitesses all have wooden faced dashes as standard. A more luxurious burr walnut was an optional extra on some models. Check for cracked, unmatched and faded veneers. A nice selling point of this well presented Mk 2 Vitesse Convertible is the original wide radio mounting with separate speaker beneath . . .

BG37. . . . as is this original tool kit.

BG38. ▶ All GT6s and all but the earliest and MkIV Spitfires have wood veneer dashboards so the same rules apply.

BG39. ▲ Seats and panels should be checked for splits. Rear seats were an optional extra on Herald Coupés. On these models, a separate and matching fixed trim panel should be revealed as the rear seat is folded forwards. On 948 cc saloons, lowering the rear seat back allowed additional access to the boot space.

BG40. Rear seats were also an optional extra on GT6s. A little cramped perhaps but OK for small children.

BG41.   As with interiors, the state of the engine bay says a lot about the owner's attitude towards the car. Rather tired engine bays like this . . .

BG42.   . . . can be turned into Concours examples like this but it takes a lot of hard work and dedication to achieve and keep it this way.

BG43.   An equally well presented GT6 engine bay with just a couple of revisions. Both Mk 2 and Mk 3 cars were fitted with alternators. All the other cars apart from Mk IV and 1500 Spitfires were fitted with dynamo charging systems as standard.

BG44.   When it comes to choosing the right type of car for you, the choice is endless from the modestly priced and fun-packed sportscar, the Spitfire . . .

BG45.   . . . to the practicality of the Herald Estate.

BG46. If choosing an early Spitfire, ensure that the hood irons are included. If not fitted to the car, they should be stored in the boot along the sides of the fuel tank and secured with a leather strap. This vehicle is fitted with a non-standard roll-over cage.

BG47. Whether it's a Herald or Vitesse Convertible or Spitfire make sure that you have a good look at the hood. Check for splits and discoloration. A hood bag and a tonneau are nice additions . . .

BG49. ▲ Overdrive is a very worthwhile optional extra to have. Whilst not necessarily improving overall fuel consumption, it makes for much more relaxed driving. It doesn't actually put much, if anything, on the price of the car, either.

BG50. ► Other optional extras on earlier Spitfires and GT6s include wire wheels. Unfortunately, the splines on these wheels are rather short and tend to wear out quickly especially on the more powerful cars and even more so if the nuts or spinners are not tightened properly. There's no doubt that they're very attractive (if kept clean) but check splines for wear (by driving the car and listening for clonks) and for loose spokes, by pushing the car slowly along, engine off, and listening

for cracks and groans. Later Spitfires were offered with bolt-on wire wheels.

BG51. Sunroofs are also a sought after extra on Herald and Vitesse Saloons and GT6s. Perhaps the best liked is an original fabric type. As with soft tops, check for ripped or cracked fabric and distorted or poorly fitting hardware.

BG48. . . . as is an original steel hardtop, the early ones being particularly stylish. Later models have opening rear side windows. Check the headlining for rips.

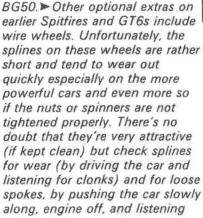

3 Bodywork

This section shows some of the tools and equipment that the author has used while working on his many projects. All of the equipment shown here is non-car specific - so I'm sure you'll forgive the lack of Triumphs in this section.

COLLECTING THE SET

You will never have a complete set of tools; there will always be something else that you need! But over the years, if you buy equipment a little at a time, as you need it, you will accumulate a surprisingly large range of items. I still use some of the same tools that were bought for me as Christmas and birthday presents when I was a teenager and, now that I'm middle-aged, I give the same advice that I was given then always buy the best tools you can afford.

Actually, having said that, times have changed and it certainly pays to shop around. Tools that you won't need to use regularly, such as an impact screwdriver or a rubbing block for use with abrasive paper can be picked up for a song and will usually have been made in China. In general, British, German and American hand tools are better made and last longer than Far-Eastern tools, although most power tools seem to be built there: just look for a reputable maker.

When it comes to large and expensive items, such as a compressor or welder, it again pays to stick to a known maker rather than to take a chance with an apparently cheap tool who you may never have heard of.

▶ T&E1. Although this chapter is about bodywork, there is often a need to remove mechanical items to enable you to get at the part to be repaired. In the worst cases, you may have to take an engine out, which is where this an engine hoist comes into its own.

▶ T&E2. This type of engine hoist has the advantage of being able to be folded into a really small space for storage.

TOP TIP!
Buy one with larger wheels than these, if you can. It's a heavy - in fact top-heavy - old lump to move around and larger wheels would make it much safer and more stable.

MIG welding see p.308-on

► T&E3. For the serious home restorer or home repairer (and many enthusiasts really are this serious!) a scissor car lift brings almost professional standards of access to the home workshop. If you have ever tried welding under the car's floor while lying on your back on the ground, and you've got a lot of repair or restoration work to do, you'll think this was made in heaven, rather than in an engineering workshop!

The only downside is that the centre of the car's underside is not accessible on many models because of the frame and supports - something to consider.

► T&E4. Where access beneath the car needs to be totally unimpeded, or for extra support when fitting and aligning sills or floorpan, Holden Vintage & Classic among others can supply these extra-tall but very stable support stands, capable of supporting the whole vehicle off the ground while you drag the scissor lift out of the way.

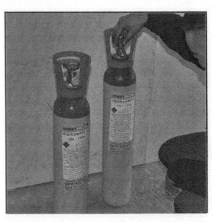

▲ T&E7. Unless you use spattery, horrible gasless MIG wire, you can't do without gas! In the UK, Hobbyweld are great for affordable gas cylinders, also available for home use. Much more economical than disposable cannisters.

▲ T&E5. For serious bodywork repairs, you won't be able to get far without the use of a welder of some sort. The type of welding that gives you the best quality while being the easiest to learn how to use (always provided that you carry out preparation immaculately) is a MIG welder. This is an inverter-type MIG from Inverter Fusion Ltd. Inverter MIGs are lighter and provide a smoother weld, which enables them to handle almost any car bodywork repairs that you are likely to encounter.
This one has brazing and even TIG-welding capabilities.

▲ T&E6. The most versatile type of welder – although it does have certain drawbacks – is an oxy-acetylene gas welding set. This is the BOC Portapack set which is capable of carrying out the smallest welding or brazing job as well as quite heavy-duty cutting through thick steel.
When the bulk of this manual was written, it's all there was but these days, a MIG welding set is something you'd purchase well before a gas welding set.

▼ T&E8. The cleanest, neatest welds of all can be carried out by a spot-welder, and you ought to think about obtaining one along with extension arms which enable you to get round all sorts of obstructions.

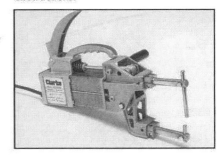

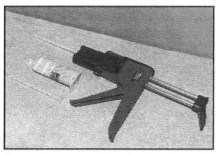

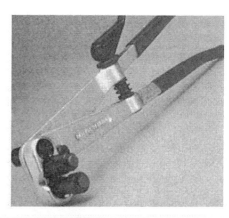

▶ T&E11. This is another Sykes-Pickavant tool, one that is invaluable if you have to cut out and replace sections of rusty steel. It pulls the edge of the sheet along between two rollers which form a shoulder on the edge of the steel. This allows you to join two flat pieces of metal with all the smoothness of a butt joint but with the strength and ease of a welded lap-joint. Wonderful!

▲ T&E9. Why, you might ask, is this 3M glue gun and two-pack epoxy resin kit shown next to the welding section? The reason is quite simple. For certain repairs, it is possible to use adhesive instead of welding and, if you doubt that it would be strong enough, remember that the entire structure of the Jaguar XJ220 supercar, capable of 220 mph, was fixed together almost exclusively with such adhesives. And we haven't heard of any falling apart yet!

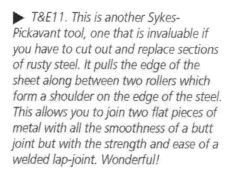

▲ T&E12. Most home mechanics will find this a little out of their price bracket but the Sykes-Pickavant folder is the best way by far to create perfectly formed bends in sheet steel. Bear in mind that you can buy ready-folded strips of steel from most bodywork parts suppliers.

▲ T&E10. Before welding steel, you will have to cut it. If you have a lot of cutting out to do, these Sykes-Pickavant cutting tools will slice through steel like nobody's business and can also cut gentle curves. For smaller amounts of cutting, regular tin snips are fine.

◀ T&E13. Another tool that you can scarcely do without is a compressor. This is a typical compressor from the bottom end of the range, both in terms of price and performance. A tiny compressor will struggle to power a spray gun but you'll be able to use it to inflate tyres and carry out other lightweight jobs.

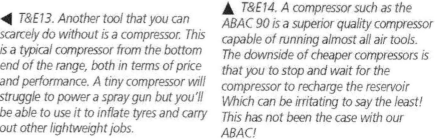

▲ T&E14. A compressor such as the ABAC 90 is a superior quality compressor capable of running almost all air tools. The downside of cheaper compressors is that you to stop and wait for the compressor to recharge the reservoir Which can be irritating to say the least! This has not been the case with our ABAC!
It's also relatively quiet, which keeps the neighbours happier...

▲ T&E15. The Clarke Raider 120 is a V-twin mobile compressor, which produces plenty of air for spraying, inflating and air tools. Mine performed well for a good few years until pensioned off for the ABAC unit. Solid performance though pretty noisy!

▲ T&E16. As you develop your spraying skills, you will undoubtedly wish to invest in a better gun and you will find them far easier to use into the bargain! There is a huge range available but you must make sure that your compressor is capable of coping with the gun you choose, and for the DIY sprayer, the dearest equipment may not be necessary.

▼ T&E17. The Clarke Air Kit 400 provides a very useful and remarkably low-cost set of air tools capable of being powered by even the smaller compressors.

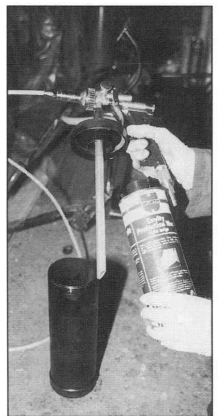

▲ T&E19. There is a range of Bosch (and other) electric random orbit (RO) sanders which will keep going when any compressor other than a large one has had to stop for breath.
An RO sander is an essential tool if you have large areas of filler to sand because it doesn't leave scratch marks or furrows. TOP TIP!
Don't use a sanding pad with took stick-on sanding discs! The surface will forever become contaminated with dust, turning them into 'fly-off' discs!
Discs such as the 3M Hookit system uses a Velcro-type of adhesion between the back of the sanding disc and the front of the sanding pad. Problem solved!

◀ T&E18. Another use to which you will be able to put your compressor is spraying cavity protection wax. This Würth injection gun is dual-purpose. It takes throw-away Würth screw-on canisters and also has its own large separate canisters for injecting any protection wax that you may want to use 'loose'. You may feel that this is an expensive piece of equipment but, in terms of protecting your vehicle against rust, it's actually very cheap!

Hand-powered, cheap-and-cheerful injectors simply don't atomise the protection wax or blast it far enough into nooks and crannies for it to be effective and then the whole exercise will have been a waste of time and money.

▲ T&E20. For hand sanding, 3M also produce a wide range of sanding blocks and papers, all using the same Hookit system. You will definitely need a hand block for sanding large areas of filler to prevent the surface from coming out wavy. 3M also produce small, disposable pads for fine finishing and their hand blocks and sheets have the facility for dust extraction equipment to be added (such as from an old vacuum cleaner) to keep potentially dangerous dust out of the air, and out of your, and other people's, lungs.

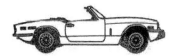

▲ T&E21. A plasma cutter can cut the most intricate shapes and, when set correctly, rapidly makes clean cuts in various thicknesses ferrous metals. of This is the Inverter Fusion iCut40 which, like the company's welders, are based on inverter technology making them much lighter in weight for the same power output. Plasma cutters utilise an electric arc and a jet of air from an air compressor.

▲ T&E24. Another invaluable tool is an angle grinder. This is the Bosch PWS 7-115. A beautifully built piece of kit which is perfect for using with grinding and cutting discs but, when used with this twisted-wire brush (available from any bodyshop supplier), scours paint and rust off steel in seconds. Always wear goggles when using an angle grinder.

MIG welding
see p.308-on

▲ T&E22. This Bosch Compact Belt Sander was produced primarily for use on wood but, with the correct type of blue belts, can be used for car bodywork and is handy for getting into small spaces, for enlarging slots and even for sharpening tools such as cold chisels and the like.

▲ T&E23. At the other end of the sanding scale is this Dremel Multi tool. It's like an electric drill but it's not! It runs at variable speeds, right up to far higher speeds than are reached by electric drills and it takes a wide range of small attachments, including this sanding head. It can be used for drilling, grinding, polishing, and almost anything else you can think of. So, if you need to remove the head from a pop rivet in a confined space, grind out rust from a recessed area or clean out a crack in plastic ready for repairing it, this is your man!

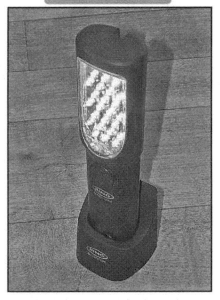

▲ T&E25. A rechargeable inspection lamp, such as a hands-free, high-power, LED lamp provides hours of energy-efficient light, a cool bulb that will never cause burning, and great resistance to breakage. Before purchase, decide which will be best for you. A wide or magnetic base? A hook for hanging?

§T&E26. One power tool with a lot of domestic applications, as well as being almost indispensable when carrying out restoration work a power washer. Be aware that cheaper washers don't use corrosion-resistant components and often fail once they have been used then left standing for a while. Kranzle power washer shown here made from highest quality materials, and will still be working when you want to pressure-wash the drive next year or the year after.

▲ T&E30. Another invaluable Makita tool is the BTD140Z 18V LXT Lithium-Ion Impact Driver. It produces 145Nm maximum torque, has both forward and reverse action and, once again, there's an integral job light. If you've never used an impact driver for dismantling and reassembly, you wouldn't believe how much time you can save. The BTD140Z shares its batteries with the BHP452RFE drill.

Note: LXT Lithium-Ion provides longer run time and a self-discharge rate that is five times lower than conventional batteries. The 45-minute charger and battery communicate throughout the charging process, using the built-in chip in the battery and built-in CPU chip in the charger. Clever stuff!

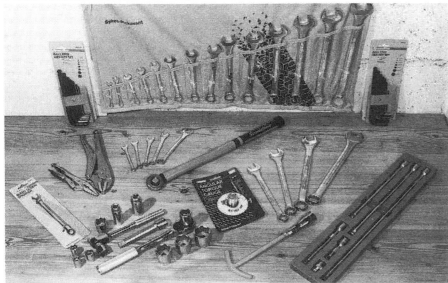

▲ T&E27. Cheap handtools just won't last and can be dangerous. Good ol' Sykes Pickavant remain one of the best-made and most utterly dependable brands of workshop tools and equipment. After 30 years, I still use these every day.

T&E28. At the top of the 'must-have' scale comes a cordless electric drill. These days, Makita li-ion drills are widely regarded as the best in the business. They are light in weight, but extremely strong. Their li-ion batteries can be recharged without damage, regardless of their state of discharge. In the background is the earlier model which I've been using - and abusing - for a good many years now.

▲ T&E31. If your budget -- or your workshop space – won't run to a stand-alone pillar drill, a portable drill stand will turn your mains-powered drill into a perfectly adequate home-user version. A hand vice is also an essential piece of equipment for gripping small workpieces.

T&E29. I've only recently 'discovered' Lok-Type socket sets from Welzh Werkzeug. They're amazing! Tough and strong as any socket sets you'll find, they even work on 90% rounded-off nuts. You'll find a few of those on any restoration project!.

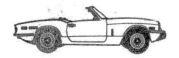

Fuel tank removal

FTR1. Set the tank pick-up pipe in the reserve position and drain the tank by releasing the fuel pipe where it attaches to the fuel pump. Separate the rubber feed pipe located at the top of the tank from the main fuel pipe. Release the fuel cap wire by undoing the single screw.

FTR2.▼ Remove the sender electrical connections.

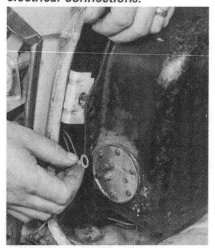

FTR3. Next release the tank securing screws at the front and back . . .▼

FTR4.◄ . . . followed by the two tank/boot lid stay screws on the top. Don't let the boot lid fall on top of your head. It's quite heavy!

FTR5. Push the wing/filler pipe seal through into the boot and withdraw the tank.

Safety

Bear in mind the correct safety procedures outlined in the Appendix when working with sheet metal. Wear thick industrial type gloves, especially when working with cut or rusty edges and wear goggles when working with sheet metal grinders or cutting equipment. Assemble grinding wheels with enormous care, following manufacturer's instructions. Beware of sparks from the grinder and hot metal when cutting away. Again, wear goggles and thick industrial gloves. Ensure that the car is securely raised off the ground in such a way that:

a) it cannot topple onto anyone underneath it, bearing in mind the amount of force that will be applied to it and

b) it will not twist or distort as old panels are cut out.

NEVER rely on the handbrake to hold a car that is on a slope or on ramps. Ensure that the wheels are chocked when using jacks or ramps. Use axle stands when working under the car, NOT the jack.

Take all the usual precautions when welding. See the appendix at the end of this book and contact your supplier for specific safety information. You should seek training in welding skills before tackling oxy-acetylene welding. Follow the maker's safety instructions carefully before carrying out electric arc welding of any kind. Wear goggles when working beneath the car. NEVER attempt work for which you are not qualified. Have a qualified specialist check over each stage of your work before you proceed. If in any doubt whatsoever, have important work such as panel and component alignment and welding carried out for you by a qualified specialist.

Tread plate replacement

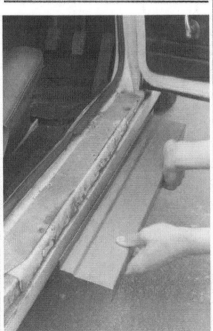

TP1.▲ *Tread plates often rot as shown. The replacement top plate is shown alongside. Where applicable, drill out the pop rivets which hold the alloy kick plate in place.*

Some models have single tread plates and some double. Replacement is much the same in either case though double skinned models tend to be more prone to rot. Here we show how to replace the tread plates on a Vitesse Convertible. Start by removing the side sills as shown in SR1-3.

TP2.▼ *Cut through the spot welds along the floor and rear edges. Air tools do help but they're certainly not essential . . .*

TP3.▼ *. . . and cut out the lower panel as necessary.*

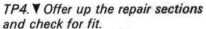

TP4.▼ *Offer up the repair sections and check for fit.*

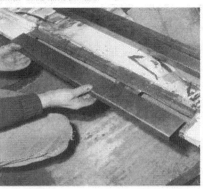

TP5. After securing the rear edge, the two panels can be further fixed in place by drilling a series of holes . . .

TP6.▼ . . . and MIG welding through. Next, weld the panels along the lower edge.

TP7. The front and rear body sections split along this seam, and normally, this joint is not welded but is simply sealed with a flexible mastic. If desired however, it could be permanently welded or brazed. ▼

Sill removal

SR1. Herald/Vitesse sills are little more than cosmetic features though do offer some improved rigidity if the lower tags are correctly screwed (or welded) to the chassis side rails. Derek Johnson takes out one of the screws holding the sill in place (sometimes you may find that the sills have been spot welded in place). As a last resort, grind off, drill out and re-tap. ▼

SR2. The sill just lifts away from the car.

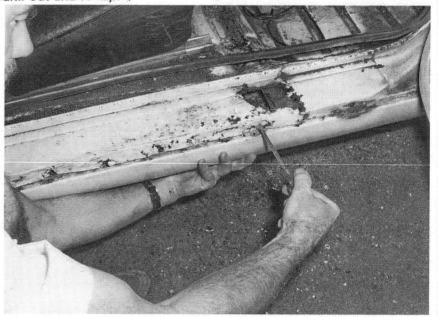

SR3.▼ Mounting straps have elongated holes to allow adjustment when re-fitting.

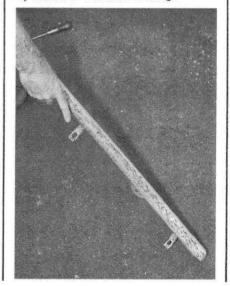

Rear over-rider removal

ROR1.▲ Before removing the rear and side valances, the rear chrome overriders need to be unbolted. The overriders are held in place by two bolts, one which screws into an upper caged nut just seen in the picture, and a second lower one which passes through the tube shown beneath the rear lamp unit.

ROR2. Unfortunately, one or both of these bolts are often locked in solid so the answer is to saw them off. If the over-rider is in generally good condition, the bolts can be removed after a good soaking in penetrating oil by gripping the caged nut/bracket in self-locking grips or similar . . . ▼

ROR3.▲ . . . and then unscrewing the bolt. You could equally well grip the bolt shaft in a vice.

Rear and side valance replacement

RVR1. On later Heralds and all Vitesses, the valances bolt on and are simply removed by unbolting. First, remove the boot rubber seal and remove the horizontal row of bolts below the boot aperture. ▶

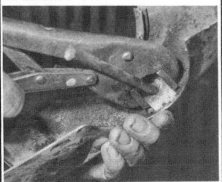

RVR2.▲ Unscrew the bolts beneath the side light assembly . . .

RVR3.▼ . . . followed by those which connect the rear to the side valance. Valances with rubber bumpers tend to rot along the line of the bumper attachment as shown here.

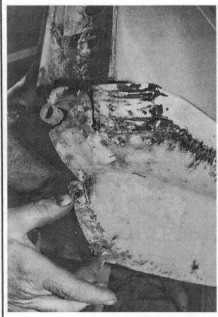

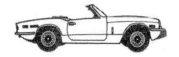 

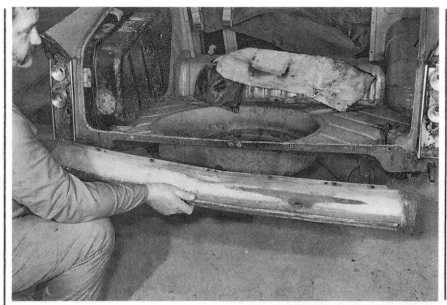

recommend that replacement valances should be bolted in place on early cars just as with later ones.

RVR9. ▼ Any small repairs can be carried out along the way . . .

RVR4. ▲ The rear valance can then be removed.

RVR5. ▼ The side valances can then be removed by releasing the self-tappers (or possible bolts) along the lower rear wing seam. . .

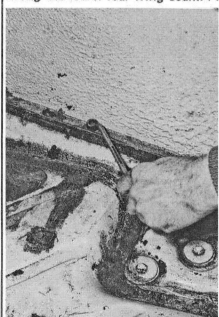

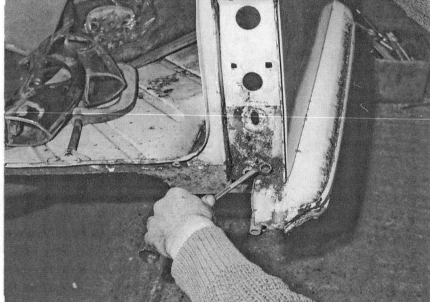

RVR6. ▲ . . . and beneath the side light unit . . .

RVR7.   . . . allowing the valance to fall away. ▶

RVR8. ◀ Early Herald valances are welded on, side and rear, and will therefore need to be chiselled and ground off. Once the main section has been removed, clean up the flange area but leave the top edge of the side and rear valances spot welded in place as these form the return lip and boot seal lips on their respective panels. Triumph used to

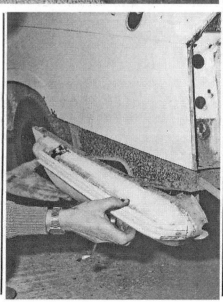

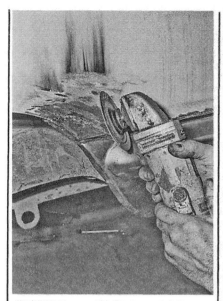

RVR13. . . . drill holes into the side valance as appropriate. Some repro panels are not pre-drilled here. These, however, fitted well and were purchased from John Kipping, Triumph Spares (see 'Specialists' section). ▼

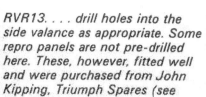

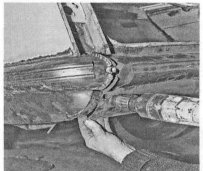

RVR10.▲ . . . and merged into the general contours later.

RVR11.   Align the new valances and simply bolt and self-tap back on. If bolting new panels onto early cars, carefully align and drill new holes in the rear wing flange as necessary. Use new clips where relevant and a flexible sealer between the side valances and the rear wing. ▶

RVR12.▼ After bolting along the top edges . . .

Rear floor repair

RF1.   Many Heralds and Vitesses show rot along the front edge of the rear inner wheel arch just as shown here. Often, the floor pan further ahead of the wheel arch will also be weakened with age. Check this out by prodding with an old screwdriver.
Foot of column.▼

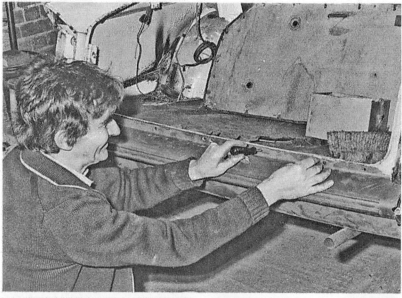

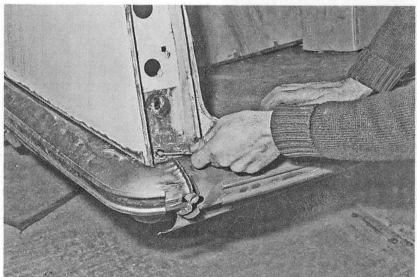

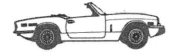

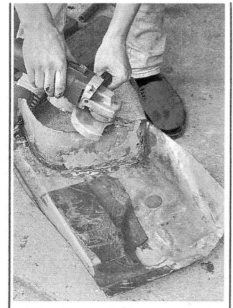

RF2. Often, the best source of repair panels will be a vehicle of similar type but well past saving. The floor section being cut to size here came from just such an abandoned shell. Although not shown here, wear gloves! ▲

RF3. Referring back to RF1, notice the absence of a body mounting bolt hole in the repair panel. The car under repair is an early 948 Herald. Later models with the Mk 2 chassis didn't have a body mounting at this particular point. ▼

RF4. Comparing the area to be repaired and the 'new' panel. ▲

RF5. Search out the rot and cut it all out. It's the only way to achieve a successful long term result. ▼

RF6. Clean the edges of the repair panel and main body section to bright metal and weld in place. At first, anchor the repair with short tacks spaced evenly around the work. These can be joined up later. There's no real need to use a totally continuous weld in these panels. The weld here looks a little rough but it's certainly strong enough. To be fair, this attempt was the first weld that Michael, the 16 year old operator had carried out. Not bad after only half an hour's instruction. ▼

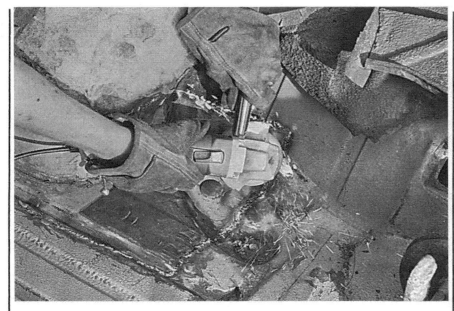

RF7. After welding, the raised beads should be ground back to make a neat job. Gloves now in use! Don't forget those goggles. Apply a good coat of paint as soon as possible. Bright new weld rusts very quickly.

Front footwell replacement

Another area that can benefit from using the same repair panel technique is the front footwell.

FF1. Cut or grind out the old footwell. In addition to wearing goggles and gloves, it's also a good idea to wear a few layers of general protective clothing and a hat – not quite as shown here. Also, cover up any areas of the car that could be damaged by the white hot sparks – especially inflammable trim and glass surfaces. ▼

FF2. Allow the old footwell to fall to the floor. ▼

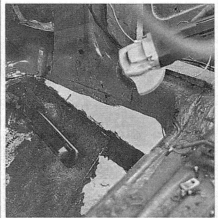

FF3. ▲ After similarly cutting out a donor panel (more than likely with a cold chisel if the donor shell is in a scrap yard) trim to size, prepare the edges for brazing or welding and fix in place. A further advantage of this type of repair panel is that it holds itself in. No clamps required. Much better than commonly available biscuit tins. Note that Mk 1 and Mk 2 chassis Herald floor pans are slightly different so the wrong one would require some modification to fit.

Rear wing repair

The rear wing often shows the effects of rust between the wheel arch and the B post. It's easily repaired with after-market repair panels which generally fit well.

RWR1. Rest (or better still, clamp) the repair panel in place and scribe a reference line. ▶

RWR2. Chop out a corresponding section of the wing allowing a small overlap for the shouldered edge of the repair to sit behind.

RWR3. ▲ Once removed, make any necessary repairs to the inner panels. This particular section can be left oversize and trimmed to match the repair panel later on.

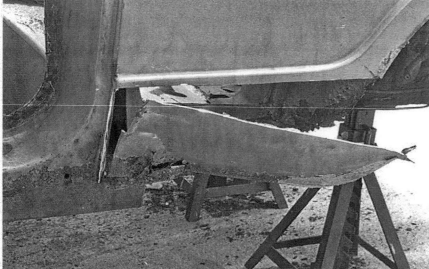

RWR4. ▲ Offer the repair into place and check for an accurate fit. Further trim the wing panel or repair section as necessary. A neat job at the front edge can be made by punching or drilling holes in the return flange and plug welding to the B post either by gas or preferably, MIG welding.

MIG welding see p.308-on

RWR5. ◀ In this case, the repair panel has been brazed in place with an arc welding/brazing kit. Quite sufficient for an unstressed panel.

TWR2. . . . and tack in the repair section. Notice the hole in the transverse chassis member showing this to be a Mk 1 Herald chassis car. Seal the joint with a flexible sealer. ▼

RWR6. ▲ Level any high weld or braze spots then finish off with a thin skim of body filler or lead loading.

Spare wheel well repair

Another quick and easy repair using either panels cut from a donor car or sheet steel is that to the rear bottom edge of the tyre well which often rots through on both Heralds and Vitesses.

TWR1. Simply cut out the rusty area and carefully grind back to clean, straight edges . . . ▼

Front wing repair panel

Most of the time, car body panels remain sound in all respects save for their lower edges. In the next few figures, the repair of the lower edge of a front wing is shown. As will be seen, repair panels are available but fitting the more complicated ones successfully is quite a skill and more often than not, replacing the whole panel, if available at reasonable cost, is an easier and in the end a more satisfactory solution.

HWP1. As normal, start by scribing a line around the repair panel and then cut out the rot as necessary up to the line.

HWP2. Tack weld or braze the repair in place on the outside . . .

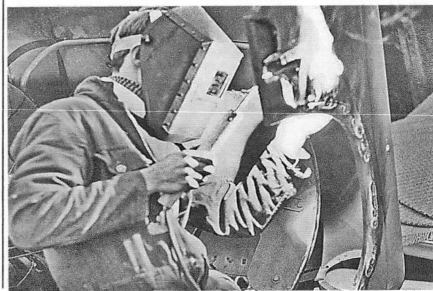

MIG
welding
see p.308-on

HWP3. . . . and inside. ▶

HWP4. After completing, clean up the surface and finish off with a little filler. ▼

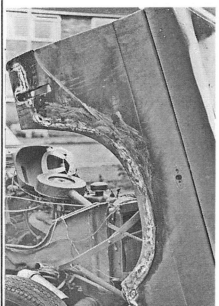

HWP5. ◀ In hindsight, the brazing on this repair was overdone which in turn resulted in excessive distortion (bear this in mind) so much so that it was decided to remove and replace the whole wing. MIG welding would have been a better technique. In addition, these repair panels are usually a poor fit and don't necessarily replace all of the rusty areas. If full panels are available, go for them every time!

Door stripdown & door skin replacement

The work in this sequence was carried out on 'Terry' Johnson's pride and joy. Her Herald Convertible is featured in several areas of this book. Repairs to Saloon and Convertible doors are identical.

HVD1.► Start by removing the door stay bracket retaining rivet with a sharp cold chisel. Replace later with a clevis pin and split pin (the same as used to retain the handbrake cables at the drums) or even a suitable nut and bolt.

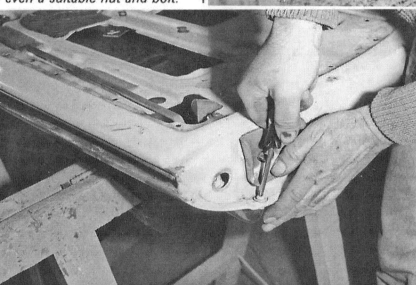

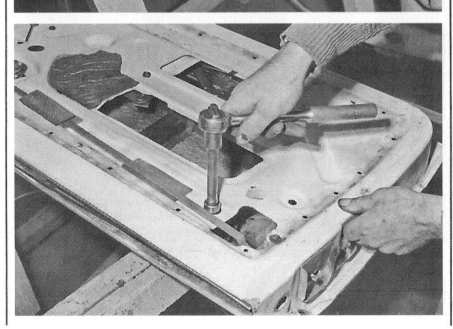

HVD2.▼ Next, remove the six door hinge bolts. Early models use two bolts and a rose headed set screw at each hinge. If the screw is overtight as was the case here, loosen off with an impact screwdriver, such as the type made by Sykes-Pickavant.

HVD3. With the door off the car, begin dismantling by removing the outer door handle screw . . .

HVD4. . . . followed by the inner bolt.

HVD5. As always, the best way to store these bolts is on the component itself.

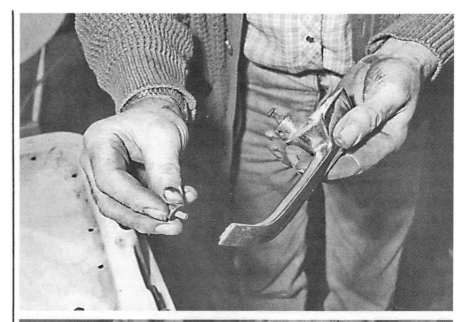

HVD6. The front quarterlight frame should now be loosened off by removing the lower . . .

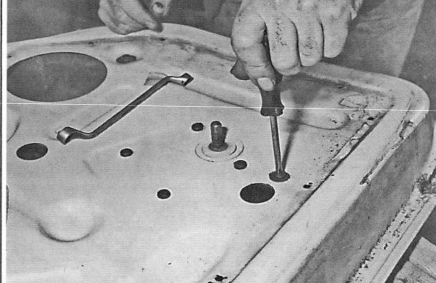

Bottom: left to right

HVD7. . . . and upper bracket securing screws and bolts on the front door glass guiding channel.

HVD8. The two at the front of the frame should also be removed, the top one should be hidden beneath a rubber grommet . . .

HVD9. . . . now removed.

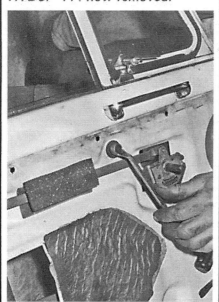

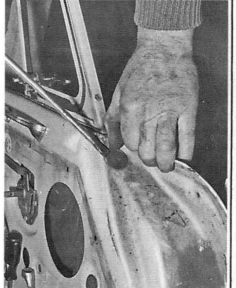

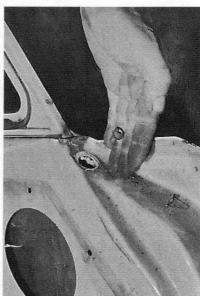

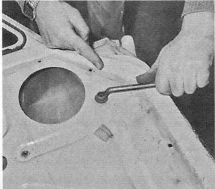

HVD10. ▲ The lower bolt is more easily spotted.

HVD11. ▼ The frame can then be pulled out slightly.

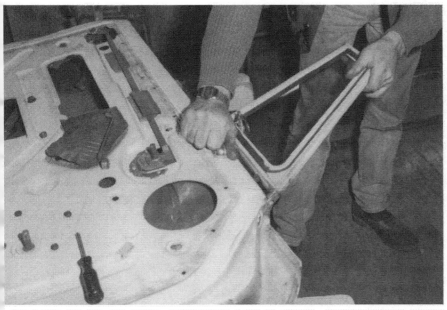

HVD14. ▲ Removing the old skin usually involves grinding so it's advisable to remove the door glasses now. Once a shower of sparks imbeds itself, the glass is forever ruined as the damage can't be ground out. The glass is held in place by these runners which slide along these slots in the door glass' lower fixing plate.

HVD12. ▼ Similarly, remove the upper and lower bolts holding the rear glass channel to the inner door frame . . .

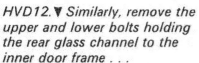

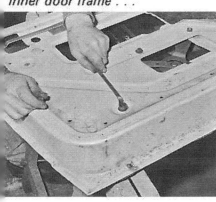

HVD13. ▼ . . . not forgetting a third fastening hidden behind another rubber grommet in the edge of the door.

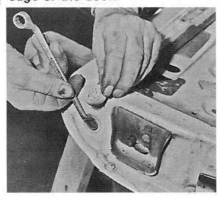

HVD15. ▲ With the door frame turned over and the skin removed, the clip over fixing washer can be seen.

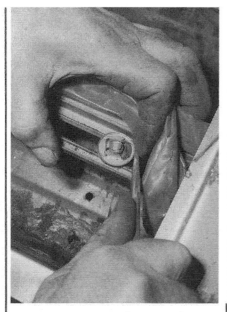

HVD16. Obviously, removing the clip in this position is easy but although a little fiddly, it's not much more difficult to remove it from the other side with the skin still on.

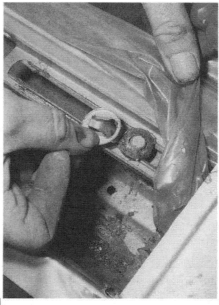

HVD17. ▲ The clip removed . . .

HVD18. . . . and the door glass lifted out. ▼

HVD20. Although it's a bit of a squeeze, the frame will come out – shown here with the lower fixing bracket.

HVD21. ▼ Using an angle grinder with a rubber pad-mounted 40-grit sanding disc, carefully sand around the frame edges – you'll see three metal edges appear (the frame itself plus the outer skin and folded over edge).

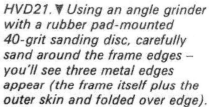

HVD19. ◄ By the same token, it's also a good idea to remove the quarterlight. To do this, the bracket on the glass runners need removing. Again easily done.

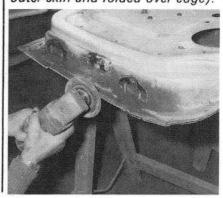

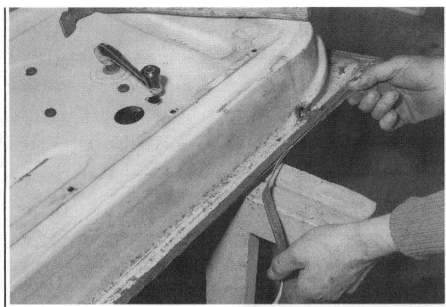

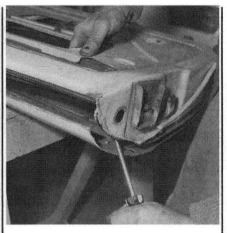

HVD25.   This allows the skin to be levered off.

HVD22.   Peel back the return edge. It comes off as a very sharp strip so unlike here, wear gloves.

HVD23.   At the top, a reinforcing plate connects the door skin with the main frame. Either drill out the spot welds (the quarterlight hasn't been removed here) . . . ▶

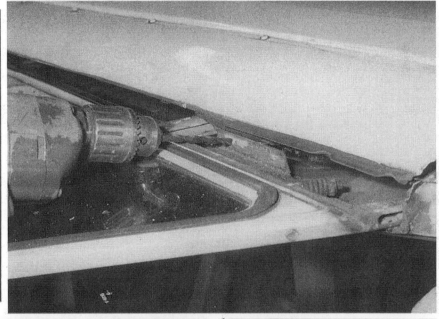

HDV24.   . . . or grind or saw around the reinforcing plate area.

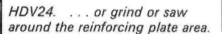

HVD26.   On the inside a tensioning strip locates into the top of the skin – simply move it out of the way . . .

HDV27. . . . and lift the skin off, unhooking the reinforcing strip at the top. ▶

HVD28. Dismantling almost complete. ▼

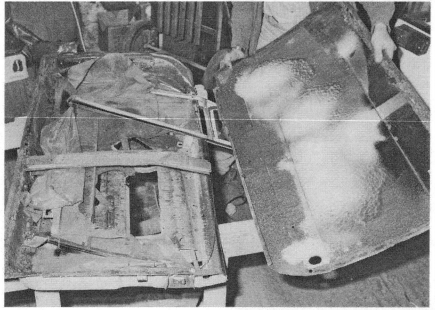

HVD30. Refitting a new skin is quite straight forward assuming that a properly fitting skin is obtained. Excellent repair panels are available from a number of stockists including the ever helpful and knowledgeable John Kippings – address under 'Clubs and Specialists'. Lay the new skin on . . . ▼

HVD29. Finish off by carefully grinding the old skin top tag from the frame as required. But do wear gloves! ▼

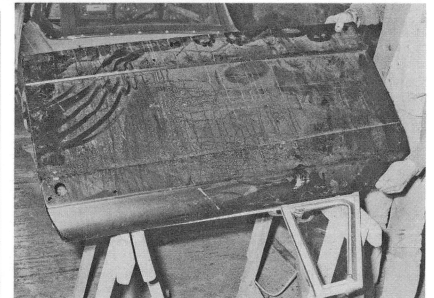

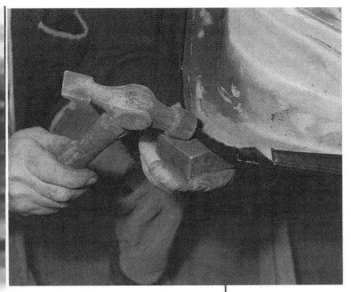

HVD31. ▲... and gradually tap over the return lip either to finish (make sure you use a supporting dolly) or tap over partially ...

HVD32. ... and finish off with a purpose made Sykes-Pickavant door skinner tool – well worth having. Make sure during fitting that the doorglass gap is correct and even all the way along (check the old door before removing the skin).

HVD34. ... at the rear top ...▲

HVD35. ... and at the bottom. But don't fully weld the door skin in place until the door has been re-hung and all surrounding panels are in place. It will be easier to twist the door back into shape and if it has gone 'out of wind' (common) and it will be possible to ease the skin position up, down, back or forth by a shade, if necessary. ▶

HVD33. Just a few welds are required to finish off the job around weak and stressed areas for example in front of the quarterlight ... ▶

HVD36.▲ A few plug welds should also be used to connect the reinforcing plates together. Get an assistant to squeeze the skin and frame together. You can either weld from inside the door ...

HVD37. . . . or through the top. It will help to drill or punch a few holes into the frame or skin plates before fitting the skin to assist welding.

It is possible to fit lower door repair panels as usually only the bottom four inches of the skin rots. However, as stated many times already, it often requires less skill and results in a better overall job if the whole panel is replaced.

General chassis repairs

If the work has been well planned in advance, it's still possible to obtain original chassis members from autojumbles or some dealers. Repro. box sections which normally fit quite well are also available. Before making any chassis repairs which will normally entail replacing side rails and/or outriggers, make quite sure that the main rails are 100% sound or else your hard work will be surely wasted.

HC1. The full range of chassis box sections is easily available from many of the Triumph specialists now operating to service parts for Herald based cars. Obtain original if possible.

HC2. ◄ The front outrigger can be replaced in the same way as the equivalent chassis member of the Spitfire/GT6 covered in the Spitfire/GT6 bodywork section.

HC3. ▶ *Side rails are secured to the body by four bolts each side (more often than not rusted solid) and by welds to the outriggers. Often the easiest way to remove them is to grind them off, here with the Black & Decker mini-grinder. On early models 3in bakelite discs separate chassis and body. Later models use rubber/fabric mountings. (Watch faces will be ruined by grinder sparks, by the way, as will screen glass not covered or masked-up.)*

HC4.   If a grinder isn't available (it really is advisable to buy one), revert to a lump hammer and chisel . . . ▼

body isn't to come off, a satisfactory job can be achieved by welding an additional plate to the top of the inner end of the outrigger so that when in place it sits over the top and overhangs the other side of the main chassis rail. An extra weld line can then be made along the top inner edge of the main rail which effectively locates the top edge of the outrigger onto the top of the chassis – not otherwise properly achievable. (Thanks to Dennis Benson of the Triumph Sports Six Club for this tip – an official Triumph repair technique).

HC5. . . . and lots of brute force. (But don't pull as the car can topple from its axle stands and **do** *wear gloves.)*

Chassis outrigger replacement should ideally be carried out with the body off so that a proper top weld can be achieved. MIG welding is ideal but an arc weld can be used here. Measure up to fixed reference points very carefully – it may be best to tack new chassis members in place before removing the body to ensure exact repositioning. If the

Roof removal

There surely can't be many cars made today in which the roof panel can be as easily removed (if at all!) as the Herald, either in its saloon or Coupé form. Here we show just how easy it is. Although the roof removal procedure is shown for the Coupé model only, removing the roof panel of a saloon follows much the same steps (take note of interior light wires where applicable) and shouldn't prove any more difficult.

RR1.   The first stage is simply to remove items of trim such as the rear and side panels, easily achieved by undoing a few screws and prising against one or two push-in clip fasteners.

RR2.   Here, Michael removes the seven nuts holding the roof to the rear deck.

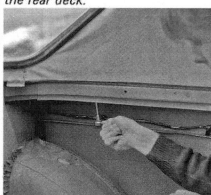

RR3.   All but the two corner bolts are held with simple nuts and washers. However, in the corners there are additional large cup washers. After removing the relevant nuts, the cup washers drop off revealing further nuts beneath. Don't undo these as they preset the final height of the roof above the rear deck. Large holes stamped into the top deck allow the roof bolts, complete with these inner nuts to pass cleanly through. ►

RR4.   As the loading on the roof panel is reduced and it begins to lift, wooden packing pieces are revealed along the top of the rear wings. ▼

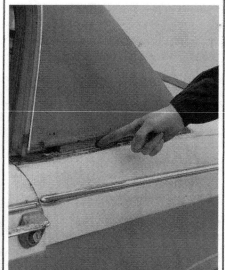

RR5. ▲ As a precaution and before removal, these were clearly marked 'F' for front. This isn't really necessary as the repositioning is fairly obvious. Still, it's wise to get into the habit of labelling how things come

apart. Weeks or even months later you just won't remember!

RR6.   Back inside the car, undo the Philips screws at each top corner. If stubborn, a sharp tap with an impact screwdriver works wonders. Note the absence of any support for the sun visor at this point. Supports weren't included on early models though were included on later cars. The fixing arrangement on later cars is also slightly different here with right-angled brackets being welded to the top of the windscreen frame. A similar bracket is also fixed to the corresponding position of the roof on later cars. Roof and frame are then fixed together at the corners with a nut and bolt rather than the simple screws shown here. ▼

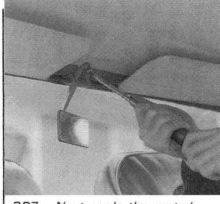

RR7. Next, undo the central holding screw . . .

RR8. ▼ . . . followed by the additional screws behind . . .

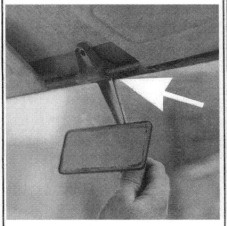

RR9. . . . which will enable the visor assembly to be removed and stored safely away.

RR10. Having released all the bolts, free the front edge of the roof from the screen rail. Due to age, this will more than likely be stuck fast. Best separated by a mixture of careful prising apart and sustained pressure. ▶

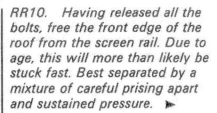

RR11. Finally, simply lift the panel off. Notice the smooth rear quarter panels of an early Coupé. Later ones were ribbed.

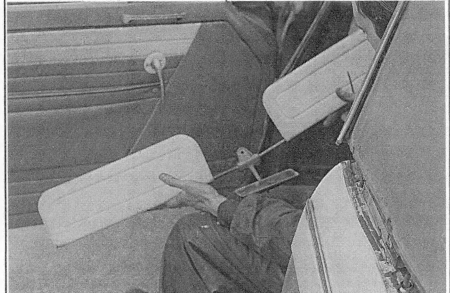

Front valance removal

Removal of the front valance of any Herald or Vitesse starts with removing the front over-riders. On 948 and 1200, 12/50 Heralds, these are held with three bolts. In the case of the 13/60 and Vitesse, only two bolts are used. These latter over-riders are handed left or right but there's hardly any difference so two rights or two lefts could well be fitted.

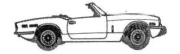

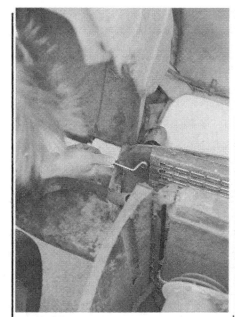

FV1.▲ On early models, remove the top and bottom over-rider bolts . . .

FV2.▼ . . . followed by the central one.

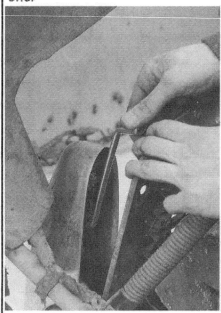

FV3.▶ This next shot shows the bolt and spacer tube layout for 948 and 1200, 12/50 Heralds. Later models and the Vitesse have shorter over-riders which don't require an equivalent top fastening. The chassis mounting is also shorter on later models.

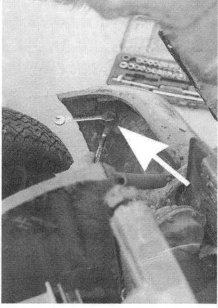

FV4.▲ Next, remove the nut and bolt which holds each valance corner . . .

FV5.▼ . . . followed by four Philips screws, one located each

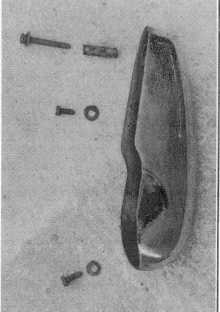

side of the bonnet pivot point. In principle, the valance can now be removed.

FV6.　However, as is often the case, the screws on this particular car were rusted in solid so after removing the bonnet (covered in the next section) the single bolt on each pivot point where the front valance brackets locates was removed . . . ▼

FV7.▲ . . . and the valance lifted free complete with radiator grille to be dismantled later on the bench with more than a little squirt of Plus gas, WD40 or similar easing oil.

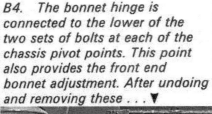

B4. The bonnet hinge is connected to the lower of the two sets of bolts at each of the chassis pivot points. This point also provides the front end bonnet adjustment. After undoing and removing these . . . ▼

FV8. If desired, the front grille can be removed first by undoing the relevant screws.

Bonnet removal

Although covered here as a simple dismantling procedure, it's worth pointing out that if any repairs such as fitting new wings, wheel arches or D-Plates are

required, it's probably a good idea to replace these first before removing the bonnet. By carrying out any repairs systematically, each one can be checked along the way by testing the bonnet fit against the rest of the car. Hence, you can ensure that all repairs will eventually lead to a well fitting and non-distorted unit.

B1. Locate the main loom to bonnet bullet connectors. Jot down which wires connect where or label the wires directly and disconnect. ▼

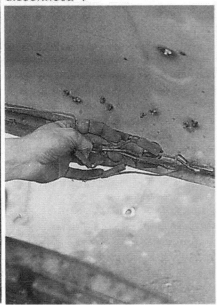

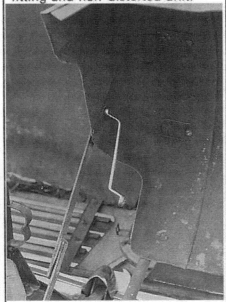

B2. ▲ Where fitted, undo the bonnet stays on the inner front wings . . .

B3. ►. . . followed by disconnecting the spring assisters on each side.

VBR3. . . . and lift off the boot. Don't forget to disconnect the number plate and reversing lamp assemblies where applicable. ▼

B5. . . . the bonnet can be swung forward . . .

B6. . . . and lifted clear.

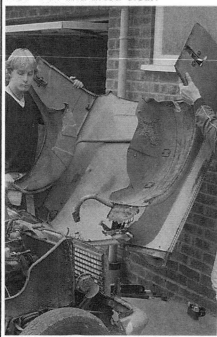

VBR1.▲ On saloons, remove the roof section followed by the doors, the latter being secured by three bolts and a 'stay' on each side.

Body removal

Some of the operations required to remove the front and rear body sections from Heralds or Vitesses are covered in more detail elsewhere but the shots below give the general idea. It really is quite easy.

VBR2.▶ Next, remove the three bolts holding each boot hinge in place . . .

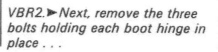

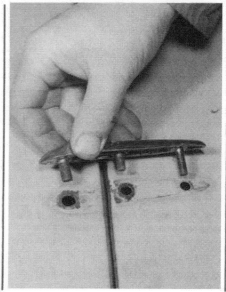

VBR4. ▲ If working on a convertible model, the overall weight can be reduced by unbolting the hood frame . . .

VBR8.   . . . and the seats removed. Rear seats can then themselves be removed. ▼

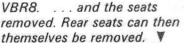

VBR9. ▲ Pull the wiring loom out of the way where necessary and disconnect at the bullet connectors.

VBR5. ▲ . . . ensuring that all rear and side fastenings have been removed followed by gently lifting free . . .

VBR6. ▶ . . . and then totally removing.

VBR10. The front section is bolted to the chassis at the front bulkheads and at body mounting points at the corner and along the two side rails.

VBR13. At the rear, the boot floor is secured by two bolts each side at the end of each rear chassis leg.

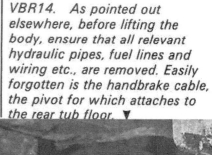

VBR14. As pointed out elsewhere, before lifting the body, ensure that all relevant hydraulic pipes, fuel lines and wiring etc., are removed. Easily forgotten is the handbrake cable, the pivot for which attaches to the rear tub floor. ▼

VBR11. There is also a row of bolts/set screws all the way across the car which connects both front and rear sections to each other and to the front chassis outrigger. ▼

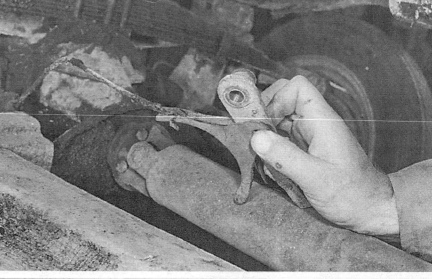

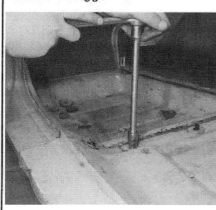

VBR12. ► Bolts also connect the rear body tub to the chassis over the top of the rear spring tunnel, further along the side rails with, depending on the model (see rear floor repair) additional bolts underneath the rear seat.

VBR15.   Split the rear tub away from the chassis . . .

VBR16.   . . . and lift it away. It isn't particularly heavy. Just rather awkward. The front section can be lifted off in a similar fashion. There's no need to remove the engine but as mentioned above, ensure that all relevant cables, pipes (steering column) etc., are disconnected first. Further tips are given under Spitfire/GT6 body removal. Thanks are due to Mike Penn of the Sparkford Motor Museum at Sparkford, whose car this is.

Bodywork: Spitfire/GT6

One of the most vulnerable and important areas on Spitfire and GT6 bodyshells are the sills and outer floor edges to which they attach. Not only do they provide essential body stiffness (especially for the Spitfire) but they also act as the anchor points for both the rear radius arms, for positive wheel location, and seat belt mountings. Their good condition is therefore vital to the structure of the car. Some cars have been found to have been ''repaired'' with any number of odd materials such as newspaper and chicken wire plus of course lots of disguising (*disgusting* when used like this!) body filler or underseal, so check the above areas over very carefully.

Production items which tend to accelerate the rotting process by trapping damp are rubber door sealing strips found on GT6s and bright metal finishing strips which push over the floor/sill edge weld on later models. If your car still has these it's advisable that you remove them or at least fill the latter with a flexible, non hardening rust proofing agent, such as the Corroless product described later.

As pointed out earlier. It's essential that any repairs to the sills should be properly carried out before any attempt at lifting the body tub from the chassis is attempted.

Have a good look at the floor and try to assess the full range of repairs required. If the floor is in really bad shape it may be a good idea to repair that before removing the sills. This will enable some structural rigidity to be maintained and also provide a reference point for the repair.

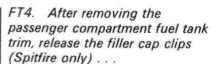

Whatever the case, make sure as shown later, that the sill area is fully supported before merrily hacking out all the rot. Most of this section was photographed at Classic Car Restorations near Worcester, who rather specialise in these cars.

Safety
As with any major body repairs involving welding or brazing torches, remove the fuel tank first and have a good capacity fire extinguisher on hand. Even supposedly empty fuel tanks are dangerous so keep well out of the way to reduce the hazard of fire. Always wear protective clear goggles when grinding or wire brushing and the correct grade of smoked glass goggles when welding. Eyes are easily damaged but not so easily repaired. Easily forgotten, make sure you keep fascinated children and the family pets out of the way. They've no idea of the danger.

Fuel tank removal

FT1.   Open the boot and remove the fuel tank trim board.

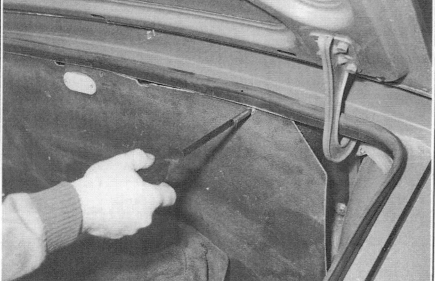

FT2.   As appropriate, remove the electrical connections to the boot courtest light . . .

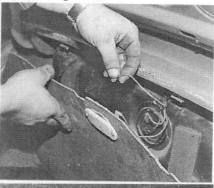

FT3.   . . . and fuel gauge sender unit.

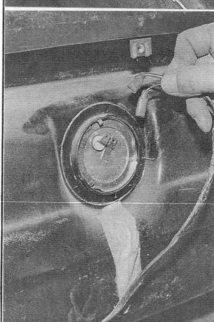

FT4.   After removing the passenger compartment fuel tank trim, release the filler cap clips (Spitfire only) . . .

FT5.   . . . and pull out the cap.

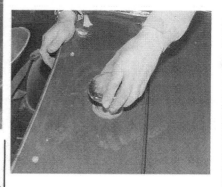

FT6.   If planning to respray the car later, you may like to remove the rubber seal at this stage also.

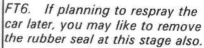

FT7. Drain the fuel lines at the fuel pump connection and remove the connections at the bottom . . . ▶

FT8.▲ . . . and top of the tank as applicable. Remove the holding screws around the tank edge and lift out the tank.

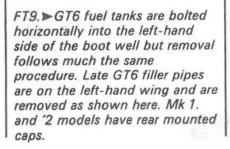

FT9.▶GT6 fuel tanks are bolted horizontally into the left-hand side of the boot well but removal follows much the same procedure. Late GT6 filler pipes are on the left-hand wing and are removed as shown here. Mk 1. and '2 models have rear mounted caps.

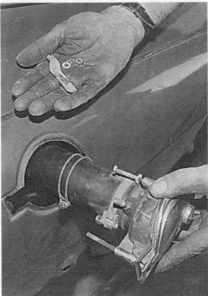

Floor repairs

FR1. In some instances, only the very lip of the floor may require attention in which case, the sills could be removed and the area in question cleaned up . . . ▼

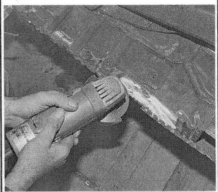

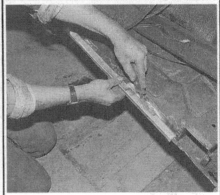

FR2.▲ . . . prior to fabricating a new lip and welding in place.

FR3.▼ More often the floor will require more extensive repairs normally up to about four inches from the sill edge and especially around the radius arm/seat belt mounting point. As usual, cut out all of the rot and clean up the area to bright metal with an angle grinder.

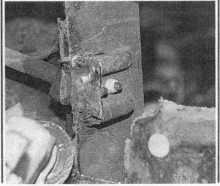

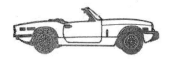

FR4. Clamp and then weld in place any necessary reinforcing plates on the left-hand side take care not to set fire to the wiring loom – remove it if possible but pull through and leave a non-flammable uncoated wire in its place so that the loom can be pulled back into place later . . .

> **MIG welding**
> *see p.308-on*

FR5. . . . before tackling the floor itself. A number of small plates may be required. ▶

FR6. Similarly remove any suspect areas further along . . . ▼

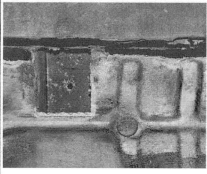

FR7. . . . and either gas or MIG weld in new sections. Obviously don't weld along the sill edge if that's to come off next. ▶

In practice, patching is likely to be an unsatisfactory way of repairing the floor for a number of reasons. If there is any more corrosion than that shown in FR1 replace the whole floorpan with a repair section. It seems more drastic but the end result will look 100 times better, last 10 times longer – and take half the time to carry out, in the end.

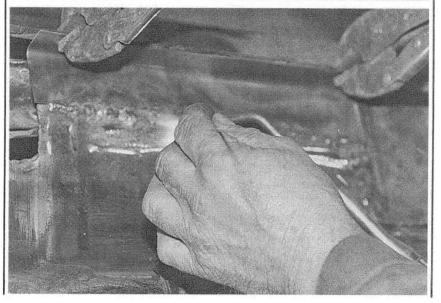

Sill replacement

SR1. Ensure that the floor is securely supported adjacent to the sill right the way along its length. ▶

SR4. Replacing the outer sill may be all that's required but more than likely, the inner sill and strengthening plates will need some attention as well. This ▼

SR2. Ken Wright, at Classic Car Restorations, removes the six door securing bolts, not forgetting to release the door stop arm first . . .

SR3. . . . and lifts out the door.

particular sill is an original Leyland pattern recognisable by the way the front top corner carries on around the front bulkhead. Always go for these. They definitely fit and are easily available if at a few pounds more than copy panels.

. . . the 'A' post . . .

SR5. ▲ With the door removed, PW uses another good piece of timber wedged inside the door opening which also helps rigidity. You could also use a purpose made body jack or even temporarily weld a length of angle iron across.

SR6. On later Spitfires drill out the pop rivets which hold the trim in place. Ken uses his Black & Decker cordless drill which is ideal for this sort of job because it requires no trailing wires. ▼

SR7. ▲ Cut through the rear sill close to the original weld point but slightly towards the front of the car.

SR8. Chisel or grind the sill away from the outrigger . . .

SR12. Often neglected, the sill strengthener is a vital part of the box section. Although often made up from flat sheet, the panel should actually have angled flanges as shown for a proper fit. Again, go for the original or properly fabricated copy. Also worth noting is the fact that the rear of the panel extends beneath the rear wing so for a proper job, part of that needs removing and replacing afterwards. ▼

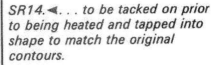

SR13.▲ With the forward end of the sill removed, more rot may well be revealed which is not covered by the repair strengthener. It should be repaired first. Here a repair panel has been made up . . .

SR10.▲ . . . and along the side and front bulkhead (and if necessary along the floor edge).

SR14.◄ . . . to be tacked on prior to being heated and tapped into shape to match the original contours.

SR11. . . . The sill can now be removed. As shown, floor repairs have already been completed on this car. The remains of the inner sill should now also be carefully removed. ▼

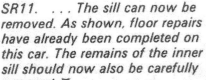

SR15. The inner sill may now be slotted into place . . .

SR20. As you might expect, spot welding makes for a very neat job.

MIG welding see p.308-on

SR16.▲ . . . and permanently welded. All sill sections are handed right and left so ensure you obtain the ones you need. Don't carry out final welding, however, until the door has been temporarily re-hung and door gaps checked and adjusted. Also check height of front and rear body relative to a flat floor – check that with a spirit level first. You must avoid distorting the body at this stage.

SR17. In principle, it may be a good idea to protect the new panels with a coat of paint though this may well be burnt off depending on the welding process and how close the weld is to the paintwork. Especially if spot welding, you shouldn't paint the flange edges, unless you use a spot-weldable paint available from some professional body shop suppliers. Würth produce a particularly suitable high-zinc-content product.

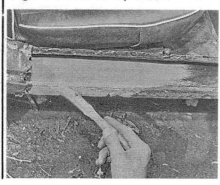

SR18.▲ The sill strengthener should then be welded at its rear edge and then tacked or clamped in place along with the outer sill and then both welded to the inner sill . . .

It's highly recommended to remove any upholstery before welding. It's quite a fire-risk!

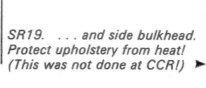

SR19. . . . and side bulkhead. Protect upholstery from heat! (This was not done at CCR!) ▶

SR21. The A post panel may now be addressed.

SR22. Clamp the new panel into place and fix in position.

SR24.➤ Ensure the surrounding area is free from underseal etc., after which clamp in position and weld on. It may be easier to tack the outer edge of the closing plate to the outer sill before the latter is fixed to the car. Make sure everything fits well by a trial fitting before finally welding in place.

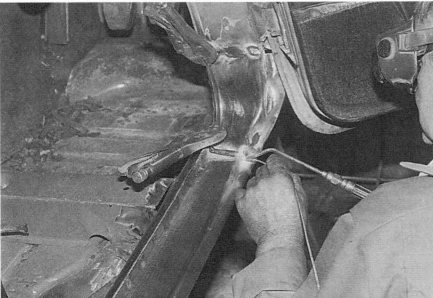

SR26.▲ Scribe mark to the correct shape before final cutting.

SR27. As mentioned in SR25, the alternative method is to obtain a repair panel like this.

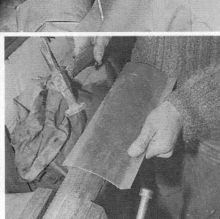

SR23. A front closing plate may then be made up (as shown here) or an original type obtained. The latter have an angular crease to enable a correct fit.

SR25.▲ Repair panels for the lower front edge of the rear wing can be obtained from many Triumph dealers or can be fabricated from sheet steel. Make a lip in a vice and bend over a suitable former.

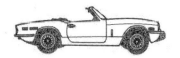

SR28.   Once a suitable section has been cut out, the new one can be clamped in place . . .

SR29.   . . . and then welded or brazed in position.

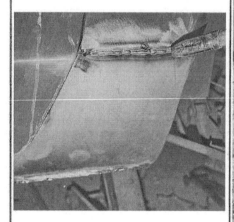

SR30.   The repair welds smoothed off and ready for painting.

Front wing replacement

As stated in the introduction, the techniques described below can be mirrored to replace not only GT6 front wings but also the front and rear wings on similar GT6s and Spitfires plus Heralds and Vitesses. Although there are some obvious differences, the basic principles apply right across the range of cars covered.

FWR1.   Not all bodywork damage is due to rust as shown here. A sad case of collision on this GT6. Although the wing top can be repaired by panel beating, it's just not worth spending the effort on the detachable lower wings.

FWR2. ▲ Start to remove the wing by first unbolting the frame attachment.

FWR3. The wing can then be chopped off below the weld seam in a number of ways including using professional air tools, hammer and cold chisel, nibbler or mini angle grinder. Be sure to wear goggles whichever technique you use.

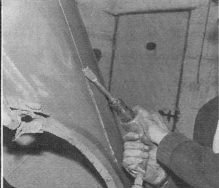

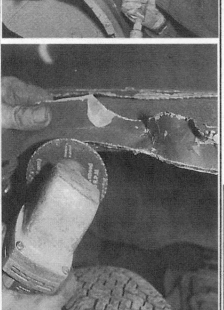

FWR4. Although not shown here, the metal edges are very sharp so wear stout leather gloves. Gardening types are ideal. The wheel arch lip can be carefully ground through . . .

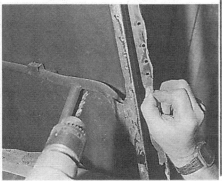

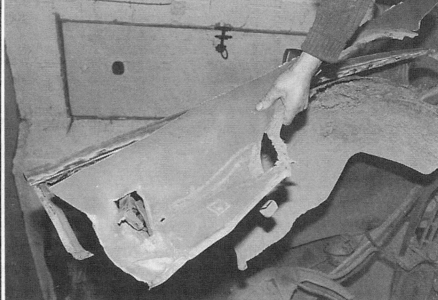

FWR5. . . . and the wing removed. As shown, leave the rear support strip attached to the bonnet. This is connected to the wing by a couple of tack welds which can be ground through before wing removal.

FWR6. Clean up the weld flange . . .

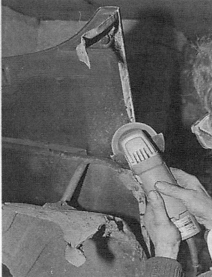

FWR7. . . . and then either drill out the spot welds or grind away in order to remove the old wing flange. Leave the bonnet one intact.

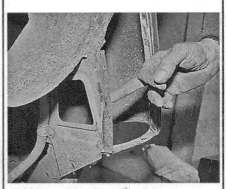

FWR8. The front and lower flanges should be tidied up in a similar way.

FWR9. Make good any distortion especially if you've used a chisel to remove the wing and double check that the new panel fits properly. Make adjustments to the bonnet as required. If the wheel arch is damaged due to impact or rust, aim to replace this also

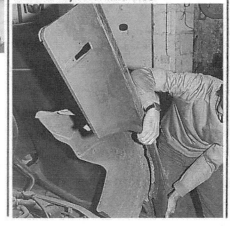

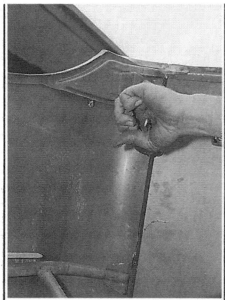

FWR10.   The new wing can then be clipped on with vice grips. (On late GT6s and Spitfires, at the bonnet frame attachment points.)

FWR11.   Tack weld the panels in a couple of places along the flange making sure of the fit. If gas welding, ensure that it's done with the minimum of distortion. MIG welding is easier for amateurs. ►

MIG welding *see p.308-on*

FWR12. ▲ Clip the rear edge strip into place . . .

FWR13.   . . . and tack weld this also. Further tack welds every couple of inches can now be carried out along the wing seams to finish the job. ▼

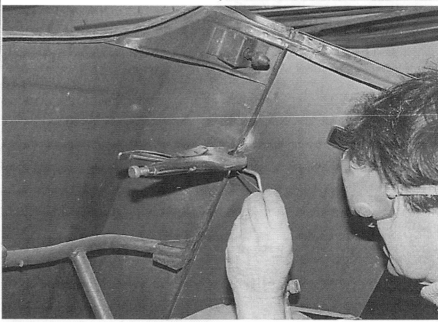

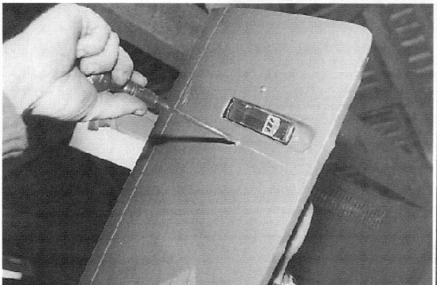

FW14. ◄ After finishing and spraying, the final job simply entails the replacement of the bonnet catch.

Wheel arch and wing lip repair

Main wing panels may often be in good condition except for the wheelarch lip and panels to replace the lip and the wheelarch itself are available. However,

inspect the wing carefully and assess exactly what work and effort is required before deciding to replace just the lip. The wing may not be worth repairing. Replacing a whole panel, although initially more expensive, is often easier for the inexperienced than attempting a repair. It also reduces greatly the risk of more rust breaking out in future.

WAL1. ► In a similar fashion to wing removal, grind the old outer wheelarch away from the inner panel taking care to keep the main flange intact.

WAL4. The panel edge may then be cut down exactly to size. Keep checking for fit and then clean up the wheelarch flange.

WAL2. ▲ Scribe around the wing lip replacement panel and grind through the damaged lip well inside of the line. The wheelarch and lip can then be lifted forward . . .

WAL3. . . . and after cutting away at the front, removed.

WAL5. Making sure that both panels will fit properly, clamp, then weld the wheelarch in place.

WAL6. Offer up the outer lip . . .

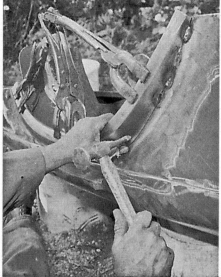

WAL8. As the lip is being welded, make frequent checks and tap the panel in place as necessary. Again, MIG welding is ideal especially for the inexperienced welder, as very little or no distortion should result to spoil the job. ◄

WAL9. Finally, weld the wheelarch and wing lip flanges together. It may help the final appearance to pre-drill or punch small holes in the wing lip flange and then plug weld through for a really professional "spot weld" finish.

WAL7. . . . and fix firmly in place.

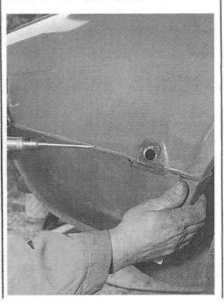

WAL15.▲ Offer in the repair and secure.

WAL10.▲ The pronounced MIG weld beads (less marked in the case of good gas welding) can be carefully ground flat afterwards.

Repairs to early cars can be carried out in a similar way.

WAL11.▼ Chop out all the rot . . .

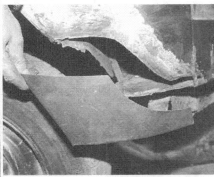

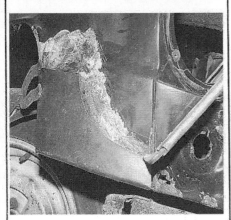

WAL12. . . . and then clamp and weld a suitable repair panel into position. ▲

WAL13.▲ At the same time, make any necessary repairs to the wheel arch.

WAL14. Clean off all old underseal and again cut out all suspicious areas.

Lower rear wing repair

Water tends to find its way into the rear wing recesses of all Spitfires and GT6s so carefully inspect this area when buying. Fortunately though, the repair is quite straight forward.

SRW1. The same basic procedure applies for both early and late Spitfires and GT6s. Initially the rear bumpers have to be removed. Make sure that any electrical wiring is kept well out of the way. Start off by scribing around the repair panel . . .

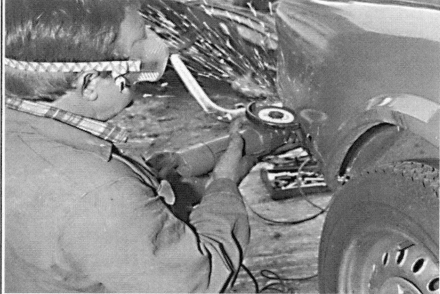

SRW2. . . . then cutting slightly undersize to allow for trimming accurately later.

SRW3. Usually some flat panel repair behind the outer panel will also have to be carried out before attaching the outer panel. ▼

SRW4.◄ Cut a suitable piece from sheet steel and hold in place. The more clamps the better!

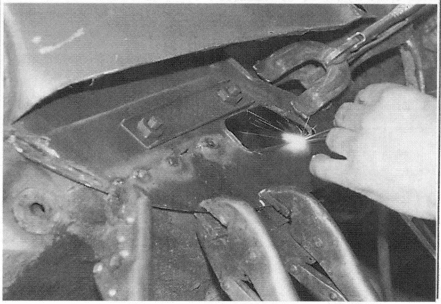

SRW5. Small tacks are quite all right here.

SRW6. Remove any old paint or underseal which would otherwise prevent you from obtaining a strong final weld. It will also prevent it from catching fire. ▶

SRW7. ▼ Clean up the outer panel with a sanding disc.

SRW8. If suitably skilled, a butt weld makes for a very neat job. However, an overlap joint with the repair panel behind (having possibly 'shouldered' the edge) provides a good serviceable repair though a little more body filler will be required to complete the work. Always aim to use the minimum amount of filler.

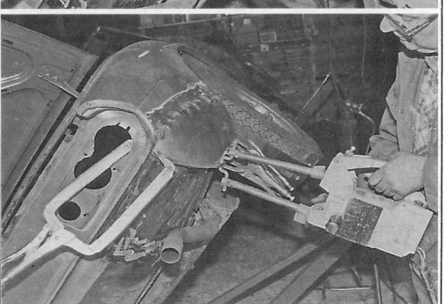

SRW9. The lower edge could be spot or otherwise welded.

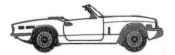

SRW10.   Finish off all weld seams by sanding the joins flat.

SRW11.   While in the area, small repairs can also be attended to around the wheel arch.

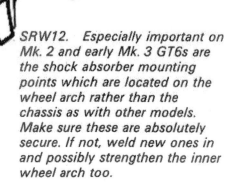

SRW12.   Especially important on Mk. 2 and early Mk. 3 GT6s are the shock absorber mounting points which are located on the wheel arch rather than the chassis as with other models. Make sure these are absolutely secure. If not, weld new ones in and possibly strengthen the inner wheel arch too.

Boot floor repair

Boot floors may show fairly extensive rust damage but usually corrosion is restricted to the side edges, as shown in SRW3, and the lower rear lip.

BFR1.   After repairing, as necessary, the adjacent area behind the lower rear wing, cut out the floor rot. The metal surrounding the bumper bracket points was in good condition so was left in place.

BFR2.   A repair panel can easily be produced from flat sheet, bent into shape and welded into position. The bumper bracket holes can then be drilled through from underneath.

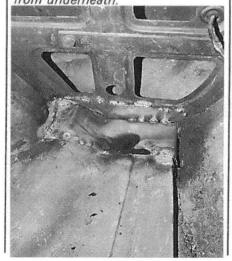

BFR3. Both the vertical and curved faces at the bottom of the boot floor flange are prone to rusting through. ▶

BFR4. This damage can easily be repaired with a suitable section. For more extensive repairs, whole boot floor panels are available so as usual, and before deciding to patch or totally replace, assess just how much work is involved along each potential route. If in any doubt whatever, replace the whole section. ▼

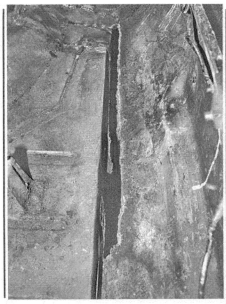

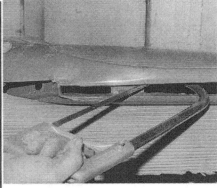

SGD2. ▲ On GT6s then, remove the skin by first sawing, grinding or drilling out the spot welds of the connecting bridge.

SGD3. ▼ The corner can also be sawn through rather than ground if desired. Again as before, it's best to remove all the glass to protect it against hot metal filings.

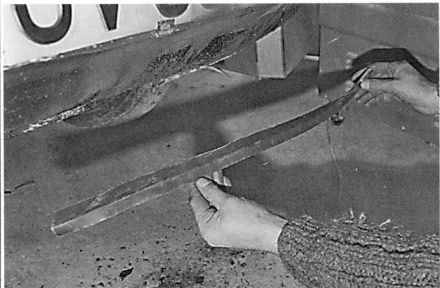

Doorskin replacement

The basic procedure for removing and replacing the doorskins on the above cars is as previously shown for the Herald and Vitesse. However, the sequence below shows a few differences between the models and alternative techniques applicable for all the cars.

SGD1. As with the Herald and Vitesse, GT6 doorskins have a bracing bar between the skin and door frame positioned underneath the quarterlight. Having full width

windows, Spitfires do not. Hence, good second-hand Spitfire doors could be used without modification in GT6s (with some loss in rigidity) but not the other way around. ▼

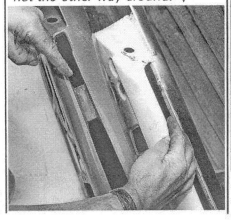

SGD4. ▲ Grind around the door skin edge just deep enough to remove the folded over edge.

SGD5.   The half inch wide return lip can then be separated from the frame . . . ▲

SGD6.   . . . and stripped off. Remember it's razor sharp so wear gloves. ▼

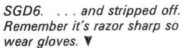

SGD8. ▲ Rather than take the chance, refit the frame into the car and double check for any distortion.

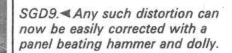

SGD9. ◄ Any such distortion can now be easily corrected with a panel beating hammer and dolly.

SGD10.   All being well, lay over the new skin and tap over the return lip as shown using a supporting dolly or use a door skinner tool. ▼

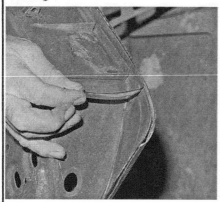

SGD7.   The outer skin can then be lifted off. ▼

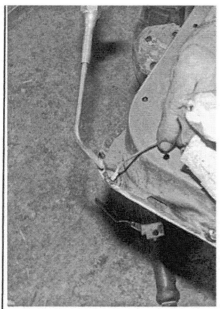

SGD11. All that's needed now is just a few weld or braze tacks made in key places around the edge. Brazing has the advantage that it can be more easily softened and the panel moved.

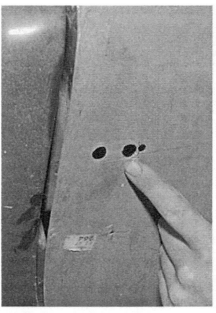

SGD13. Suitable start holes can then be drilled and joined up to complete the desired cut out with a file . . .

SGD14. . . . after which the door can be resprayed and the handle refitted . . .

SGD15. . . . and tightened home. ▼

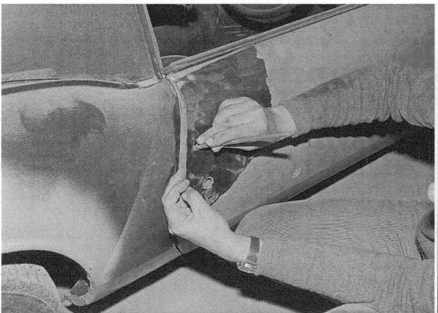

SGD12.▲ Nowadays, most doorskins come complete with lock and handle holes already formed. If there aren't any, a good way to ensure correct placement is to chop out a section from the old skin (avoiding distortion) and mark around the inside of the relevent holes.

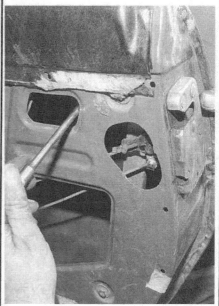

SGD16.◀Once back on the car, the door fit can be adjusted by slightly loosening the securing bolts . . .

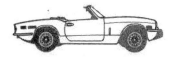

SGD17. . . . and levering up and down . . .

SGD18. . . . and backwards and forwards with a suitable length of wood before finally retightening the bolts.

SGD19. Incidentally if, as is likely, the door frame base has corroded, you could fabricate (using a Sykes-Pickavant bench folder) a repair section, letting it into the new door skin as the skin is fitted . . .

SGD20. . . . then welding or brazing it in place after the door skin is in place. MIG welding would be better. ►

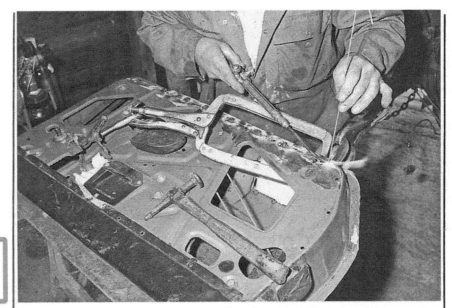

MIG welding
see p.308-on

Front chassis repairs

Front outriggers especially are prone to the ravages of rust. They can be replaced either with the body on or off the chassis. If replacing with the body still attached to the chassis, the fuel and brake lines should ideally be removed and the engine and all ancillaries covered over with a damp sheet. Have an observant friend and a fire extinguisher on hand just in case.

SCR2. ► Comparing the old and replacement chassis members, this one obtained from good old John Kipping.

SCR3. ▼ Make good any rust damage to the main rail before fitting the new panel, but remove any adjacent fuel or hydraulic lines before doing so.

SCR1. ▼ Remove the old outrigger by chiselling or grinding at the inboard end and by removing the central and end body bolts. Inspect the main chassis rail for additional damage.

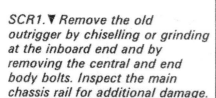

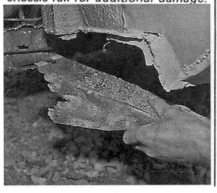

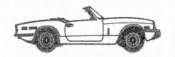

SCR6. Before cutting off the old member, make lots of measurements to a number of fixed reference points to ensure accurate realignment. ▼

SCR4. ▲ *Clamp and weld the new panel into place. Fitting the body bolts will ensure correct alignment.*

Repairing the chassis with the body off requires a little thought towards panel positioning but follows the same basic procedure.

SCR5. As can be seen, with the body off, the true extent of the damage is visible. Ken Wright of Classic Car Restorations takes over . . . ▼

SCR7. Remove the old outrigger and clean the chassis rail back to bright metal, as Ken points out.

SCR8.   As before, make good any repair to the main rail before welding on the new panel.

SCR9.▶ Fit the new outrigger in place with a couple of weld tacks and double check all the previous measurements . . .

SCR10.   . . . before finally welding in place.

Rear chassis repair

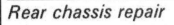

RCR1.   Typical rear chassis rot can appear around the differential mounting area and shock absorber mounting points. As with the front outrigger repair make a series of measurements before the work begins. Also shown here is a patch repair about to be completed on the transverse chassis member.

RCR2.▲ Chisel off the damaged section. Wear stout gloves and fit your chisel with a hammer stop grip for safety. Ken forgot; just look at that thumb!

RCR3.► Make up a repair section of the correct gauge steel. This itself may need welding together before fitting. Make frequent checks for fit along the way. It is a remarkably complex shape to fabricate, as LP found when he made one! Make it first in thin card, fixing the 'folded' edges with masking tape. Open out the card and scribe round it onto your sheet steel.

Front chassis crossmember and bonnet mountings

FCR1.   Front chassis rails do sometimes rot on all the cars. This shows a rather sad example on a late Spitfire.

FCR2.   In this case, the easiest solution is to replace the whole of the rail and to fit new chassis bonnet mountings.

FCR3.   Assuming the main rail ends are serviceable, it should be a simple case of grinding off the old and welding on the new.

FCR4.   While you're about it, check out the state of the bonnet. Splits can occur . . .

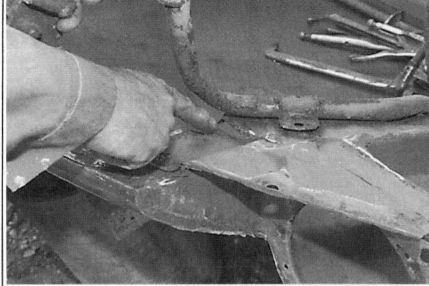

FCR5.   . . . and can take extensive work to rectify, there being no repair panels available at the time of writing. Weld in a new section(s) and grind back.

FCR6.   If fitting new bonnet mountings, clean back the new or old rail to obtain bright metal, especially if MIG welding.

FCR7. Take care to position the bonnet as accurately as possible. The rear height is adjusted by screwing the rubber cone stop either in or out and then retightening the locking nut.

FCR10. If the old ones are unserviceable, new blind nuts may be welded in place on the bonnet adjustment/location plate.

FCR11. The plate can then be bolted in position. As shown, the slotted plate offers some degree of bonnet positioning forwards and backwards. ▼

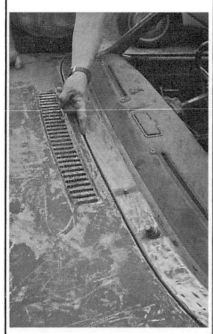

FCR8. The top of the bonnet should be level with the base of the windscreen frame with about a quarter of an inch gap.

FCR9. ▶ Even gaps should also be present along the door edge and sill (as shown later, prop up the front of the bonnet with a suitable length of wood – the correct height should have been noted before originally removing the bonnet).

FCR12. Having correctly set the bonnet, offer on the chassis mountings and tack weld in place.

FCR13. Final welding can be carried out with the bonnet off the car.

FCR14. The bonnet can then be refitted and final adjustment to height and front/back alignment carried out, as Ken Wright demonstrates.

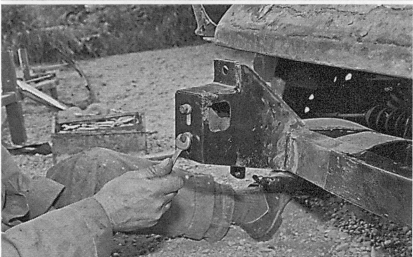

Front valance replacement

Front valances unfortunately do rot, especially the double skinned panels on later models. Steel replacement units are available for all models although not surprisingly, those for early models are quite rare so you may have to hunt around for them. Also, Spitfire 4, Mk 2 and GT6 Mk 1 valances are slightly different from those found on Spitfire Mk 3 and GT6 Mk 2s.

Good quality fibreglass replacements are available if you shop around. If originality is important, new steel panels are a must but for everyday motoring good fibreglass replacements are not a bad idea. Usually, replacing steel panels with fibreglass involves a little more work than just bolting original metal ones back on so we're covering the former here. In the end it's down to personal choice.

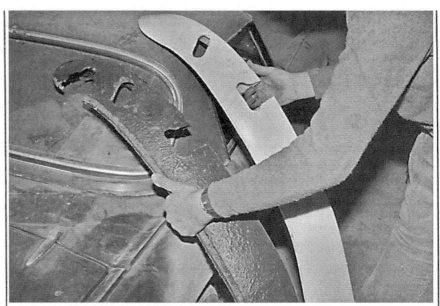

FV2. On Spitfire 4, Mk 2 and GT6 Mk 1 models you also have to remove at least one of the front bumper irons which pass through the oval holes at each end of the valance. These holes can easily be seen in this shot which compares the old rusted steel valance with a new fibreglass panel. Apart from these extra holes, Spitfire Mk 3 and GT6 Mk 2 panels are identical to the earlier versions.

FV3. Hold the replacement panel in place and then mark and drill holes to match those in each mounting bracket. On new original steel panels a strip of metal, left on during the manufacturing process, bridges the gap between the top mounting hole pairs. This strip needs to be removed before the valance can be fitted.

FV1. Soak all bolts/brackets in penetrating oil and unbolt at each end and at the front chassis mounting points.

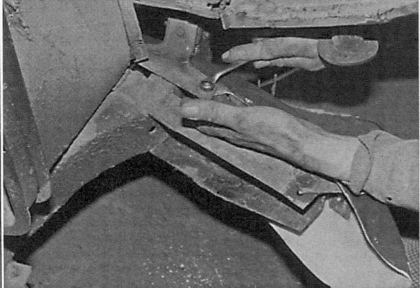

FV9. . . . plus further bolts through lower and side brackets.

FV4.▲ Once everything is in order, tighten the securing bolts . . .

FV5.▼ . . . and refit the bumper iron removed earlier.

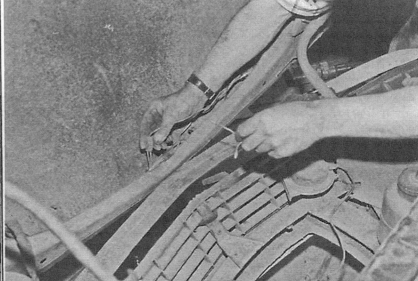

FV6.▲ On later models, start by disconnecting the sidelight wiring at the central bullet connectors.

FV7.◄ The sidelight may be removed now or after the quarter valance has been removed.

FV8.► The valance is held by a bolt through the front bumper assembly . . .

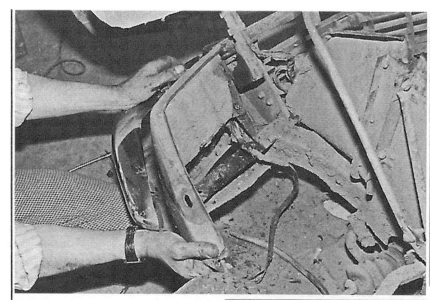

Below:
FV13. Offer in the replacement panel and check for fit.

Bottom:
FV14. It's a lot easier to spray these panels off the car prior to refitting. Clean out the mounting holes . . .

FV10. Once undone, the section can be lifted out.

FV11. If fitting fibreglass, you'll probably have to drill sidelight fixing and general mounting holes. Use the old panel to make a template to ensure correct positioning.

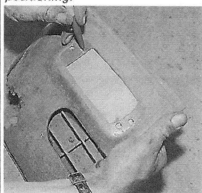

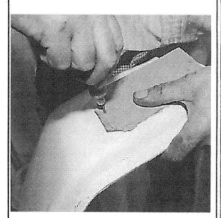

FV12. Holes can then be accurately transferred.

110

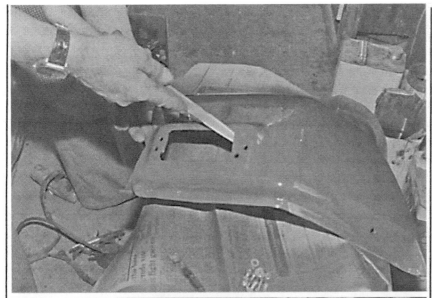

FV15. . . . and make any last minute corrections – these should really be sorted prior to spraying.

FV16. The sidelight back plate can then be screwed back into place followed by the lens assembly . . .

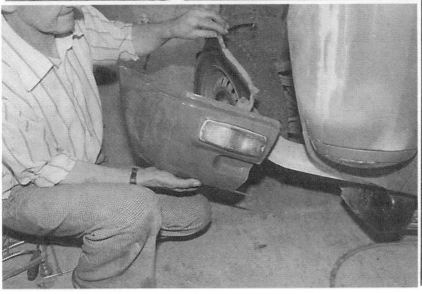

FV17. . . . and the complete unit offered into place.

111

FV18. Simple brackets should also be made as required, or they may be available from your specialist supplier, or the old ones may be re-usable.

FV19. Final tightening. Reconnect the wiring (depending on the panel involved, fitting fibreglass may also entail adding an extra earth wire) and the job's done. ▼

Body removal

Removing the body shouldn't present problems unless bolts have rusted themselves in solid, in which case grind or cut them off then drill and re-tap later. Fortunately, there are few bolts holding the tub in place and the shell isn't particularly heavy so if you haven't any lifting gear just ask a few friends round. One on each corner will be quite sufficient. There's no particular order in which the following operations should be carried out but the main ones required for removing the body tub are illustrated below.

Safety
The dangers from broken glass should be self-evident. Tape up screen vent holes. If the screen breaks, glass particles can be blown out later when the blower is turned on.

SBR1. Not particularly necessary but this shot shows an accepted method for removing the windscreen without damaging it using firm, steady pressure from a number nine boot. Don't kick at the glass. Have someone around to help catch it when it pops free. Never attempt to lever it out as the screen will more than likely shatter. Apply steady pressure, working from one side first, to the other . . .

SBR2. . . . and it should come free. Alternatively (and more safely) if the windscreen appears to be stuck fast or the seal is due for replacement anyway, the screen can be removed after cutting out the retaining rubber as shown earlier for the Herald Coupé rear screen HR1. Bear in mind that the screen rubber will probably require replacement in any case. Fresh rubbers are far less likely to allow leaks when the screen is re-fitted.

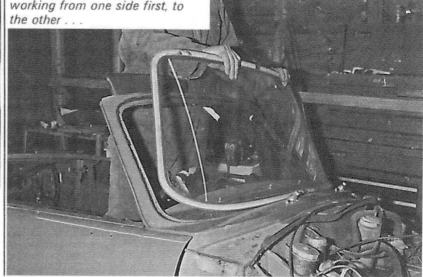

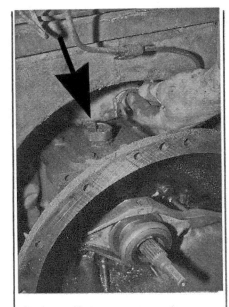

SBR3. Make sure that all wiring, earth cables, gearbox reverse and overdrive leads etc., are removed. Double check prior to lifting the body. There always seems to 'e just another one.

SBR5. If the hydraulic pipes are to be used during the rebuild, it's useful to plug each pipe as it's disconnected to ensure they're not contaminated with general muck. However, new pipes aren't expensive so preferably throw the old ones away and consider fitting non-rusting new ones such as Kunifer or 'Handy' copper sets as shown in a later section.

Tip! Use 'vacuum hose caps' from eBay.

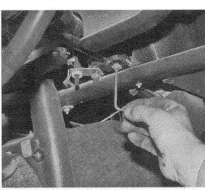

SBR4. Brake and clutch pipes should be disconnected and freed from the body. Drain the systems first. ▶

SBR6. Prior to cleaning up the top bulkhead, brake cylinders etc., will have to be removed. Often, due to leaking fluid, this area will be rusty as paint is stripped off under the attack of brake fluid. To free really locked in nuts, a sharp tap with a cold chisel is often the answer.

SBR7.◄ Continuing around the engine bay, disconnect the steering column by first loosening the two clamp arrangements inside the car – this shot shows the top one (earlier models are a little different) . . .

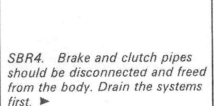

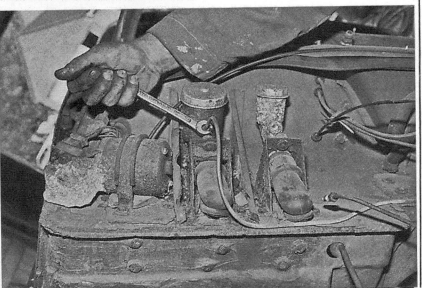

113

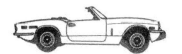

SBR8. `... followed by removing the lower bolt which secures the bottom universal joint.

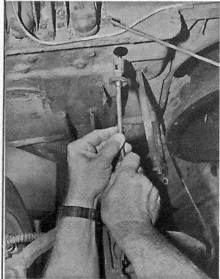

SBR9. The column can now be slid out of the way.

SBR10. Don't forget to remove the speedometer and throttle cables. In this sequence the engine has already been removed so choke cables etc., have been disconnected previously. However, the engine doesn't have to be removed to lift the body off. ▼

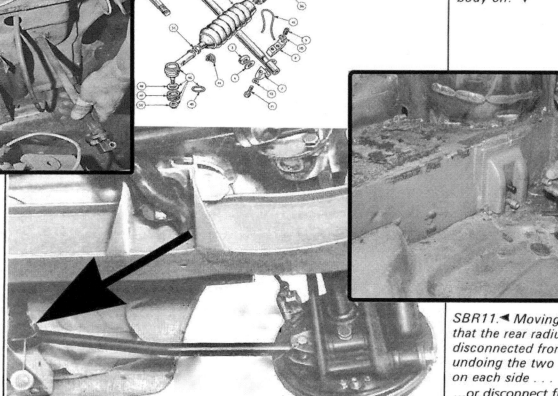

SBR11.◄ Moving inside, ensure that the rear radius arms are disconnected from the body by undoing the two securing nuts on each side ...
...or disconnect from beneath (Herald/Vitesse shown).

SBR12. ▶ *. . . and tapping the bolts through.*

SBF13. ▼ *The brackets could be totally removed as shown here or left on the ends of the radius arms – in which case, the other end of the arms would have to be disconnected from the rear vertical link.*

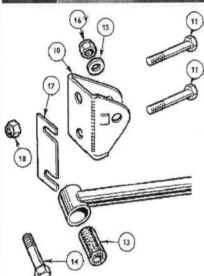

SBR14. ▲ *Off the car, the shims(17) used between the radius arm bracket and body are clearly seen. Due to tolerances during manufacture, different cars will have different numbers of shims each side of the car. Label!*

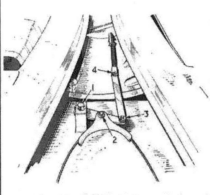

SBR15. ▲ *Don't forget to disconnect the handbrake assembly.*

SBR16. ▼ *Twelve bolts secure the body on the chassis. One each side on the front bulkhead brackets and inside the Herald footwell...*

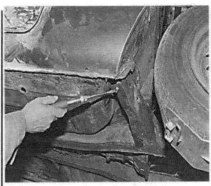

SBR17. ▲ *. . . with a further bolt at the end of each front over-rider. Once loosened or cut off . . . .*

SBR18. *. . . these bolts can be tapped into the driver and passenger's footwells.*

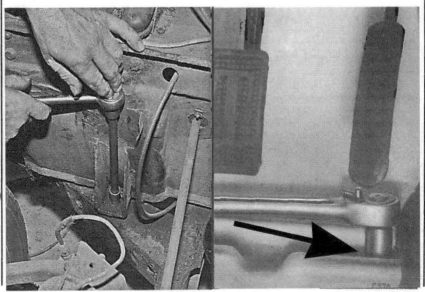

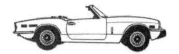

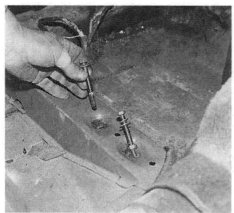

SBR19.　A further pair of bolts are found on each side, just forward of the seats. These bolt into the chassis' central stub outriggers. ◄

SBR20.　Moving back, the inner seat belt mountings also bolt into the chassis so remove these followed by the final two bolts situated on the transverse stiffening bridge. ►

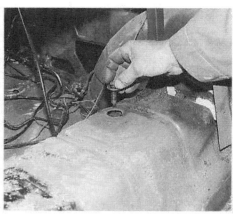

BONNET CATCH BRACKETS

Holes (A) 9/32"d 3/4" centres

HERALD Sill strengthening bracket

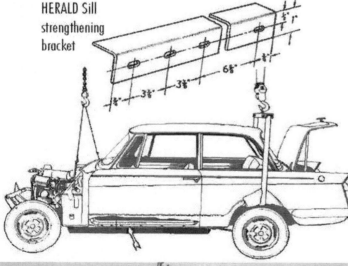

DISCONNECTION CHECK-LIST

KEY: (H) = Herald/Vitesse

(S) Spitfire and some GT6

(H) The body may be removed from the frame as a unit or by removing individual sections

CABLES FROM: Battery; Front lighting cable at connectors on top of air duct; Coil; Generator ; Oil pressure switch; Temperature sender; Engine earth cable; Tacho. drive from distributor; Horn/s; Stop lamp switch.

DISCONNECT: Drain coolant, disconnect hoses from heater; Carburettor controls; Connection between brake master cylinder and 3-way connector; Handbrake cable; Accelerator relay lever (1 mills pin*** + split pin with washers); Handbrake cable from compensator; (H) Speedo drive cable from rear of instrument panel, pull cable into engine bay; (H) Gearchange knob, gearbox cover.

REMOVE: Bonnet (4 bolts); Seats; Facia support bracket to floor (4 bolts); (S) Fuel tank; (H) Fuel pipe from tank.

(H) Both sill panels and fit reinforcement plate shown (4 bolts).

RELEASE wiring loom from chassis, withdraw clear of engine. Release lower steering clamp bolt, push column up and clear.

DISCONNECT radius arms from body.

REMOVE Grommets then 12 bolts securing body to floor.

•1 each side, in engine bay; •1 each side of front toe board.

•2 each side of body in line with front of prop. shaft; •1 each side, front of seat pan; •1 each side spring access cover. Protect the body against chafing. Make up lifting brackets as shown (S), remove bonnet catch bracket and fit brackets to body. (S) Use safety harness eyebolts adjacent to rear wheel arches. Lift the body clear of the chassis.

*** Mills pins, also known as groove pins, are re-useable, very strong, steel dowel fasteners. Similar to but NOT the same as roll pins.

SBR21. As mentioned above, lifting the main tub doesn't require specialist lifting gear but one way to do it could be to lift the chock up the back end using a bar passed through where the transverse spring sits followed by lifting the front end.
The rolling chassis could then be pushed out from underneath and pulled out of the way.

Refitting the body

It is very important to bear in mind that **THE BODY TUB MUST NOT BE RESTORED WHEN OFF THE CHASSIS.** If it is, it is highly unlikely that you will ever get it back on again! It will be fairly difficult, in any case, to align all the bolt holes easily.

RTB1. This chassis is the one shown being repaired in an earlier section. Whether repaired or not, the opportunity should be taken to pressure wash the chassis (see the Clarke pressure washer under "Tools and Equipment") and to paint it with Corroless rust-inhibiting primer and extraordinary tough top coat. Here Gordon Ashford, proprietor of Classic Car Restorations uses the Corroless paint. The "correct" finish is body colour, but your choice of paint will depend on whether you want to be show-original or go for ultimate longevity.

RTB2. After painting, but before refitting, use a tap to clear all the mounting threads. Fit the body and insert each bolt a couple of times. This will enable you to lift, shove and lever the body until all the bolts can be inserted. You can swear, too, if it helps . . . .

117

Rustproofing

With the bodywork repaired, it's important that new metal is protected as soon as possible as if allowed to, freshly welded panels and patches can take on a rusty surface very quickly. A good quality paint system such as that produced by Corroless is essential.

RP1. ►Two good coats of rust stabilising primer should be applied to panels showing any remnants of surface rust. Although many manufacturers claim that only loose rust needs to be brushed off, you should really aim to ensure that all rust is removed before painting. You don't often get something for nothing. Suppliers such as Fertan and Corroless supply excellent primer in either a brush . . .

RP2. . . . or spray finish. Both types of paint contain, uniquely, a rust killer. ►

RP3. Once dry, follow up with a further two coats of top coat. Corroless top coats are available in a range of colours. They contain tiny glass beads which make the paint surface incredibly tough. ▼

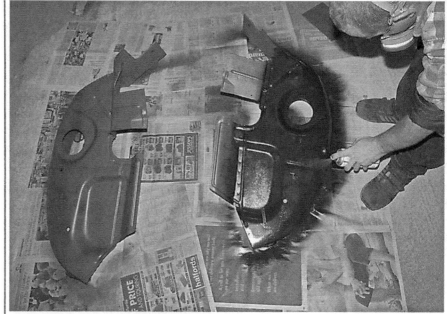

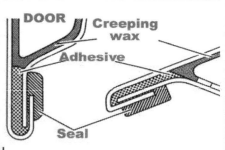

RP4.▼ More often than not, box sections and cavities rust from the inside out. Access for spraying rust preventing cavity waxes is usually very easy through existing holes such as in Spitfire and GT6 sills (from outside and inside the car) . . .

RP5.▲ . . . and behind the door trims on all models. Wax should also be sprayed into chassis box sections again achieved through existing holes. Bonnets too suffer around the light pod and outer wheel arch areas and should be well protected with a few good coats of paint or wax. During the winter especially, give the car underbody regular and thorough hose downs to remove general water retaining mud and salt.

RP6. Stone chips can be irritating but unless the car is wrapped up in the proverbial cotton wool, they're bound to occur. Corroless also market a handy paint chip kit which has its own internal wire brush for preparing the surface. ▼

RP7. Once a key has been made, apply a drop of paint followed later by body colour top coat. This primer also contains a rust killer. ◄

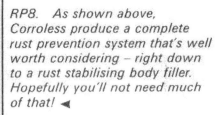

RP8. As shown above, Corroless produce a complete rust prevention system that's well worth considering – right down to a rust stabilising body filler. Hopefully you'll not need much of that! ◄

RP9. Applying underbody sealer, especially by spraying can be a very messy business so protect yourself and the rest of the car before starting.

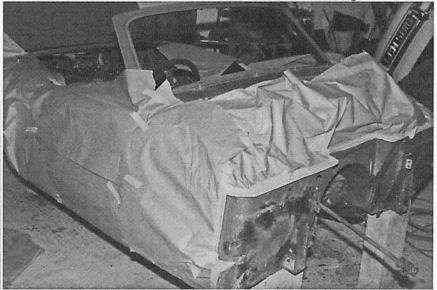

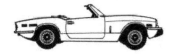

In the author's opinion, nothing really beats a well prepared and serviced paint finish for both outer body and under body surface. Mud and grime can be relatively easily hosed off and stone damage etc., can easily be seen and touched up. However, for the more 'do it and forget it' inclined, a good coating of an underbody sealer such as Body Schutz is a lot better than leaving repairs to the elements.

RP10. Particularly vulnerable areas include all wheel arches . . .

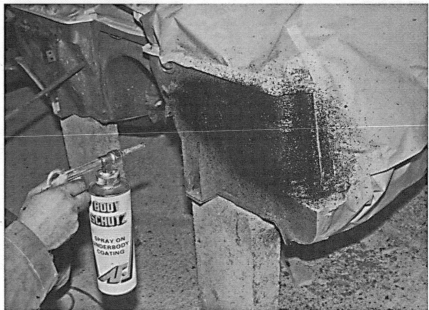

RP11. . . . and front bulkheads. Even underseal can benefit from a coat of paint afterwards. Plastic Padding market 'Stonechip Protect' in aerosol cans. It can be painted afterwards, dries to a smooth finish but gives the surface the toughness and flexibility to do as its name suggests.

Paintwork

With the bodywork complete, the time usually comes when you have to decide whether to respray the car yourself or to have it carried out professionally. Quotes for professional resprays can vary widely from a low price for a quick 'blow over' to £1000s for a money no object 'Rolls-Royce' finish. Quality has also been known to vary and one doesn't always get what one pays for. Certainly, as the final shine (literally) on all your efforts in restoring the car's bodywork, the quality and value offered by the professional sprayer should be carefully looked at. In the end the decision is down to personal choice not forgetting available finances. Where you intend having a professional respray, it's always best to shop around and better still, to use someone with whom you or other enthusiasts have had close contact.

Having said the above, it's certainly within the capabilities of most DIYers to undertake and achieve a high quality spray finish at home. The key word is 'preparation'. Without a really good base to lay the paint onto, a good result just won't be achieved. A high gloss paint finish brings out even the smallest of surface imperfections. It is rather beyond the scope of this book to describe all the different techniques available but certainly attention to the points given below will enable a very satisfying result to be achieved. A much more in-depth treatment regarding home spraying and car bodywork in general is given in Lindsay Porter's book, *The Car Bodywork Repair Manual*, also published by Haynes.

Tool box

Spray gun/compressor: hired, borrowed or bought. Preferably high pressure, with a reservoir tank but excellent results can be achieved with even basic machines given patience. Sanding block and various grades of wet and dry paper. Though not essential, a random orbit, D/A (Double Action) sander reduces the preparatory elbow work considerably.

Paint Systems

Nowadays, there are many different types of automotive paints available including cellulose, synthetics and acrylics. More modern paints may be classed as having high gloss from the gun whereas certainly with traditional cellulose enamel, some after spray compounding will be regarded as the norm in order to achieve the final desired result. Again, different paints require different setting conditions with some classed as air drying and others needing a low temperature bake. This obviously makes the latter unsuitable for the home restorer. A further paramount issue to the home resprayer is that of safety. Fumes from modern two-pack iso-cyanate containing paints, as implied by the name, are deadly poisonous and should only be used in conjunction with full safety breathing systems usually well beyond the amateur as outlined below. Hence the only type of paint we can recommend for the DIYer to use is cellulose. Even with this paint a proper charcoal filter mask should be worn and other general safety aspects adhered to.

Safety

Cellulose paint

The spray is volatile and so are the fumes from the paint and thinners – keep away from all flames or sparks. Thinner dampened rags are also a fire hazard. The spray can cause you to lose consciousness if inhaled in a confined area. Always use a suitable filter mask (check with your paint supplier) and ventilate the work area. Simple cotton masks are simply not good enough (handkerchiefs over the face are worse than useless). Protect hands with a barrier cream or wear protective gloves when handling paint (ensure that any gloves are not themselves dissolved by the paint solvent). Keep well away from eyes.

'2-pack' paint

Spray from this type of paint is toxic to the degree that it can be lethal! (The hardened paint on the car is not dangerous, of course!) Only use with an air fed mask from a clean, isolated compressed air source (i.e. not from within the spray area) and never use this type of paint where the spray could affect others. It can also cause eye irritation and eye protection should also be worn. Protective gloves should be worn when mixing and handling paint. Those who suffer from asthma or any other respiratory illness should have nothing to do with this (or possibly any other) type of paint spraying! There is also a fire risk with peroxide catalysts. In short, this type of paint can be seen to be totally unsuitable for DIY use and should be left entirely to the professional.

General

Don't eat, drink or smoke near the work area. Clean hands after the work is complete, but never use thinners to wash paint from the skin. Always wear an efficient particle mask when sanding down. **OBTAIN AND THOROUGHLY READ THE MANUFACTURERS DATA AND SAFETY SHEETS BEFORE USE. TAKE NOTICE OF THEM.**

PF1. To carry out a quality job and to reduce the amount of masking required, all ancillaries should be removed. In this case, the rear quarter windows from a GT6 may be detached by carefully drilling out the heads of the simple pop rivet fastenings.

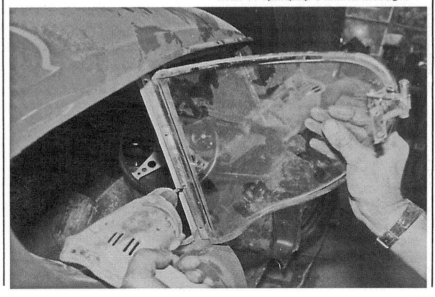

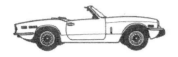

PF2.   Other items such as the rear deck soft top securing clips on a Spitfire 4 can be unbolted.

PF3.   For best results the old paint should be removed. (If spraying over old paint, you may have to apply a separate layer of a special isolating paint as different paints can show disastrous reactions if sprayed on top of one another. Check for this effect first by wiping over a small area of old paintwork with the new paint thinners. If wrinkling occurs the two paint systems are incompatible and an isolator will be required. Check repaired and pre-primered areas too). Make sure that the areas where you don't want stripper are adequately masked over. Old newspaper is OK, but since newsprint 'leaching' out into new paintwork is not unheard of, strong brown wrapping paper is better. Here, paint stripper is being applied to Dr. Cruse's GT6. Unlike the operator in the figure, ensure that you wear gloves (and wear safety glasses) in case of spills etc. Stripper, as you might expect, is very corrosive and will damage eyes and skin if splashed on to them. Read the safety notes that come with the stripper before use.

PF4.   Let the old paint wrinkle up and then remove with a metal scraper. You must still wear gloves and goggles!

PF5. A better idea than that shown in PF3 is to remove the doors at an early stage, masking over the door opening straight afterwards. This will certainly help keep stripper (if used) and paint dust out of the car. Paint overspray really does get everywhere if not protected against. As shown, always use proper masking tape. ►

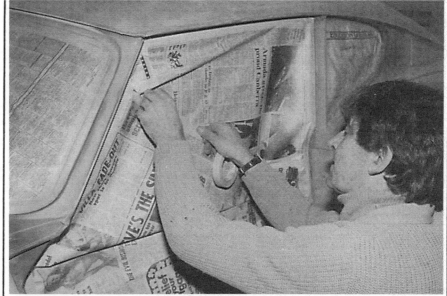

PF6. ► If the old paint is to be left on, it should be rubbed down starting with 240 grit paper ending up with 320. If rubbing down by hand, use a block to hold the paper and keep the paper wet to reduce clogging. Once the paint over the whole bodywork has been 'flatted' off, inspect each panel carefully. Slide your finger tips all over to detect any imperfections and repair before going any further. Here a skin of filler is being applied to the doorskin of Mrs. Terry Johnson's Herald featured earlier in the book.

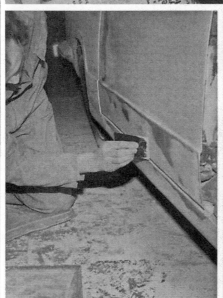
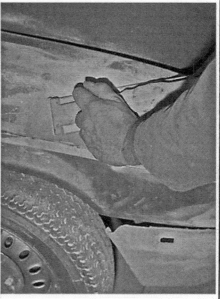

PF7. ▲ Where the panel surface is sharply curved as at the base of the windscreen pillar, abandon the paper holding block and apply directly by hand.

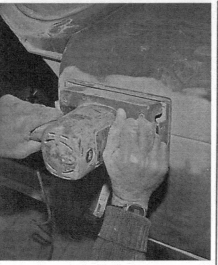

PF8. ▲ For larger surfaces, a double handed block should be used, to avoid creating undulations in the panel.

PF9. ◄ Alternatively, an electric sander of this type is fine for initially levelling filler. However, due to its action, scratch marks and ripples can be left behind which could show through the final paint finish. In this case, it's best to finish off by hand. Better still, and to obtain less effort, scratch-free sanding, you could use a random orbit sander. An example of one of these produced by Black and Decker is illustrated at the start of the chapter.

123

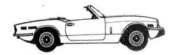

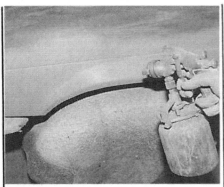

PF10. With the old paint removed or flatted down and totally dry, the first double coat of primer (or thicker primer surfacer) may be applied. Degrease the surface first using Berger spirit wipe which is made for the job. As always, ensure adequate ventilation. If applying to bare metal consider using a self-etch primer first to ensure a good key. **Check with the paint manufacturer's instructions concerning any special precautions necessary. As stated earlier not all paints are suitable for DIY application.** *As illustrated below, Berger produce an excellent range of paints well recommended for the home restorer. Paint/thinner ratios vary from paint to paint and depend on the spraygear used. Ideally the paint mix as recommended by your supplier should be checked with a viscosity cup – simply a funnel with a calibrated small hole. Fill it up and time how long it takes for the paint to empty out. A 50/50 mix is generally OK for high pressure equipment for all but perhaps the final top coat which is often thinned more. When applying the paint, keep your wrist locked and move the gun with an arm action so it always keeps at a right angle to and the same distance away from the work. To prevent edge build up, start moving the gun before pressing the trigger. Overlap each paint stroke by 50%.*

PF11. After applying primer coats, flat down again using 600 grade wet-and-dry used wet, again wrapping it around a block for support. Don't rub down too hard over edges as paint over corners is easily removed. One of the best ways to highlight surface irregularities is to use a guide coat over the primed surface. That is, apply a very thin dust coat of a contrasting colour paint (of the same type). After flatting down, highs and lows are contrasted where the guide coat remains. ▼

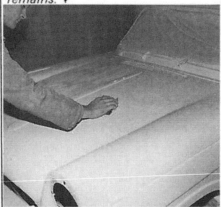

PF12. ▲ *Minor imperfections can then be corrected. Cellulose putty as shown here can sometimes shrink back. The best type to use is Two-Pack Stopper*

PF13. ▲ *After each flatting down, washing with clean water and drying session, and before applying the next coat, wipe over the whole car with a 'tack rag' to remove any surface dust. These wipes are slightly sticky and serve to remove any surface particles. To reduce airborne dust, dampen the floor of the work area with water.*

PF14. ▼ *Always start by spraying door shut openings and any other awkward areas such as around Spitfire headlamps, where, to delay when spraying the complete car could cause a run to occur. Detachable panels such as doors, valances, etc., are often best sprayed off the car. If the paint does start to sag at any stage, don't try to correct by immediately applying more paint. It'll only make it worse. Allow the paint to thoroughly dry and then carefully flat it back. This is one of the times when patience plays a great part towards achieving a good result.*

PF15. ◄ *With awkward areas out of the way, paint the roof next, starting with a central line running from front to rear and*

working outwards towards the gutter. Once complete, go around to the other side of the car and repeat for the remaining roof area again working from the centre outwards. The choice is then yours. Start at one corner of the car and working on one panel at a time with horizontal strips work your way all around. About three double coats should be sufficient. For best results, each double coat should be allowed to dry and then rubbed down wth 400 or preferably 650 grade paper used with lots of water. As mentioned before, ensure that all seams are totally dry before applying the next coat and use a fresh tack rag just before painting. For best results before applying the final coat, remove all the old masking and apply fresh. This ensures that any dust trapped in the masking isn't incorporated in the final finish.

PF17. ▲ **HMG** produce an excellent range of automotive paints such as Two-pack which gives the most durable finish though is strictly for professional use only.

PF18. At the same time, some still produce cellulose paint which is a high quality, high gloss vehicle paint suitable for use by the DIYer provided he/she always wears a charcoal mask when spraying and remembers to properly ventilate the work area. (See 'Safety' notes).

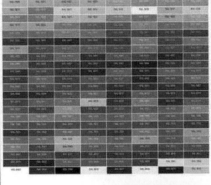

PF19. For spraying, the Clarke 'pioneer' is a very popular 'first time buyer' compressor, capable of completing a full respray, and fine for smaller jobs including use for other purposes such as tyre inflating, etc.

PF20. Going further up the scale, the ABAC 27 Hp 2 is probably larger than the average DIY user will buy but would cope easily with a full paint job or for powering professional air tools.

PF16. As suggested in PF14 it's a good idea to spray large removable objects such as doors, bootlids etc., off the car, preferably with items such as door handles removed. With the car now painted, allow it to dry for at least a week before compounding. If the final spray finish needs heavier treatment to achieve a good gloss, rub the paint down with 1200 grade paper used with soap and lots of water. Obviously, treat the paintwork very gently at this stage then finish off with fine compound and polish.

4 Mechanical Components

Tool box

Fortunately, the Herald, Vitesse, Spitfire, GT6 range does not demand the use of many special tools. Where special processes are required, they can invariably be got round by using the techniques described here and in the relevant *Haynes Owners Workshop Manual.* There is one for every model of car covered in this book and it is intended that the Haynes Manual will be used in association with this book.

TBI. To complement the Sykes-Pickavant tools shown elsewhere, there is a range of S-P mechanic's tool boxes and chests which enable you to store your precious gear in a tidy and secure manner. ▼

TB2. Some "special tools" are really a part of the keen mechanic's kit. You'll probably need an oil filter remover, a piston ring compresser and feeler gauges. Other S-P and Speedline tools shown here include an electrical circuit tester, a boon when rewiring or re-assembling electrics, spark plug (cylinder head) thread chaser and top-left, a cylinder head stand for those who want to get it "absolutely right". ◄

TB3. When the engine rebuild is complete, a dwell-tach tester, 7-function analyser and timing aid marketed by Sedan, will enable you to get the engine settings spot-on. ▼

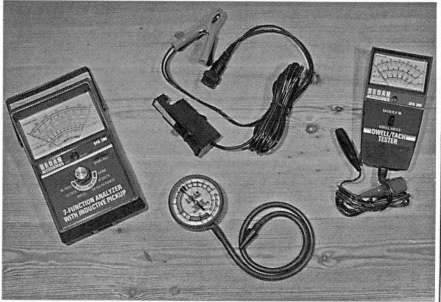

Front suspension and front brake overhaul

Apart from spring rates, the fitting of drum or disc brakes and other minor differences, all Herald based cars share the same front suspension components. Repair and replacement of ball joints, trunnions and bushes etc., are all straightforward and shouldn't cause any difficulty to the home restorer.

Drum and disc brake removal

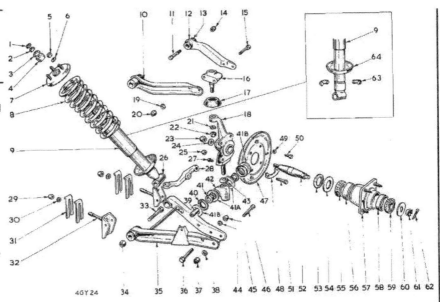

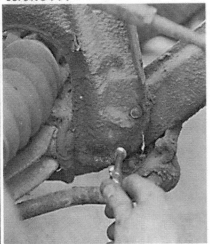

FSO1. For full dismantling, begin by removing the engine bay splash guards. On Heralds and Vitesses, this involves removing two front lower set screws . . .

FSO2. . . . plus bolts each side of the suspension turrets. The hose on models with drum brakes also needs to be removed . . .

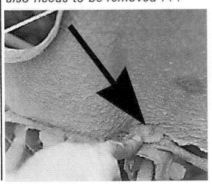

FSO3. . . . before the splash guards can be lifted free. As shown, this early Herald Coupé is fitted with drum brakes . . .

. . . whilst the majority of cars were fitted with discs.

FSO4.

FSO5. On both types, disconnect the steering rack ball joints by removing the lower nut and splitting the joint.

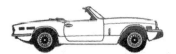

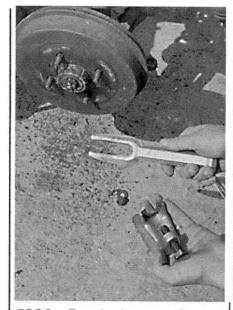

FSO6. Two basic types of splitters are available, those with a screw pressure action and other simple wedge types. Once again, the most reliable are those made by the better UK, German or US firms.

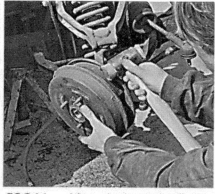

FSO11. After slackening off the brake shoes and removing the two locking screws, the drum and hub assembly may be tapped off . . .

FSO8. On drum brakes, prise off the grease cap and straighten out

FSO9. . . . and withdraw the locking split pin.

FSO12. . . . followed by the felt grease seal.

FSO7. The wedge-in types are very effective though ensure that you don't damage the brake slave cylinder nipples if the cylinders are to be used again. This is probably a false economy anyway especially during a full rebuild. Throw away and buy new.

FSO10. On disc brakes a different grease cap is fitted. Screw in a wood screw and pull off. Behind lies the same nut and thick washer as found on drum units.

FSO13. Disc calipers and hubs are removed by releasing the two locking bolts behind.

FSO14. . . . sliding the caliper off (place the caliper on a box so that no weight is taken by the hydraulic hose) . . .

FSO15. . . . and withdrawing the hub complete with attached disc. The disc may be refitted by releasing four bolts on the opposite side of the hub. The outer bearing can be slid free at this stage . . .

FSO16. . . . and the disc dust shield lifted off.

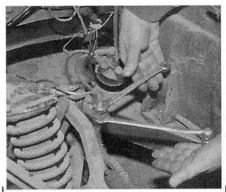

FSO17. To remove the caliper from the car, simply unscrew and release the brake hose.

FSO18. To further dismantle drum brakes, tap back the locking tabs on the lower 9/16in bolts . .

FSO19. . . . and unscrew. This bolt is fixed with a nut on the other side. The other screws directly into the vertical link. Next, remove the two 1/2in bolts above.

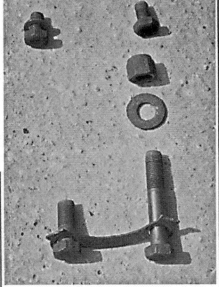

FSO20. The bolts and nut revealed.

FSO21. The back plate can now be tapped free from the link.

Front trunnion replacement

FTR1. Loosen off and remove the front trunnion bolt. Note the felt grease seal cup on this model.

FTR2. The vertical link may then be removed by either splitting the top ball joint as described previously . . . ▼

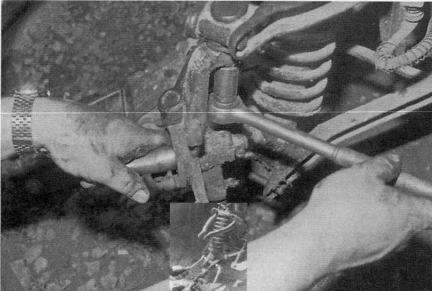

FTR3. ►. . . or by releasing the joint's two transverse bolts as shown here.

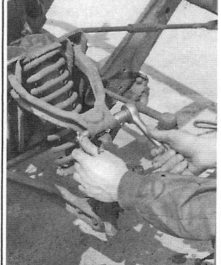

FTR4. ▲ It helps to loosen off the lower shock absorber bolt in order to withdraw the link.

FTR5. ▲ Once off the car, the vertical link can be brushed clean . . .

FTR6. ◄ . . . and the trunnion unscrewed from the link. Examine the link threads for wear and especially check that the lower end is straight and not bent due to accident damage (usually due to 'kerbing').

FTR7. The full kit of parts for replacing both axles with trunnions, seals and bushes. The trunnion threads are handed and will only fit on their designated side. ▼

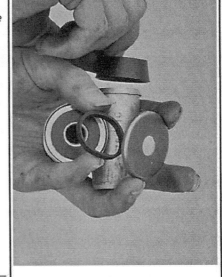

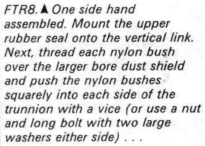

FTR8. ▲ One side hand assembled. Mount the upper rubber seal onto the vertical link. Next, thread each nylon bush over the larger bore dust shield and push the nylon bushes squarely into each side of the trunnion with a vice (or use a nut and long bolt with two large washers either side) . . .

FTR9. . . . followed by the metal inner bush, rubber sealing ring and outer dust shield. The trunnion should be screwed to the end of its travel onto the link so that the top rubber seal seals without great distortion. Unscrew just enough so that when moved from side to side, the trunnion moves comfortably through its full arc of travel under normal operating conditions. Fill a grease gun and fill the trunnion with EP90 gear oil. DO NOT USE GREASE of any description. It's just not suitable. It's also best to have an extra grease gun filled with this oil for routine servicing in any case.

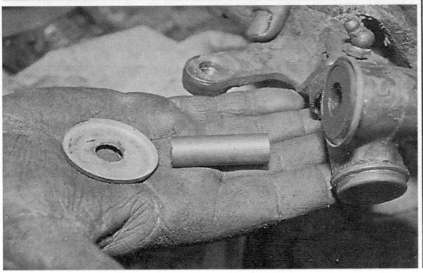

Wishbone and shock absorber dismantling

WSD1► *Following removing the vertical link, remove the shock absorber complete with spring by removing the top three nuts.*

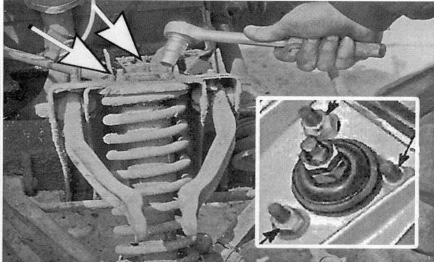

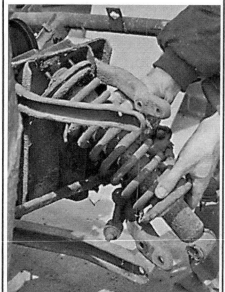

WSD2.▲ *Removing the spring/shock absorber unit. No special tools are required at this stage. However, if planning to separate or fit new springs and shocks, the proper spring compressor tool MUST be used. Home built lash ups are deadly dangerous. There's an awful lot of stored energy in such a spring, so take care. Read your Haynes manual for full information on spring removal.*

WSD3.► *Upper wishbone arms may be removed by undoing a single bolt each side. On reassembly, burn out the old bushes with a blow lamp – they don't easily push out cold. Have a fire extinguisher close by in case the flames threaten to get out of hand! Don't breath in the fumes. Squeeze in new ones using a vice. A spot or two of washing up liquid is a good lubricant.*

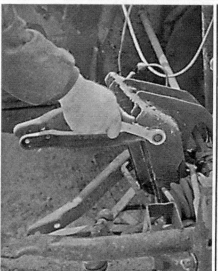

WSD4.▲ *Detach the anti roll bar mounting arm either with spanners or if necessary saw through. The rubber insert will often be perished so fit new ones on reasembly.*

WSD5.▼ *At the other end, remove the nut or stud holding the link to the bar.*

WSD6. ▶ *The lower wishbones are removed by undoing the nut the other side of the chassis . . .*

WSD7. ▼ *. . . and removing complete with brackets. On the bracket side (arrowed) the bolts are arranged in such a way as to not allow their removal before the wishbone is removed from the car. Note the spacer plates. There may be none or more than one of these and the number may vary at each bracket so make a note of the number and location now! Or even take a photograph – not a bad general technique. Check the trunnion and shock absorber mounting bolt holes for wear and renew the wishbone if any are oval.*

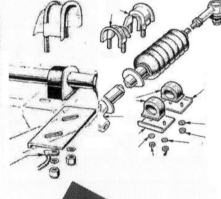

Steering rack removal

SRR1. ◀ *Early Herald brackets used solid alloy mountings. All later models employ brackets with rubber inserts which tend to soften with age due to oil contamination. As applicable, fit new inserts on reassembly.*

SRR2. *The steering rack can be removed by undoing two brackets and four nuts.*

WSD8. ▲ *The correct spring compressing tool mentioned is WSD2. This particular version, made by Sykes-Pickavant, is ideal for the home restorer or even the small garage as the compressors*

are very strong and well made. Ensure that they are located correctly at opposite sides of the spring and that they are tightened or removed evenly.

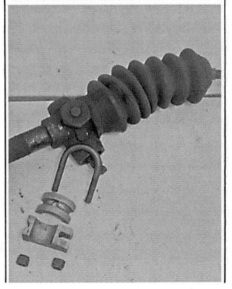

133

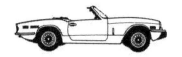

Front wheel bearing renewal

FWB1. Inspect both outer and inner bearings for wear. If showing pitted or stained surfaces or if at all doubtful, replace. ▶

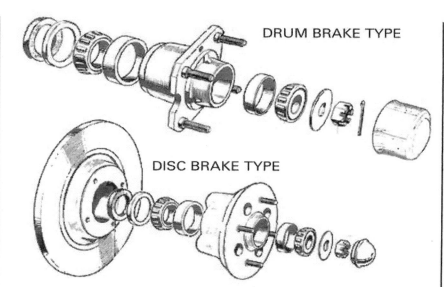

DRUM BRAKE TYPE

DISC BRAKE TYPE

FWB2. Clean the hub of all old grease . . .

FWB4. ▲ The inner race removed.

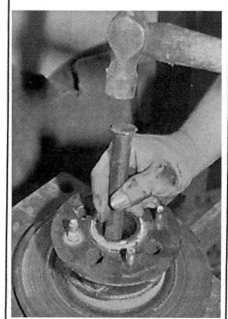

FWB3. ▲ . . . drift out the inner races.

FWB5. A new bearing and race together. Inners and outers are different sizes.

GT6 Mk 3s with rotoflex drive shaft couplings. Basic dismantling is much the same though. The work in this section is again shown being carried out on Richard Swinfield's Spitfire 1500 at Classic Restoration Centre, other than that which relates to the car with body in place.

FWB6. Drift in the new bearing race evenly, preferably with a SOFT faced hammer (unlike shown here) or with the aid of a piece of wood. Repeat for the other side.

FWB7. On reassembly don't forget to fit and pre-grease both sides of the felt grease seal. Carefully inspect the stub axle for wear, replace as necessary and refit packing the hub and bearings with high melting point grease. Tighten the outer nut so that the hub tightens up and then loosen off until a new split pin can be fitted while making sure that the hub turns freely. You should loosen off the minimum amount from the 'tight' position, compatible with the hub turning freely and the split pin finding its 'home' position.

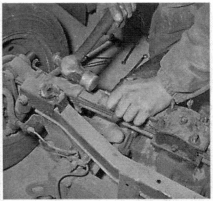

RED1.▲ With the body off, everything is open and easy to get at. It's not much more difficult with the body on. Differential nuts can sometimes seize but can often be chiselled free . . .

RED2.▼ . . . and spannered off or removed with a nut splitter. Late Spitfire and GT6 swing springs are attached with four studs. All other models are fitted with six.

Rear end mechanical assembly dismantling

The rear suspension of Heralds, Vitesses, Spitfires and GT6's are all remarkably similar. In fact the only major differences exist for all GT6 and Vitesse Mk 2s and early

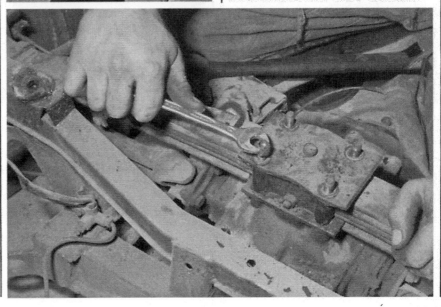

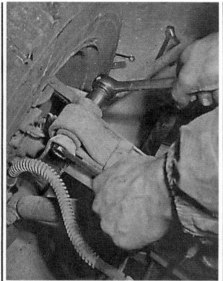

RED3. Unscrew the spring eye bolt . . .

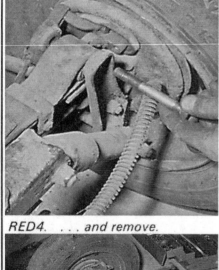

RED4. . . . and remove.

RED5. The spring can then be levered off. Keep clear until the spring is clear.

RED6. With the body still on the car, jack up the car (ensure it's securely chocked) and set on stands or ramps under the chassis. Take the load off the spring with a spring lifting tool and drift out the spring eye bolt. Keep fingers well out of the way of the spring's expected travel as the bolt is being withdrawn. A very convenient place to keep the tool in position is to secure the handle on top of an axle stand. The spring's tension keeps it there during the work. Alternatively take the load off the spring by jacking under the vertical link. Take care that it doesn't slip off.

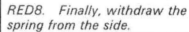

RED7. Using a stud extractor or the double locknut technique shown here, remove the six (or four) holding studs.

RED8. Finally, withdraw the spring from the side.

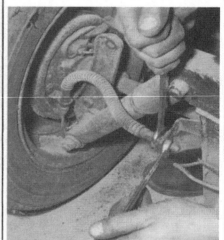

RED9. Brake hoses should also be removed.

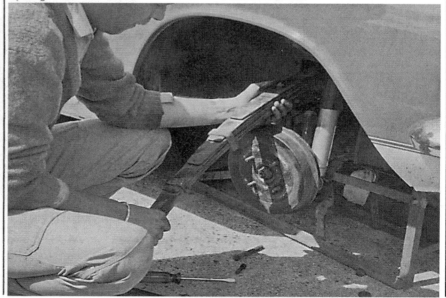

RED10. Followed by the top shock absorber bolts. On rotoflex drive shafts, the top shock absorber mountings are fixed to the inner wheel arch.

RED11. Four bolts and nyloc nuts secure each driveshaft to the differential. Fit new bolts and nuts on reassembly.

RED12. With the chassis on blocks, the driveshafts complete with vertical links and hubs can now be removed and dismantled on the bench.

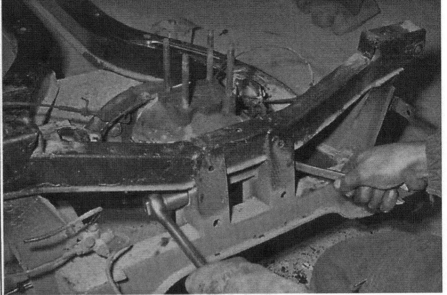

RED13 On all but the earliest Herald models, the differential unit is held with a single long bolt at the back which should be loosened off . . .

RED14. ◄ . . . and removed. Early models employ two bolts.

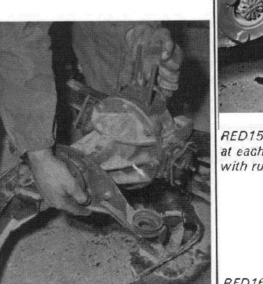

RED15. ▲ The unit is suspended at each side by two further bolts with rubber bushes.

RED16. ◄ Remove these and lift the differential out.

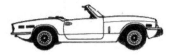

Rotoflex coupling replacement

In general, few improvements are gained without some drawback and having the improved rear suspension set-up on a Mk 2 Vitesse, or a Mk 2 or early Mk 3 GT6 is no exception. It's not surprising, considering the load placed on them, that the rubber rotoflex couplings used on these models do wear out, usually by the rubber becoming detached from the inner metal plates.

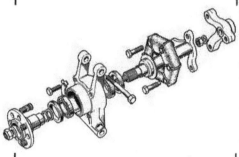

RCR4.   The main components revealed.

RCR2.   Replacing the coupling firstly involves pushing the outer drive shaft out of the hub. Use a suitable tool. The one shown here is actually home made but commerically produced tools should be available for hire or alternatively, take the drive shaft to your friendly neighbourhood garage and ask them to push the shaft out for you. Ensure that the outer shaft threads are protected. Here, they've been taped over and an old universal joint bearing cup is being placed over the top.

RCR5.   The rotoflex can now be removed by undoing six bolts. Always fit new bolts when reassembling. New rubber couplings are fitted with a metal compression band which MUST be left in place until all the bolts have been replaced – to a torque of 65 – 70 lb ft. The band can quite easily be left in place until the drive shaft is back in the car then sawn through.

RCR1.   A lightly worn rotoflex coupling.   Even when not totally detached, the rubber can nearly all come away from the metal sections to which it was originally bonded. Usually wear is noticed by an increase in vibration which can sometimes be mistaken for a worn universal joint.

RCR3.   Fix the tool in position and screw in the central operating bolt. As shown here, a lever threaded through the coupling helps stop the whole of the drive shaft from rotating.

In principle the drive shaft can be put back together as a straight reversal of dismantling, ending by tightening the (new) hub nut to a torque of 100 – 110lbf ft. The aim is to achieve a smoothly rotating hub but one which is not over loose. If fitting new bearings, different shims will probably need to be fitted which can sometimes be a difficult business to get just right without access to special tools. If in doubt on this final point, whether fitting new bearings or not, it may be best in this case to revert to your local specialist.

Engine removal (cylinder head in situ)

Due to the excellent front-end accessibility, there's probably no other production car which presents such easy access for engine removal as those of the

Herald family. Engines from all models can be removed either separately or complete with the gearbox.

Considering that the bonnet can be removed in about ten minutes, and that once ancillaries have been removed, the

engine/gearbox is held in place by just four bolts, it's probably easier even when tackling removing the gearbox alone to take both the engine and gearbox out together and dismantle on the bench. This is especially true when removing the heavier 6-cylinder units.

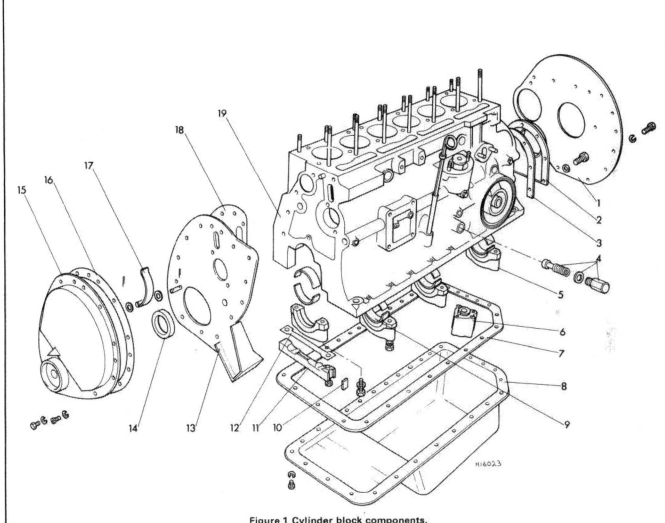

Figure 1 Cylinder block components, 6-cylinder engine

1 Back plate	8 Sump	14 Timing case oil seal
2 Rear oil seal and housing	9 Bearing shells	15 Timing case
3 Rear oil seal housing gasket	10 Front sealing block wedge	16 Timing case gasket
4 Relief valve	11 Front sealing block	17 Timing chain tensioner
5 Main bearing cap	12 Gasket (later models)	18 Front plate gasket
6 Oil pump body	13 Front plate	19 Cylinder block
7 Sump gasket		

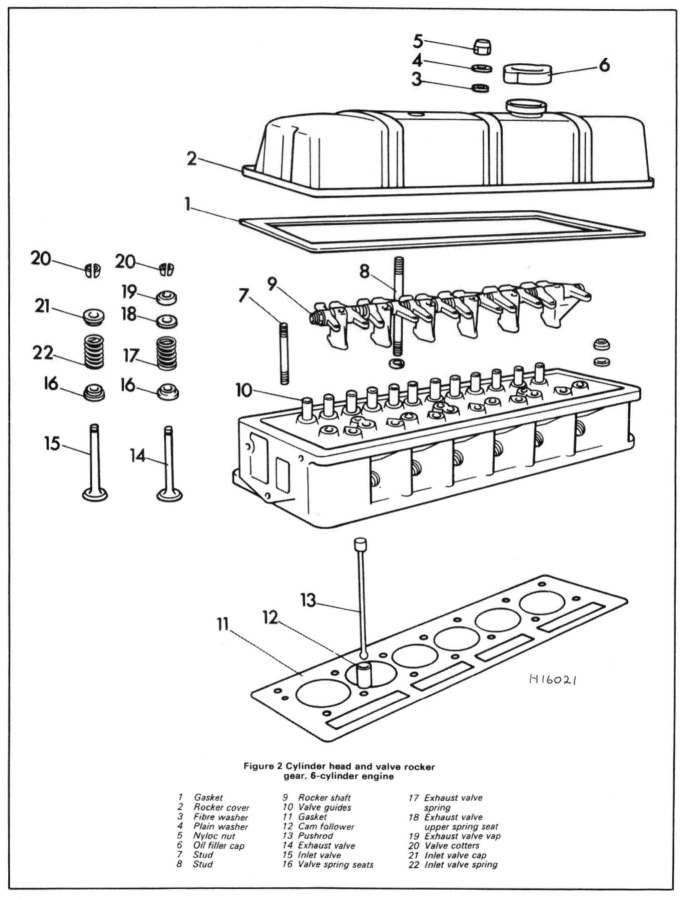

**Figure 2 Cylinder head and valve rocker
gear, 6-cylinder engine**

1 Gasket	9 Rocker shaft	17 Exhaust valve spring
2 Rocker cover	10 Valve guides	
3 Fibre washer	11 Gasket	18 Exhaust valve upper spring seat
4 Plain washer	12 Cam follower	
5 Nyloc nut	13 Pushrod	19 Exhaust valve vap
6 Oil filler cap	14 Exhaust valve	20 Valve cotters
7 Stud	15 Inlet valve	21 Inlet valve cap
8 Stud	16 Valve spring seats	22 Inlet valve spring

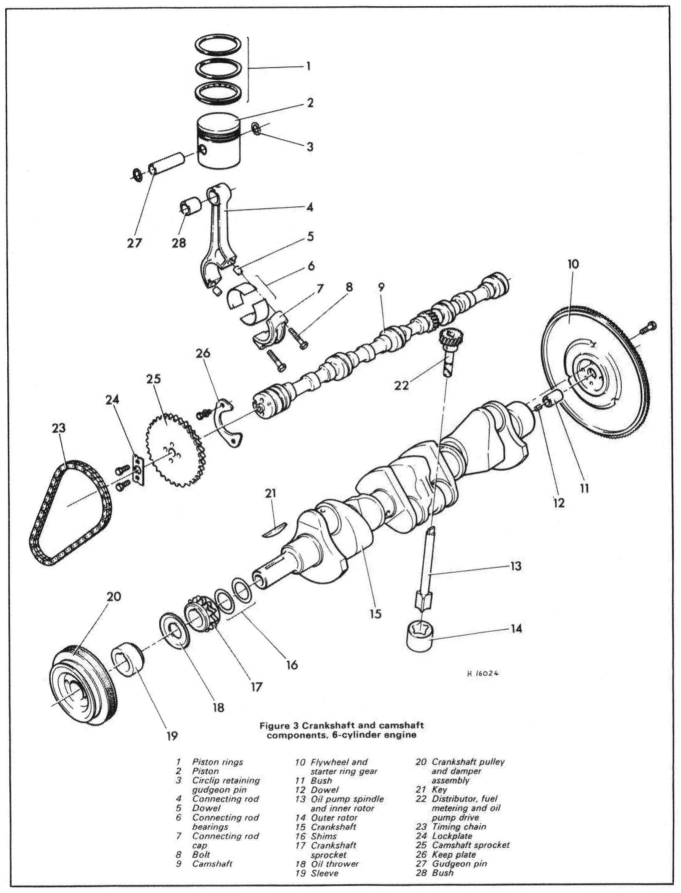

**Figure 3 Crankshaft and camshaft
components, 6-cylinder engine**

1	Piston rings	
2	Piston	
3	Circlip retaining gudgeon pin	
4	Connecting rod	
5	Dowel	
6	Connecting rod bearings	
7	Connecting rod cap	
8	Bolt	
9	Camshaft	
10	Flywheel and starter ring gear	
11	Bush	
12	Dowel	
13	Oil pump spindle and inner rotor	
14	Outer rotor	
15	Crankshaft	
16	Shims	
17	Crankshaft sprocket	
18	Oil thrower	
19	Sleeve	
20	Crankshaft pulley and damper assembly	
21	Key	
22	Distributor, fuel metering and oil pump drive	
23	Timing chain	
24	Lockplate	
25	Camshaft sprocket	
26	Keep plate	
27	Gudgeon pin	
28	Bush	

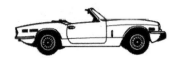

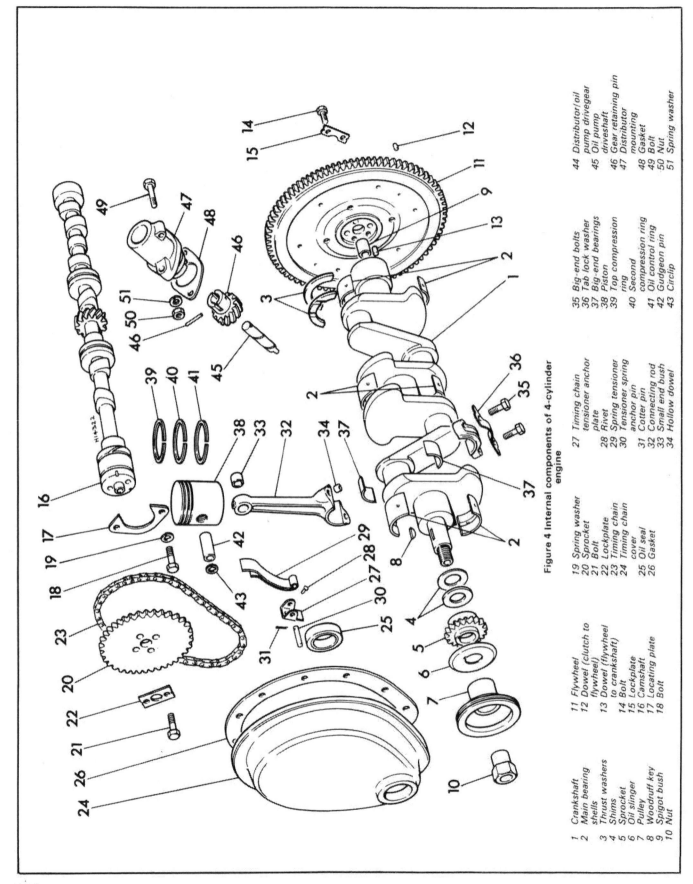

Figure 4 Internal components of 4-cylinder engine

1 Crankshaft
2 Main bearing shells
3 Thrust washers
4 Shims
5 Sprocket
6 Oil slinger
7 Pulley
8 Woodruff key
9 Spigot bush
10 Nut
11 Flywheel
12 Dowel (clutch to flywheel)
13 Dowel (flywheel to crankshaft)
14 Bolt
15 Lockplate
16 Camshaft
17 Locating plate
18 Bolt
19 Spring washer
20 Sprocket
21 Bolt
22 Lockplate
23 Timing chain
24 Timing chain cover
25 Oil seal
26 Gasket
27 Timing chain tensioner anchor plate
28 Rivet
29 Spring tensioner
30 Tensioner spring anchor pin
31 Cotter pin
32 Connecting rod
33 Small end bush
34 Hollow dowel
35 Big-end bolts
36 Tab lock washer
37 Big-end bearings
38 Piston
39 Top compression ring
40 Second compression ring
41 Oil control ring
42 Gudgeon pin
43 Circlip
44 Distributor/oil pump drivegear
45 Oil pump driveshaft
46 Gear retaining pin
47 Distributor mounting
48 Gasket
49 Bolt
50 Nut
51 Spring washer

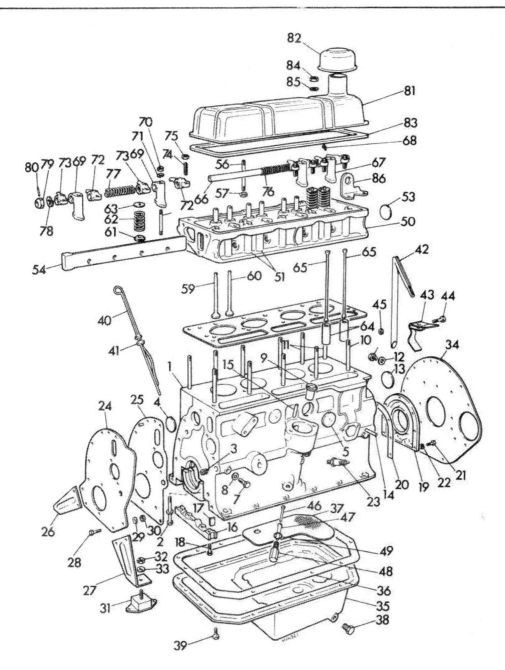

Figure 5 Exploded view of typical 4-cylinder engine

1 Cylinder block	15 Distributor mounting stud	28 Bolt	45 Nut	60 Exhaust valve	73 Rocker arm
2 Bolt and lockwasher	16 Front sealing block	29 Spring washer	46 Oil pressure relief valve plunger	61 Spring lower seat	74 Ball pin
3 Oil gallery plug	17 Filler piece	30 Nut	47 Plunger spring	62 Valve spring	75 Locknut
4 Welch plug	18 Screw	31 Engine mounting pad	48 Retaining plug	63 Valve spring upper seat	76 Rocker shaft spring
5 Welch plug	19 Oil seal retainer	32 Nut	49 Washer	64 Tappet (cam follower)	77 Rocker shaft springs
6 Welch plug	20 Gasket	33 Spring washer	50 Cylinder head	65 Pushrods	78 Spring washer
7 Oil gallery bolt	21 Bolt	34 Engine rear plate	51 Pushrod tubes	66 Rocker shaft	79 Collar
8 Washer	22 Spring washer	35 Sump	52 Valve guide	67 Drilled rocker pedestal	80 Roll pin
9 Oil pump shaft bush	23 Oil pressure switch	36 Gasket	53 Core plug	68 Bolt and lockwasher	81 Rocker cover
10 Cylinder head stud	24 Engine front plate	37 Oil strainer gauze	54 Coolant distributor tube	69 Undrilled rocker pedestal	82 Oil filler cap with breather
11 Cylinder head stud	25 Gasket	38 Oil drain plug	55 Rocker pedestal stud	70 Nut	83 Rocker cover gasket
12 Coolant drain plug	26 Typical engine mounting bracket	39 Bolt	56 Rocker cover stud	71 Lockwasher	84 Nut
13 Fibre washer	27 Typical engine mounting bracket	40 Dipstick	57 Nut	72 Rocker arm	85 Plain and fibre washers
14 Fuel pump stud		41 Felt washer	58 Gasket		
		42 Breather pipe	59 Inlet valve		
		43 Deflector			
		44 Bolt			

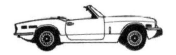

Tool box

General range of sockets, screwdrivers and spanners. Engine hoist or a few friends.

Safety
NEVER work or stand beneath an engine suspended on a hoist, or have an arm or hand in a position where it could be crushed. Even the sturdiest of hoists could give way or ropes or chains slip. When attaching to the engine, try to use mechanical lifting fixings rather than tying ropes. Always have someone with you to lend a hand.

With the engine out of the car ensure that when working on it that the block is securely chocked and that there's no danger of it toppling over. Don't trust anything but the stoutest of benches. Hire a purpose built stand or work on the floor.

Below, the general steps for removing a late Spitfire engine are shown. Owners of all the cars will note the obvious similarities to their model.

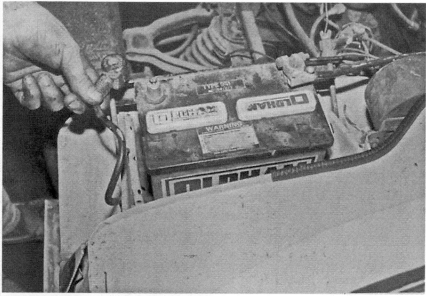

ER1.▲ If it hasn't been done already, remove the battery. Earth lead first (replace last).

ER2.◄ Remove ancillary cables such as choke and throttle cables (and tacho where applicable) and of course drain and remove fuel lines. Other models feature mechanical throttle mechanisms. Also remove electrical wiring to the coil etc. Don't forget the earth straps especially the one underneath the engine to the steering rack.

ER3. Ancillaries such as carbs, water pump etc., can be left on but to reduce the lift load can easily be removed. Here, the carbs have been removed and the manifold nuts are just being released. Alternatively, release the exhaust manifold nuts and allow the exhaust to fall to the floor. Note the engine lifting eye on the cylinder head to the rear of the engine.

ER4. Removing the bonnet, covered in section B1-6 makes life a lot easier. After draining the cooling system (and oil while you remember) remove the heater and radiator hoses followed by the radiator itself . . . ▶

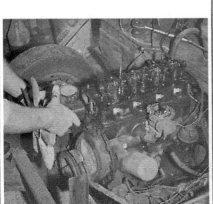

ER5. ▲ . . . and the water pump. (Although the rocker cover has been removed, this obviously isn't required unless carrying out cylinder head work whilst the engine is on the car).

ER7. ◀ Again, if just working on the cylinder head perhaps while just carrying out a decoke, the head can be removed after gradually releasing the stud nuts. If the head sticks, don't be tempted to lever it off by inserting a chisel or screwdriver between head and block. Shake it free by firmly striking with a SOFT-faced hammer.

FRONT

Herald 1200, 12·50 or Spitfire rocker assembly

1 Rocker shaft	7 Pedestal, rear	13 Centre distance spring
2 End cap	8 Shakeproof washer	
3 Mills pin	9 Phillips head screw	NOTE: The Vitesse rocker
4 Locknut	10 Rocker, L.H.	assembly is similar but has
5 Rocker, R.H	11 Distance spring	12 rockers, 6 pedestals and
6 Adjusting screw	12 Pedestal	5 distance springs.

ER6. ▲ If desired, the rocker gear may be removed by undoing the pedestal nuts – release each a little at a time. As push rods are removed, push each through a numbered 1-8 (or 1-12), front to rear, piece of card or purpose tray to enable replacement in the same order as removal. Inspect for wear and replace as necessary.

ER8. Take the weight of the engine on a hoist and undo the bell housing bolts (sturdy, secure axle stands supporting the gearbox are an absolute MUST here) followed by the engine mounting nuts. Double check that all cables have been removed. The engine should then be lifted slightly forwards and upwards to release the engine/gearbox splines and then winched free. Although shown here with the cylinder head removed, it's really easier to lift the engine out with it still in place, making use of the lifting eye shown in ER3.

As mentioned previously, it's probably easier, especially if carrying out a full restoration, to remove the engine complete with gearbox. In this case, leave the bell housing bolts connected but ensure that the top bolts holding the clutch hydraulic pipe and electrical earth strap, and starter motor wires have been removed. Next, release the rear gearbox mounting points and undo the speedo cable and any associated overdrive wiring. Both units can now be removed intact.

ER9. Not necessarily recommended for everyone but it is quite possible to man-handle at least the four-cylinder versions out though it's probably more sensible to use a stout timber across the car coupled with lifting chains. ...

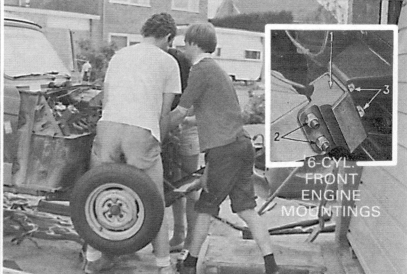

ER10. ... But do remember that there's a real risk of putting backs out, doing it this way. You have been warned!

ER11. These are:

A. The Spitfire 1500's engine mounting points plus the USA model's Engine Restraint device (arrowed).

B. Vitesse/GT6 engine lifting points as recommended by Triumph.

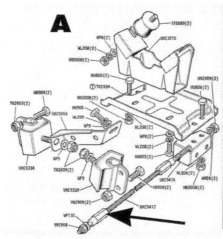

146

Engine stripdown

It doesn't necessarily save you money to carry out your own engine stripdown although you will have the satisfaction of doing it yourself and you will also undoubtedly take more personal interest in its rebuild than the 'professionals'. In fact, the engine shown here had to be done again because of a fault in the block that was missed the first time the work was done . . .

Toolbox

Additional tools: extra large socket or adjustable wrench for front crankshaft pulley nut.

Engine back plate

ESBP1. ▼ Once the engine flywheel is removed, by knocking back the locking tabs and undoing 4 bolts, the engine back plate securing bolts can be released . . .

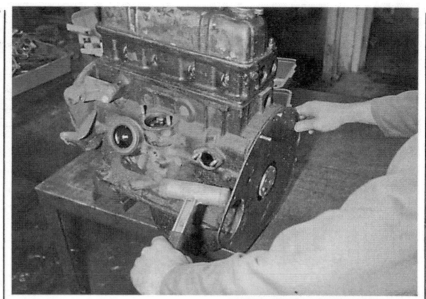

ESBP2. ▲ . . . and the plate itself tapped off with a soft-faced hammer.

Cylinder head removal

CYR1. ► Undo the two or three rocker cover fixings and remove.

CYR2. ▼ Gradually release the rocker gear pedestal nuts . . .

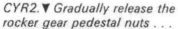

CYR3. ▲ . . . and lift off.

147

CYR4.► Lift out the pushrods and store as suggested in ER6.

CYR5.▲ Next, undo the cylinder head nuts little by little: in general starting from the centre and working symmetrically outwards. Sometimes the whole stud will lift out rather than just the top nut. This doesn't present any problems.

CYR6.▲ The cylinder head may then be lifted off. As mentioned above, if it sticks, don't insert a screwdriver or similar between head and block and try levering it off. Damage may well result. Be patient. Use plenty of releasing fluid around the studs and apply firm taps with a SOFT-faced hammer or mallet to shake the head free. It will eventually come off.

CYR7.▲ Remove the head gasket. Don't even consider re-using it. However, it may well be worth keeping for a while to act as a reference for the new one. Note which way up the gasket should be replaced by referring to the bore edge reinforcing material. Not all new gaskets are stamped 'top'.

CYR8.► Either with a stud extractor as shown or using the double lock nut technique remove the head studs. The engine can now be turned over.

Sump and oil pump removal

SPR1.▼ Start by undoing and removing the series of bolts which secure the sump pan to the block.

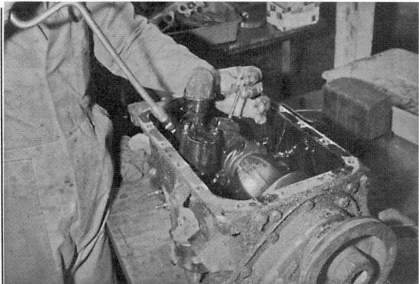

SPR3.▲ Remove the three oil pump securing bolts . . .

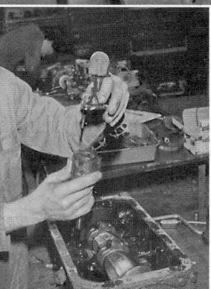

SPR4.◄ . . . and lift the components clear.

SPR5.▼ Keep the components together by wiring up.

SPR2.▲ If it sticks, as with the cylinder head, free it by tapping with a soft-faced hammer or mallet. On replacement and before fitting a new gasket, ensure that any traces of the old gasket have been removed to ensure a leak tight seal.

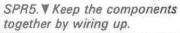

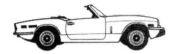

Crankshaft removal

CR1. With the aid of a large socket or adjustable wrench loosen off the front pulley nut. A sharp tap on the wrench is often the best method rather than relying on steady leverage. Early models may have a toothed starting handle dog nut. To stop the crankshaft rotating, wedge in a stout piece of timber. This nut was actually seized solid and only came off after the application of much heat and unorthodox thumping.

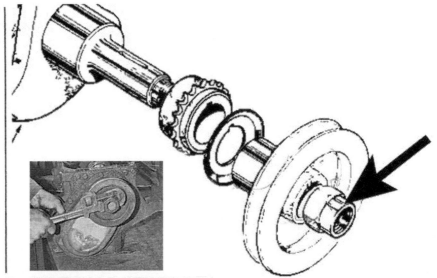

CR2. ◄ Remove the nut and tap off the pulley.

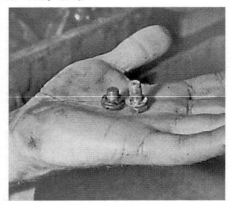

CR4. ▲ . . . and screws holding the timing cover in place . . .

CR5. ▼ . . . which can now be carefully prised off. Don't distort the cover as this could lead to leaks on reassembly.

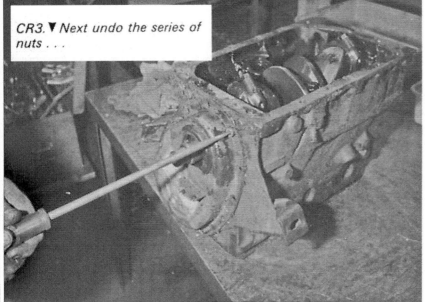

CR3. ▼ Next undo the series of nuts . . .

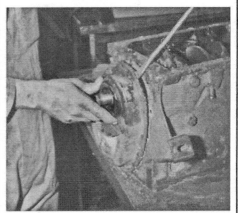

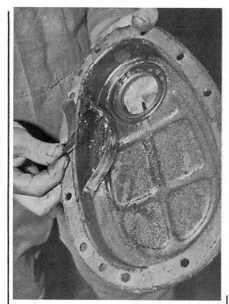

CR6. A noisy timing chain assembly could be due to a broken spring tensioner as shown here.

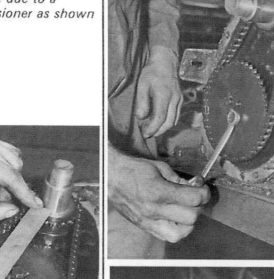

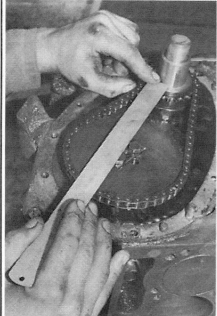

CR7. With the cover removed and number 1 piston at top dead centre (as shown), check that the sprocket alignment marks are clear.

CR8. ▲ Tap back the two locking tabs on the main timing wheel . .

CR9. ◄ . . . and release the machine screws.

CR10. ▼ The timing wheels and chain assembly can now be simply slid off.

CR11. Note the shim remaining on the end of the crankshaft which effectively sets the two timing wheel faces level with one another. This can't be removed until the Woodruff key (arrowed) is tapped out. Remove the camshaft securing plate nuts . . .

CR12. . . . and remove the plate.

CR13. The front engine plate can now be removed by releasing the remaining bolts and screws . .

CR14 ▲ . . . and tapping free the front engine plate.

CR15.◄ Similarly, remove the two front sealing block screws . . .

CR16.◄ . . . tap loose . . .

CR17 . . . and remove. ▼

CR18. ▶ Before removing anything else, clearly mark all big-end . . .

CR19 . . . and main bearing caps with centre-punch marks in such a way as to allow them to be replaced in EXACTLY the same place as they were removed. The adjacent sets of three dots can easily be seen for con-rod number three in the figure. Also note which way round the con-rods face in the block.

CR20. ▲ The next step is to remove the rear oil seal assembly. In earlier models, the rear of the crankshaft has circumferential grooves which direct oil back into the engine. Later models, as in the case here, employ an internal rubber oil seal. Earlier models may also have either aluminium or steel seal assemblies. Crankshaft clearances for these differ as described later under engine assembly.

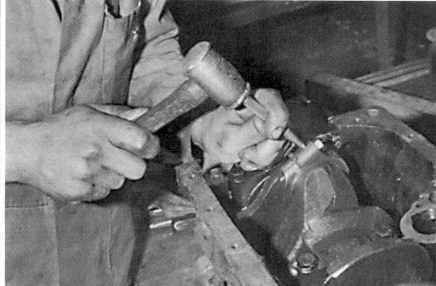

CR21. ◀ Release the con-rod bearing cap . . .

CR22. . . . and main bearing cap bolts and remove the caps.

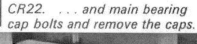

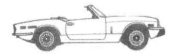

CR23.▲ The crankshaft can now be lifted out. Note the oil way holes clearly visible on the big-end bearings.

CR24.   This next shot shows the positions of the two thrust washers which sit above and each side of the rear crankshaft main bearing. Each washer has oil grooves on one side only which, in each case, face away from the bearing. Oversize thrusts are available, to set the correct crankshaft endfloat on reassembly. The size you will require depends on the amount removed from the crank by the reconditioner. ▼

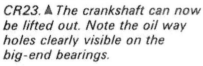

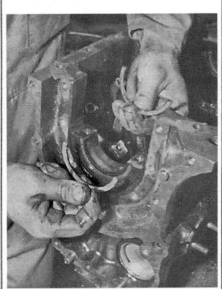

CR25.▲ Following the crankshaft removal, the pistons complete with con-rods can be pushed out with the aid of a suitable length of wood as illustrated . . .

CR26.◄ . . . and then all old bearing shells slid out of their respective housings. It may be very obvious but worth saying that it's just not worth even thinking about not replacing these shells however new looking they appear. Con-rods should be checked for straightness and big-end ovality by your specialist. They can go 'out' in either area.

CR27.◄ Apart from their size, the other major difference in the design of main and big-end bearing shells is that mains have an oil groove and pick-up hole running along the inside face whereas big-end bearings are smooth. Both have end location tabs.

Camshaft and oil pump removal and inspection

CSRI1.   After righting the engine, the removal of the remaining engine components can be carried out including removal of the cam followers . . .

CSRI2.   . . . which allows the camshaft to be carefully slid out. Take care not to mark the cam lobes or the bearings in the block as it's being removed.

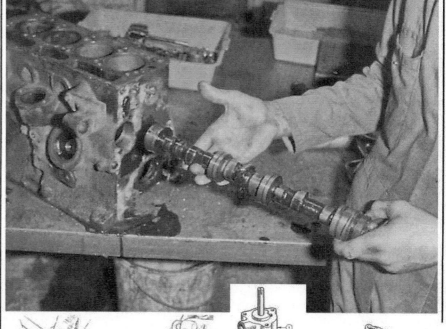

CSRI3.   Inspect the cam lobes for wear. If worn, a new or reprofiled cam is the answer.

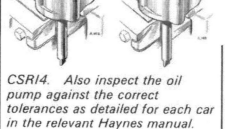

CSRI4.   Also inspect the oil pump against the correct tolerances as detailed for each car in the relevant Haynes manual.

4-CYL

6-CYL

CSRI5.   The pump itself is easily dismantled . . .

CSRI6. . . . for cleaning. Its operation is really quite simple and ingeneous.

CSRI7. Timing wheels as well as the timing chain wear – easily spotted in this case by worn, excessively pointed teeth.

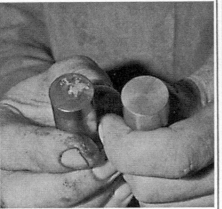

CRSI8. The wear on this cam follower is evident when compared to a new one on the right.

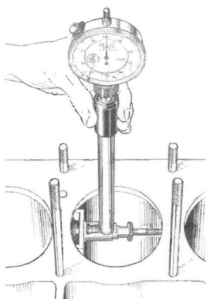

CRSI9. A well worn engine will show a marked ridge just below the top of the bore. Have it properly measured with the correct four point micrometer gauge at the reconditioner's premises. If a rebore is required, make sure of the new bore dimensions before buying expensive new pistons.

CRSI10. Over the years, a lot of sludge can build up which should be removed by a thorough degreasing.

CRSI11. Once on the bench, the crankshaft can be inspected for any obvious sign of excessive wear to be checked over later at a specialist.

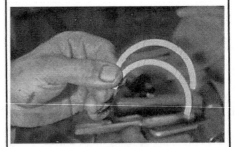

CRSI12. As with pistons, oversize thrust washers (and undersized shell bearings) are best bought after any crank grinding has been carried out. These can usually be obtained from the same place as where the crank grinding is being undertaken.

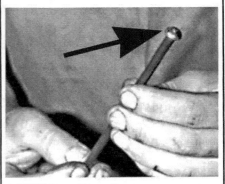

CRSI13. Often forgotten, push rods too can show signs of age.

Rocker gear

RG1. ► *With the rocker shaft assembly on the bench, check the rockers for wear. If the rockers are worn, the best long term remedy is to renew them rather than grinding worn rocker pads flat. Also, try twisting them on the shaft. There should only be a very small amount of movement.*

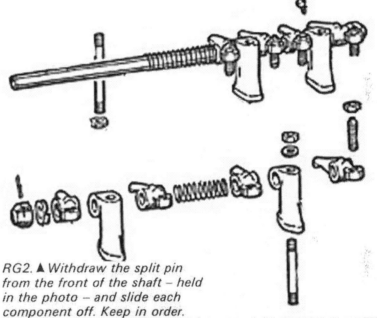

RG3. ▼ *Release the screw which locates the rear pedestal and slide off. Some models have a split pin at each end.*

RG2. ▲ *Withdraw the split pin from the front of the shaft – held in the photo – and slide each component off. Keep in order.*

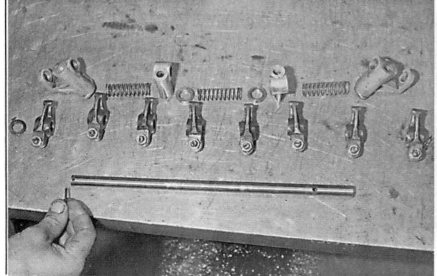

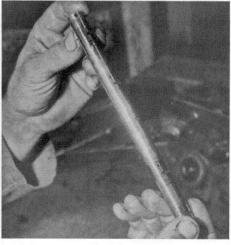

RG4. Inspect the shaft itself for wear and replace if necessary.

Cylinder head overhaul

Safety
Always wear goggles when using a power driven wire brush or grinding wheel.

*CHO1.▶ Release the valve spring split collets, or sliding collars **B** on other models with suitable compressor.*

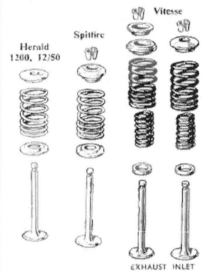

CHO2.▲ The components revealed. Some models have twin springs, others single.

CHO3. Clean carbon deposits from valves with a rotary brush. Another way is to hold the valve stem in an electric drill with the wire brush static.

Wear goggles. Don't have loose clothing anywhere near a rotating wire brush – most dangerous! Also, protect fingers by supporting the end of the valve being worked upon with a wooden support.

CHO4. Replace any valves with bent stems or badly pitted or burnt heads. If only slightly worn, the old valves may be lightly reground back into the seats or refaced, as appropriate, by your specialist.

CHO5. Cylinder heads are bound to show some baked-on deposits which can be chipped off then given a thorough brushing, preferably with a soft metal brush.

CH06.   When complete, inspect for damaged valve seats.

CH09.   Finally, grind each valve into its own valve seat. Use a clockwise then anti-clockwise action and use as little grinding paste as necessary . . .

CHO7.   Check the valve guides for wear by inserting a new valve and rock the valve within the guide. If the head of the valve moves side to side more than a tiny fraction, renew the guide. Guides can be removed by tapping a new one through like this but it's much better to use the proper screw action press tool. Ensure each guide is set at precisely the correct height above the block.

VALVE SEAT RECUTTING TOOL

CHO8.   As necessary, have the seats recut, take as little metal away as possible, or have valve seat inserts fitted. If fitting new seats, always do this after the guides have been fitted as guide centres may vary slightly.

CHO10.   . . . to obtain a thin even matt grey band all the way around the valve. If this band is too wide, the effective seal pressure is reduced so don't overdo it.

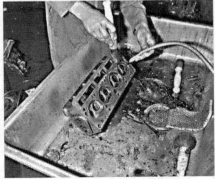

CHO11.   Afterwards make sure everything is scrupulously clean with all traces of grinding paste removed.

Bottom end rebuild

BER1. *Ensure all components are almost clinically clean. Fit new main bearings into the crankcase, ensuring that oilways in the bearing match with those in the engine and that the tags shown positively lock into their recesses. Generously lubricate moving parts with fresh oil. Additionally, use some special assembly lubricant if available.* ▶

BER2. ▼ *Carefully lower the crankshaft into the block.*

BER3. ◀ *Slide new thrust washers around each side of the rear main bearing so that they sit on top of the crankshaft (engine right side up). Ensure that their oil grooves face outwards and that the bearings positively locate.*

BER4. *Fit the front and centre main bearing shells and caps and tighten to the correct torque. (See Haynes manual). Ensure everything turns freely.*

BER5. Check the crankshaft endfloat at the rear of the crankshaft by levering against any slack (about 0.005 in – check the exact tolerances in your Haynes manual). A dial gauge would be useful here if available. Next, fit the rear main bearing and cap and tighten to the correct torque. Double check that the crankshaft rotates smoothly. Six-cylinder engines are very similar; it's just that they have an extra bearing.

BER6. Fit the main bearing shells to the correctly ordered caps taking the same care as detailed in BER1. Tighten to the correct torque. The endfloat could also be checked now. Fit the front sealing bridge. Fit the small paper gaskets shown with a little sealing compound. If it hasn't been done already, remove the old wooden seals – one is shown here still in the end of the bridge and compared with a bright new one. ▶

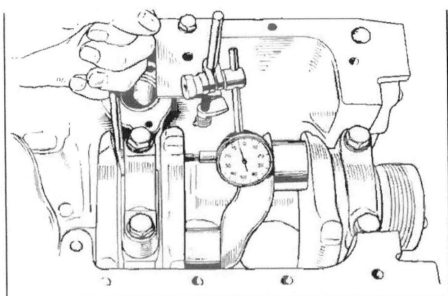

BER7.▲ Screw down the bridge, making sure while doing so that it lies flush with the face of the crankcase. A good metal straight edge is useful here. Coat each wooden block with a smear of jointing compound and tap in. They'll remain a little proud of the surface . . .

BER8.◀ . . . so trim off the excess, flush with the top of the block, with a chisel. You may have found it easier to insert the wooden blocks at the same time as the sealing bridge.

If desired, the rear engine seal could now be fitted though in this particular rebuild, the timing gear and pistons were fitted next.

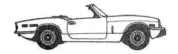 

Refitting timing gear and pistons

TPG1. Thoroughly lubricate the camshaft and thread inside the block.

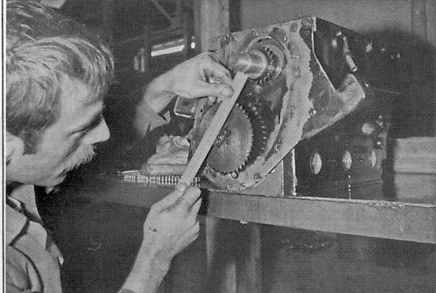

TPG3. Temporarily refit the timing sprockets and check that the two wheels are in exactly the same plane. Adjust by fitting different shims behind the crankshaft sprocket.

TPG2. Refit the front engine plate with a new gasket and a coating of jointing compound. Fit the camshaft holding plate and check for endfloat. Endfloat (about 0.005 in depending on model: check in your Haynes manual) is adjusted by fitting a new plate.

TPG4. Once the correct shims have been fitted, refit the crankshaft Woodruff key.

TPG5. If fitting new con-rod bushes, ensure that the oilway in the bush matches the oilway in the top of the con-rod. Have the bush reamed to size. Make sure that the pistons and con-rods are the correct way around to fit into the block – note the offset in the con-rod.

TPG6. Once assembled, lock in the gudgeon pin with new circlips noting that the load on the clips should be taken on the flat, not the curved side. Ring gaps, as measured with the rings in the bore, should be checked against specification and adjusted as necessary. When fitting to the piston, stagger each ring gap around the piston.

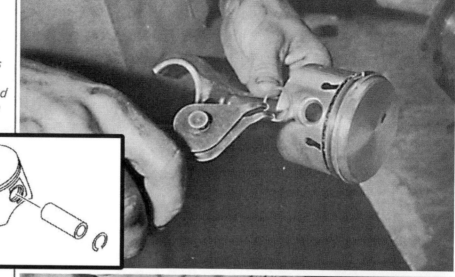

TPG7. Using a proper ring compressor tool (it's not worth trying without), tap the piston and con-rod assembly into the bore. Fit new big-end shells making sure that the tags locate in the con-rods and caps. Where relevant, refit locking tabs and tighten the new bolts to the correct torque. As necessary, tap over the locking tabs.

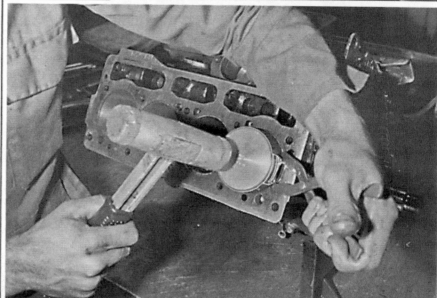

TPG8. ▲ All in place.

TPG9. ▶ Referring to the workshop manual, especially if fitting new timing wheels, refit the timing gear complete with new chain. Fit a new locking tab plate, tighten the wheel bolts and bend over the locking tabs.

Oil pump refitting

OPR1.   *Assemble the components, prime with oil . . .*

OPR2.   *. . . and bolt into place.*

Rear oil seal replacement

ROS1.   *Tap out the old seal with a suitable drift . . .*

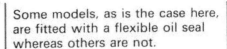

Some models, as is the case here, are fitted with a flexible oil seal whereas others are not.

ROS2.   *. . . here shown removed. You'll have to 'find' the edge of the seal cup with the end of your drift, tight against the seal housing.*

ROS3.   *Carefully push in a new seal . . .*

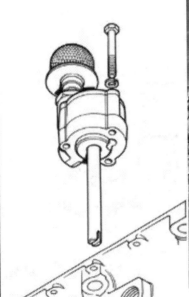

ROS4. . . . and tap squarely home. Don't allow one side to go in and then try to hammer down the other side to match, it won't!

ROS5.▲ Fit a new gasket.

ROS6.▼ Oil the seal and then carefully offer the assembly onto the block without damaging the seal lip. Hold in place finger tight with two opposing bolts. Rotate the crankshaft, adjusting the plate until it is properly centred.

Engines without this flexible seal may either have the seal plates made from cast iron or aluminium alloy. Both types should be centred in the same way as above but the seal should be centralised by inserting a feeler gauge between the seal and crankshaft journal. The gap should be 0.002 in in the case of cast iron housings, but 0.003 in for engines with aluminium housings. Tap the housing with a soft-faced hammer until the correct gap is obtained. Double check and then fit the remaining bolts.

Sump replacement

SR1. Ensure mating surfaces are free from all debris – not that there should be any around. Smear both sides with a little jointing compound and fit a new gasket. ▼

SR2. Offer on the sump and tighten evenly down.

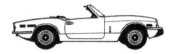

Top end replacement

TER1.► Refit new cam followers.

TER2.▲ Replace the head studs with the correct tool or use the double lock-nut technique.

TER3.► Fit a new gasket. Often, it will be embossed with "TOP". If not, compare against the old gasket as removed.

TER4.▲ The cylinder head can now be lowered into position.

TER5. For the sake of a 'few pennies', replace the old stud nuts and washers with new ones. This is a complete set from Rimmer Bros.

TER6.◄ Tighten in the correct sequence (from the centre working out) to the correct torque. The latter varies from model to model.

TER7.▲ Refit the push rods in their respective holes . . .

TER8.◄ . . . followed by the rocker gear. Don't overtighten the pedestal nuts. They're made of alloy and may crack if treated roughly! Again check for the torque required.

TER9. Finally set the rockers to the correct clearance. 0.010 in for both exhaust and inlet valves.

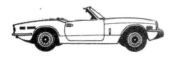

Timing chain cover fitting

TCC1. ▶ *Tap out the old oil seal taking care not to distort the cover.*

TCC2. ▲ *Tap in a new seal and fit a new spring tensioner.*

TCC3. *Slide on the oil thrower with its dished side outermost, ie., so that the thrower is pointing towards the engine.* ▶

TCC4. *Having fitted a new gasket, loop a piece of thin wire or string around the spring tensioner and, pulling it towards the side of the cover, locate the cover on the block. With the cover just off the block, the string can be pulled out having done its job.*

TCC5. *Secure the cover fixing screws, fit the pulley . . .*

TCC6. *. . . and replace the front nut to the correct torque. Fit locking tabs if relevant, eg., early cars with starting handles.*

Back plate and flywheel replacement

BPF1.   Relocate the backplate and secure. Ensure the crankshaft spigot bush is fitted.

BPF2.   Offer up the flywheel, locate on the crankshaft dowel, making sure that that is in good condition. ▶

BPF3. ▲ Tighten up the fixing bolts . . .

BPF4.   . . . and torque down. If the starter ring is worn, have it replaced by your specialist. Check that it is seated tight on the shoulder of the flywheel.

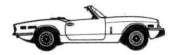

Clutch renewal

In order to fit a new clutch, either the engine or gearbox has to be removed from the car. In order to protect a 'good' car's interior, it's probably best to remove the engine.

CR1. Fitting a new clutch with the engine in or out of the car, is quite simple and shouldn't cause any problems. The component parts of friction plate, pressure plate and release bearing are shown in the figure. Early models use a coil spring loaded pressure plate rather than the diaphragm type shown.

CR3. Finally and with the alignment tool still in place, tighten the securing bolts. Later Spitfires use Allen bolts as shown; earlier models use standard bolts.

CR2. Offer up the friction and pressure plates with the two plates located on an old input shaft (the best and cheapest tool for the job – usually easily available at Club autojumbles), alternatively buy or borrow a general purpose alignment tool. A universal model is produced by the S–P 'Speedline' brand. It's not worth trying to make one from a rod of wood because the hassle involved in an engine refusing to mate with its gearbox is disproportionate to the cost.

The aim is to centralise the clutch splines with the engine such that the gearbox input shaft will pass smoothly through. Also ensure that the friction plate remains free of grease and that it locates properly on the flywheel. Friction plates are normally clearly labelled "Flywheel Side". If put on the wrong way round, the pressure plate might or might not fit but the clutch just won't operate so the job would have to be done again.

Early coil spring units also feature an adjusting mechanism to take up clutch lining wear. This is adjusted by unhooking the return spring, slackening the locknut on the operating rod to allow free travel and turning the adjusting nut until a clearance of 0.080 in is obtained between the nut and the abutment with the rod being pushed into the clutch housing. After completion, tighten the lock nut against the adjusting nut without moving the latter and refit the spring.

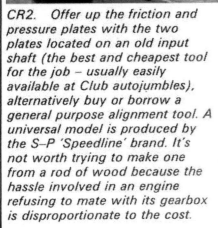

Gearbox removal

As suggested above, if carrying out a full restoration it is actually easier to remove the gearbox complete with the engine but if desired, the gearbox can be removed separately.

Tool box

As for engine removal. Good quality sturdy axle stands are an absolute must. Never depend on any type of jack, hydraulic or otherwise when working beneath a car. The risk is just too high.

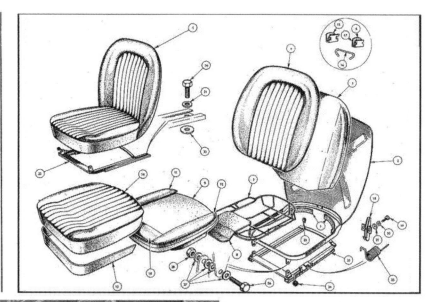

GBR1. ▲ It's not absolutely essential, but it only takes a few minutes to remove the seats. Slide the seat fully back and remove the front two securing bolts. Then, slide the seat fully forward and repeat the exercise at the other end. If the seats aren't removed be sure to cover them up as gearboxes tend to become covered in thick greasy deposits. These include 'Spitfire Low-Back Seats and Fittings' from Rimmer Bros.

GBR2. Next, but only for GT6s and Spitfires, remove the gearbox surround 'A' frame by removing two chromed bolts each side of the base of the frame . . .

GBR3. . . . followed by the two screws at the top. Behind should be caged nuts but on some cars, you may have to thread a spanner behind. Make absolutely sure that the battery has been removed before doing this.

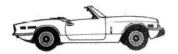

GBR4. ▲ The frame can now be removed. As necessary, any radio or tape players should also be withdrawn beforehand.

GBR6. ▲ If carrying out a full rebuild, of course all the trim will come out. If just removing the gearbox, only the central trim pads need be removed.

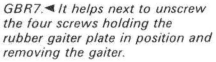

GBR7. ◄ It helps next to unscrew the four screws holding the rubber gaiter plate in position and removing the gaiter.

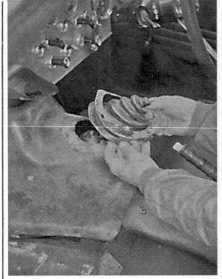

GBR5. ▼ On this GT6, the gearbox carpet is split at the back, being connected by a ribbon and press stud arrangement.

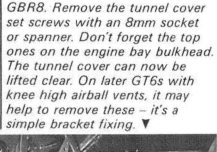

GBR8. Remove the tunnel cover set screws with an 8mm socket or spanner. Don't forget the top ones on the engine bay bulkhead. The tunnel cover can now be lifted clear. On later GT6s with knee high airball vents, it may help to remove these – it's a simple bracket fixing. ▼

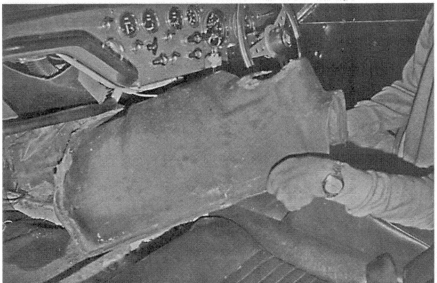

GBR9. ►The sound deadening often comes out rather worse for wear but can be repacked as shown in GR5.

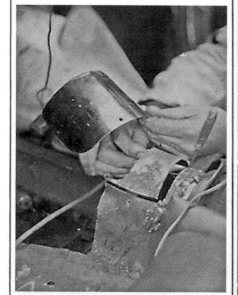

GBR10. ▲ Overdrive gearboxes are longer than non-overdrive units and in the former case, the propshaft tunnel is provided with an extra screw down plate. Remove this where relevant.

GBR12. ▲ Late Spitfire propshafts are fitted with a rather odd looking 'baked bean tin' front end.

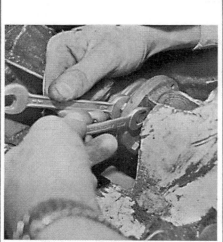

GBR11. ▲ Next, undo the four nyloc nuts holding the front propshaft flange (fit new nuts on reassembly).

GBR13. The flanges can now be separated.

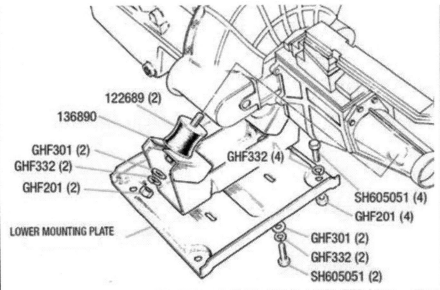

122689 (2)

136890

GHF301 (2)

GHF332 (2)

GHF201 (2)

LOWER MOUNTING PLATE

GHF332 (4)

SH605051 (4)

GHF201 (4)

GHF301 (2)

GHF332 (2)

SH605051 (2)

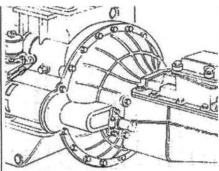

GBR16.▲ The bellhousing bolts should now be removed. Start underneath the car – note the use of axle stands. Also for safety and convenience aspects, try to arrange for someone else to be around.

GBR14.   With a non-overdrive box, release the nuts securing the two cotton reel gearbox mounting rubbers (these are Rimmer Bros part numbers)...

GBR15.   ... or in the case of an overdrive box remove either the top two mounting bolts shown here, or perhaps easier, the two lower bolts which hold the mounting rubber to the chassis plate.

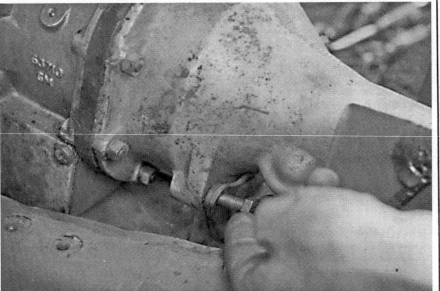

GBR17.▲ Take the weight of the engine on a suitable jack. Spread the load on the sump with a block of wood.

GBR18.   Remove the clutch slave cylinder. If the gearbox alone is being removed, leave the cylinder connected to the master cylinder but hook it out of the way.

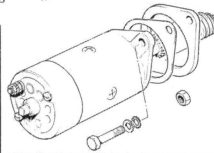

GBR19. ▲ Removing the starter motor bolts can be a bit fiddly but they do come out!

GBR21. ▲ Finally, remove the speedo cable by releasing the outer cable's knurled nut.

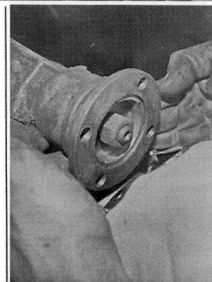

GBR22. The front of the gearbox can now be lifted clear and over the top of the propshaft tunnel edge.

GBR23. ▼ Angle the gearbox into the passenger footwell and slide it off the clutch splines. It helps if someone else levers items of trim out of the way at the same time.

GBR20. The remaining bolts can now be removed. Having someone else holding a spanner on the outside is a great help.

GBR24.   With a few more twists and turns, the unit can now be removed from the car.

GBR26. ▲ If removing the propshaft, the exhaust will have to be dropped at the rear to allow the shaft to be slid out of the propshaft tunnel. Sometimes the front flange snags within the tunnel so be prepared for this. It'll just need pushing back in and twisting round a little.

GBR27. ► Overdrive propshafts are a few inches shorter than non-overdrive ones.

GBR28. ▼ Similarly, mounting plates differ.

GBR25.   If the clutch hasn't been changed for a while, it's a good idea to do it now. If you don't, you'll probably wish that you had later on.

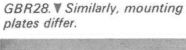

Gearbox replacement. Hints and tips

GR1. It's simple and cheap to replace worn cotton reel mounting rubbers and not much more to renew overdrive ones.

GR3. Sometimes, reversing lamp switches fail to operate because the gasket between the top of the gearbox and the switch is too thick. Simply use a smear of sealing compound instead. Unfortunately, this isn't the cure for a faulty switch or wiring fault.

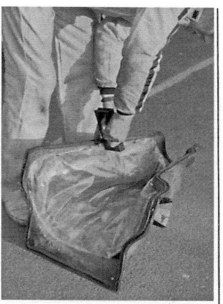

GR5. Old tunnel cover sound deadening material can easily be repackaged in good quality polythene and stapled back on.

GR2. Before replacing, tap out the old and drift in a new bellhousing oil seal using the back of a suitable size socket. When threading the housing back over the gearbox input shaft, temporarily tape over the splines to avoid damaging the seal.

GR4. When re-attaching the gear lever to the remote extension, applicable to most of the range of cars, ensure that the bolt head is on the left-hand side. If not, the threaded end will foul the inner side of the alloy extension and fourth gear engagement will be almost impossible.

GR6. Once separated, inspect the friction plate for wear. Badly worn units may have worn down rivets. This one is new.

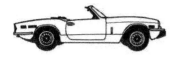

Gearbox dismantling & Inspection

Although detailed gearbox rebuilding is beyond the scope of this book (it is covered in detail in your *Haynes* manual), the following figures show the basic route for doing so. Unfortunately, obtaining spare gearbox parts tends to be difficult unlike those for engines which are relatively easy to find. All of the photographs for this section were taken at Nicol Transmissions in Kidderminster, Worcestershire. Nicol do a splendid job with Triumph boxes since they specialise in them. (See *'Clubs & Specialists').*

GD1. On all Herald-based cars except later Spitfires, the gear selectors, after being removed from the top of the gearbox, look like this. Inspect for obvious signs of wear. These particular ones were clearly worn explaining a rather sloppy gearchange.

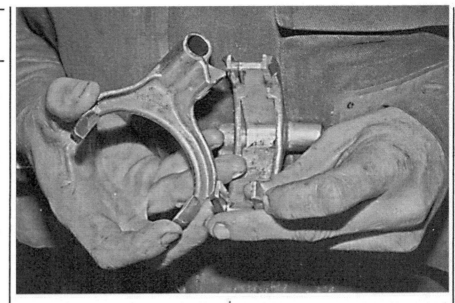

GD2. ▲ *Late Spitfire gear selectors look like this.*

GD3. ► *Slide off the pressure release bearing and unclip the actuator arm. These differ from model to model but the principle is the same. The old bearing can be tapped off and a new one pushed on in a vice. Apply a smear of copper grease to the bearing face on reassembly.*

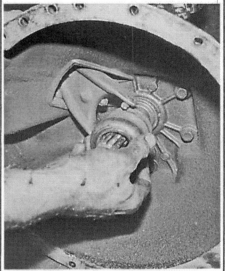

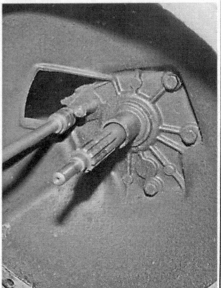

GD4. The cast iron or alloy bellhousing, depending on model, may be removed by undoing 5 bolts. As the lower bolt actually threads into a hole open to the gearbox sump, this is fitted with a copper washer. Make sure that it is replaced. In very early Heralds, the bellhousing is cast with the main gearbox sump, all being made of alloy.

GD5. Pulling off a separate bellhousing. Where relevant don't lose or forget to replace the three layshafts loading springs. ▶

GD6. The propshaft flange can be removed with a socket plus either a locking ring lever . . .

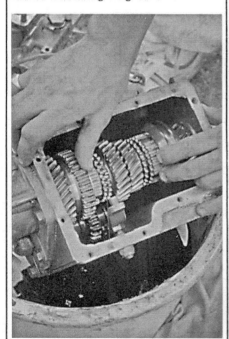

GD7. ▲ . . . or if one isn't available by locking the cogs into first and fourth gear at the same time hence locking up the box. Simply slide the two selectors away from each other and into mesh with their respective gears.

GD8. ▲ With the nut removed, gently tap off the alloy extension. Take care not to damage the mounting point lugs. They're quite fragile.

GD9. In the case of an overdrive box, undo the extension plate nuts . . .

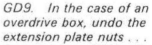

GD10. . . . and slide the unit off. This is a J-Type overdrive.

GD11. The gearbox internals may now be further dismantled by extracting the layshaft. Push a dowel or similar rod through the layshaft hole forcing the shaft out the other end. Make the rod length just a little shorter than the inside dimension of the casing. Some models have layshaft roller bearings and this rod helps them stay in place. Not necessarily required during dismantling (if new bearings are to be fitted), but certainly a great help during assembly in which case bed the bearings into the layshaft cluster with Vaseline. Popping the layshaft cluster with bedded-in bearings into the fridge for a short while also helps them from falling out during gearbox reassembly.

GD12. The input shaft can then be tapped out from the inside . . .

GD13. . . . and following the removal of the main rear bearing, the mainshaft complete with this array of gear cogs can be lifted out. Inspect the teeth for wear. Lift out the layshaft cluster.

Overdrive servicing

Once again, the work shown here was carried out by Nicol Transmission, in the main.

OS1. The majority of overdrives fitted to Herald based cars are D-Type units as shown here (though not an option originally on Heralds themselves). ▶

OS2. Poor overdrive operation can often be cured by very simple servicing such as removing the side cover plate and cleaning the filter. Four rubberised ring magnets are arranged around the base of the filter in order to collect any metal particles present. In doing so the main oilway can become blocked so clean thoroughly and replace. ▶

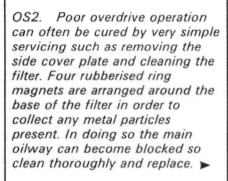

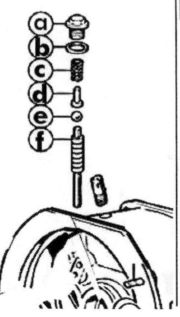

◀*OS3. The operating valve (f) can also become clogged. Release any residual pressure by operating the solenoid on and off a few times, engine off, ignition on. Undo the top nut (a seen in OS1) and hook out the components. The top ball bearing (e) can be removed with a magnetised screwdriver. Ensure the valve is clear by blowing through it and replace.*

OS4. ▶*A worn O-ring in the pressure relief valve can also cause intermittent problems. Undo the large nut adjacent to the solenoid . . .*

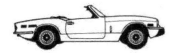

Some of the following operations can be carried out with the unit still in the car.

OS5. . . . to reveal the internal components.

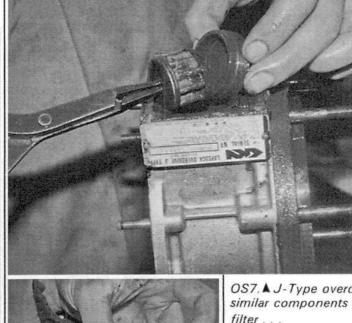

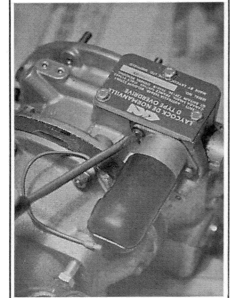

OS6. ▲ The solenoid too can be removed if found to be faulty. Service operations to this are given under 'Electrical Components'.

OS7. ▲ J-Type overdrives have similar components such as filter . . .

OS8. ◄ ...and pressure relief valve.

OS9. Once dismantled, J- and D-Type units may need attention to the O-rings around the operating pistons or even replacement of the internal clutch unit which lurks behind. ▼

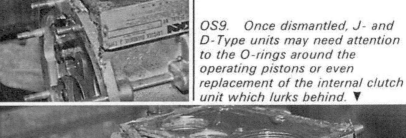

5 Electrical Components

The following 'Tool Box' and 'Safety' notes apply generally to auto-electrical work and are relevant to every section of this chapter.

Toolbox

B.A. spanners sometimes needed for earlier cars. Engineers and long-nosed pliers. Soldering iron and prefluxed solder. Selection of new electrical connectors. Insulation tape.

Safety

ALWAYS disconnect the battery before working on any electrical system. An electrical short circuit can destroy parts of the wiring system in a second or cause a car wrecking fire.

The vast majority of car breakdowns occur because of electrical faults, so it pays to give regular attention to your car's wiring and electrical components. This section gives an overview of some of the most important areas in the maintenance or rebuilding of a car's electrical system.

Wiring and wiring loom-general

The wires used in the Triumph Herald, Vitesse and GT6 range are colour coded, so rewiring one is fairly straightforward provided that a correctly colour-coded loom is used. Each lighting component already has a coded tag of wire coming from it so all you have to do is link it to the relevant part of the loom with a connector.

The seven basic colours are:
Brown – battery and dynamo alternator circuits.
White – ignition
Blue – headlamps
Red – side and tail lamps
Green – auxiliary (accessories, etc.) circuits protected by fuse terminal 4, and only live with ignition 'on'
Purple – other auxiliaries not wired through the ignition switch.
Protected by fuse terminal 2.
Black – earth wires

With care, an older cloth-covered loom can be cleaned to make it appear fresh and new. CAREFULLY remove the loom, noting the location of the clips which hold it in place and, to speed up refitting, fold a piece of double masking tape, but leaving an inch at the end single and sticky. Wrap this around the end of each wire as it is disconnected and write its location on the masking tape. Wire brush the clips and repaint them with a hammered metal finish paint. Coil the wiring loom and place it into a shallow pan with warm soapy water. SQUEEZE BUT DO NOT SCRUB the loom until it is as clean as it will get before it begins to unravel, then hang it in the garage until completely dry. PVC covered wires can be cleaned to almost new lustre by spraying a rag and the wires with aerosol carburettor cleaner, and wiping the sludge and grease from the wires.

As a rule, the wires themselves do not fail. The connectors may lose contact with the wires but the wires themselves rarely break unless they are physically damaged. Any splicing or correction to the loom should be made outside the wrapping. There should be no connections within the loom itself. If changes are made in the loom, solder Lucas bullet connectors to the wires and use the black female connectors of the type used with the rest of the system. NOTE: Prior to removing the loom from the car, remove ALL the black female connectors as they impede the free movement of the loom through the bulkhead, boot etc. Prior to

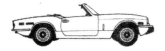

refitting the loom in the car, clean each bullet connector with fine emery paper to ensure a good connection.

The interior light switches in the door pillars become bent and corroded so that they do not work. Remove them from the pillar and from the purple/white wire. Wire brush them so that they will make good contact with the pillar and with themselves.

Straighten bent plungers with pliers.

If you decide to fit a new loom, start by laying it out alongside the car to work out its general layout in comparison with the existing loom. The new loom comes in two parts: the front section goes back through the bulkhead to the back of the car and includes the front light wires which cross the car

beneath the radiator area; the electrical control wires, which cross the car between bulkhead and dash; and the electrical component wires which run down the front of the bulkhead. Use a new special type of screw-on grommet at the bulkhead, not just a rubber electrical grommet. The rear lighting section is a separate section of loom.

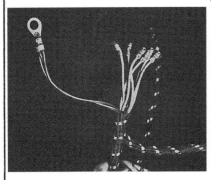

W1. ▲ Making all the right connections is easy by referring to the wiring diagram and the wiring colours shown there and comparing them with the colours on the loom.

If you're removing the old loom, snip the wires a couple of inches from where they join the component so that you have an instant cross-referencing colour code to hand.

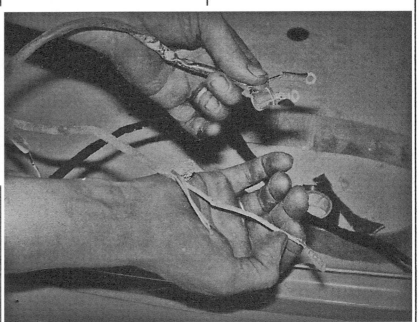

W2. ▲ You may simply wish to repair the existing loom, in which case many terminals will probably need to be renewed. Sometimes they are corroded and hanging on by a thread of dangerous bare wire.

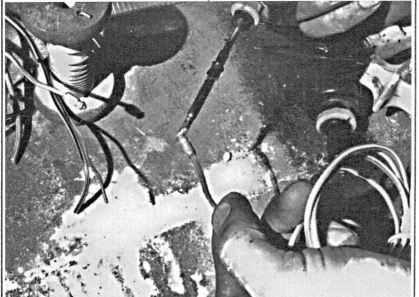

W3. You really need three hands to solder bullet connectors onto the ends of wires: one to hold the wire, one the iron and one for the solder itself! Cleanliness is the key to obtaining a good soldered joint. Remember the solder will tend to be drawn towards the heat and try not to heat for so long that the wire's insulation melts. When fitting new spade-type connectors, do remember to push on the plastic insulator before soldering the spade in place!

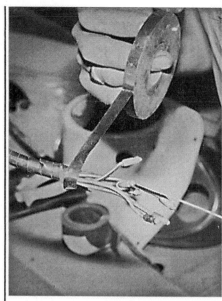

W4. You can tape up any additions, or replacement sections, with plastic insulation tape wrapped around the wire in a spiral, each wind covering about half of the one that went before.

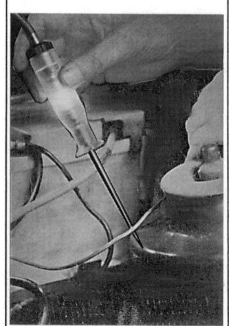

W5. The Sykes-Pickavant circuit tester has a sharp probe at one end for checking current flow within cables, an 'earth' clip at the far end of its connecting wire and a bright, clear indicator lamp invaluable when re-connecting components, fitting new wiring or investigating electrical failures.

Distributor overhaul

Figure 1 The component parts of the Lucas distributor.

1 Distributor cap
2 Brush and spring
3 Rotor arm
4 Condenser
5 Terminal and lead
6 Moving baseplate
7 Fixed baseplate
8 Cam screw
9 Cam
10 Advance spring
11 Earth lead
12 Contact breaker points
13 Driving dog
14 Bush
15 Clamp plate
16 Cap retaining clips
17 Shaft and action plate
18 Bob weights
19 Vacuum unit
20 O-ring oil seal
21 Thrust washer
22 Taper pin

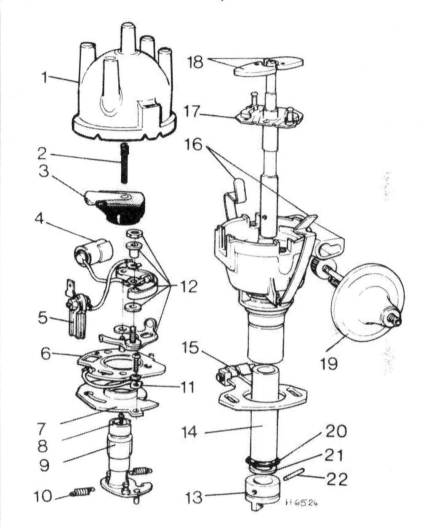

Many parts of the distributor can wear and malfunction. In particular, the following points should be checked (for component identification see Figure 1).
1) The vacuum advance unit perforates and no longer functions (check by releasing the pipe from the carb, suck it and look and listen for distributor base plate movement).
2) The plates holding the points wear, allowing the points to contact the distributor cam at an angle and causing the vacuum unit to work jerkily.
3) The mechanical advance screw seizes.
4) The cam develops sideplay on the distributor shaft.
5) The distributor shaft wears where it fits the body bush, which also wears.
6) The points and condenser fail.

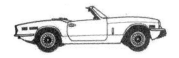

DO1. Wire insulation inside the distributor is inclined to disintegrate and cause a car-stopping short. Replace the wire with a new piece.

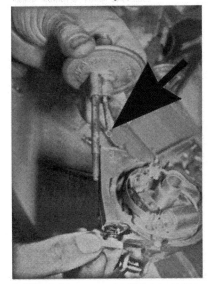

DO2. ▲ To remove the vacuum advance on the distributor, lever off the clip that holds the advance/retard finger nut (held in right hand here) in place, disconnect the spring from the baseplate (arrowed) and unscrew the nut completely before withdrawing the advance mechanism. Don't lose the spring from behind the knurled nut.

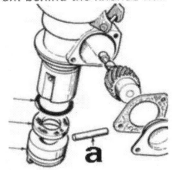

DO3. ▲ The Lucas distributor shaft assembly is held in place by a pin (a and see page 185) which must be driven out with a pin punch, after which the distributor components can be pulled apart. Note: when reassembling the distributor, make certain that the drive dog is offset relative to the position of the rotor arm as shown on page 185 or the ignition spark will occur 180° out, i.e. the wrong plug will fire.

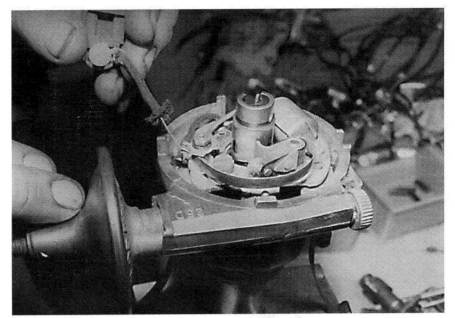

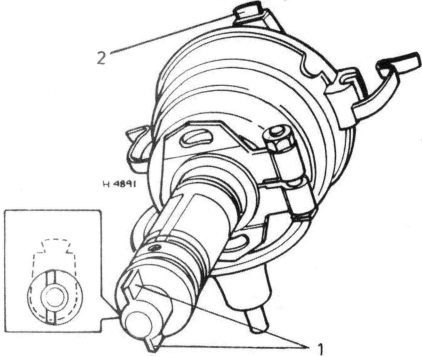

H 4891

Figure 2   Correct relative positions of drive dog end rotor arm.

1 Offset drive dog 2 Rotor arm tongues

DO4.   When refitting the distributor, make sure the clamp plate is not distorted; if it is it can damage the distributor mounting flange, like this.

Headlamp removal

Although outer surrounds may differ, once these are removed, subsequent removal of the front headlamps are very similar for all of the cars.

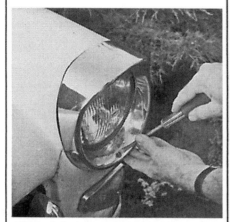

HR1.   On the earlier Heralds, the headlamp peak surround is secured by a single screw indicated here. Early Spitfires and GT6s have a push-over chrome rim. If buying new surrounds for these models, make sure you obtain the correct type as other similar rims of the same diameter as used on different cars may use a different fixing method.

HR2.   With the screw removed, the chrome peak may be lifted off. Early cars had a peak which was six tenths of an inch longer than later items though short and long peaks will fit equally well.

HR3.   On later Spitfires and Mk 3 GT6s, access to the light unit is achieved by removing three nuts and then lifting off the light surround panel. If simply changing a lamp unit, just undo the three self-tappers which locate the outer chromed securing rim and remove the lamp. A new lens unit can then be set in place without further need of adjustment.

HR4.   After removing the lamp surround peak, the ring found beneath can be removed . . .

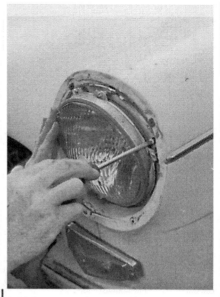

HR5.   . . .followed by the main assembly securing screws.

HR6.   The whole assembly can then be removed following disconnecting the relevant wires.

Rear lamp assemblies

RL1. The rear lamp assemblies on Heralds and Vitesses are surrounded by push-over chrome trims. These should be removed by carefully tapping them off with a piece of wood or similar.

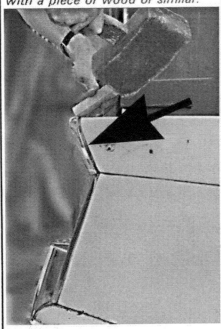

RL3. All Heralds and Vitesses use similar rear lamp assemblies with some differences as indicated under 'Production Modifications'.

RL5. Later Spitfires also use a strip-type of rear lights assembly, again secured with nuts and fixed studs, unlike earlier units which consisted of separate lamps held in place with self-tapping screws.

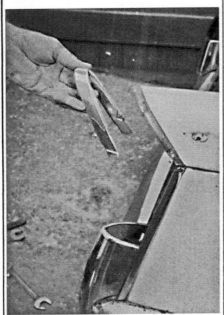

RL2. Early models employed a chrome-over-brass one piece unit. Later models as indicated here used a three piece, top inverted 'V' plus twin vertical strips, arrangement.

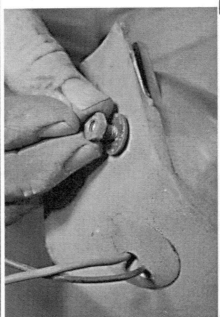

RL4. Later models used a nuts and fixed studs arrangement whilst on earlier models the assembly was held in place with self-tappers only accessible after first removing the outer lens. Put nuts and fittings back in place when stripping units off the car.

RL6. A Spitfire rear lamp assembly removed – also showing the backing plate which protects the lamp's back and is fitted inside the boot.

Windscreen wiper motor removal and park setting

WW1. The wiper motor is fixed by three simple bolts within small suspension rubbers (early cars). **NOTE:** Different models; different angles - same principles.

WW3. Undo the retaining nut between drive cable and motor body followed by the four 6mm casing securing set screws.

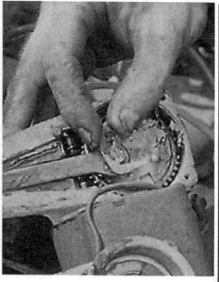

WW5. After removal, replace the piston, rotor and clip to avoid loss.

WW1, contd. ...while these are the fixing components for later Spitfires.

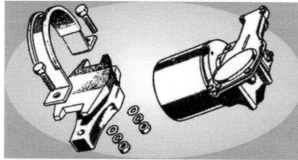

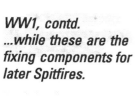

WW2. Once undone, the motor can't be removed from the car until the drive cable is released.

WW4. Remove the top casing complete with contact cap and slide off and remove the brush clip and rotor arm contact. The drive cable can then be lifted away from the operating piston.

WW6. Within the contact cap there's a segmented 'no contact' region and it's the position of this relative to the motor body which determines the final wiper park position. If wipers park evenly but they're either too high or too low there's no need to remove the wiper arms to change the park position. Simply loosen the top casing slightly as shown in photo WW3 and rotate the cap. Operate the wipers on and then off. The cap position can then be adjusted until a satisfactory park is achieved.

Overdrive solenoid and inhibitor switch

Overdrive solenoids especially on D-type units can often cause problems. Often these may be due to quite simple faults such as loose spade or bullet connectors or a repairable fault within the solenoid itself.

OS1. To inspect the solenoid from a D-type unit, carefully pull off the rubber sleeve and unscrew two small screws which hold a protective plastic casing around the terminals and points.

OS2. D-type units have two parallel coils. One, the main switching coil, works for a short time only at high current (20 amps) and the other, the holding coil, works at a continuous low current (2 amps). As soon as the main coil has pulled the operating piston clear, a set of points connecting the coil to the power supply are opened thus switching the high current path off. These points as indicated on the figure can become very worn and hence might impede efficient operation. By realigning or building them back up, the life of the unit could be prolonged if this is what is causing a problem.

A further problem is that the thinner, holding coil leads often become detached near to the terminals. This may show up as the solenoid oscillating on and off rapidly as the main coil switches on then, points open, switches off and then is immediately switched back on again, repeatedly, due to the lack of a holding coil. Often the holding coil wire can be resoldered back on. If, however, the coil is broken internally, as indicated with a standard multimeter or a simple battery and bulb circuit test, a new solenoid is the only real solution. As mentioned earlier, check external wiring first.

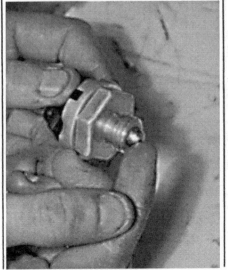

OS3. ◄ Sometimes the inhibitor switch becomes dirty or sticks. Try cleaning it with electrical switch cleaner. In other cases they have been found to operate well when cold but become sloppy and intermittently fail to operate as the gearbox and surroundings warm up. Try adjusting the operating cam (early skeleton versions) or test if suspected whilst driving along by holding the gear lever further over to the right-hand side – effectively pushing the switch button further in. If found to be faulty, a new switch is in order.

6 Interior and Trim

Spitfire seat cover fitting

SSC1. ▼ Removal of the seat base cover follows removal of the seat base from the frame by unclipping a series of hog rings with a pair of pliers. The cover can then be peeled back from the foam base to which it is glued. Take care not to damage the foam when doing this. Before fitting the new cover, it may be necessary to repair and strengthen the base foam and replace the sackcloth between the foam and metal frame.

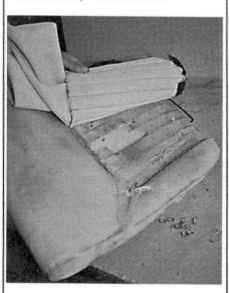

SSC2. ▲ The next step is to secure the new cover to the foam with an impact type adhesive. A spray type is ideal but as with all such adhesives, take care to ensure good ventilation.

Rimmer Bros Seat Diaphragn for Herald/Vitesse.

SSC3. ► Push down firmly and allow to dry for half an hour.

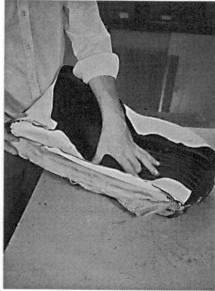

SSC4. ▲ The cover can now be turned over and pulled into position . . .

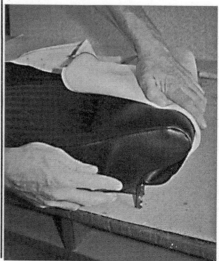

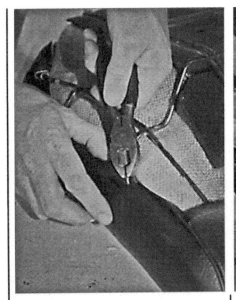

SSC5. . . .and fixed in place with new hog rings – as supplied with each seat cover kit by Newton Commercial who supplied the trim kits for this section.

SSC7. With the outer cover released, the inner flap which helps give the seat back its shape is revealed.

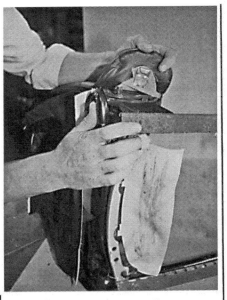

SSC9. . . .and release the cover sidebands by pulling the ends downwards to release the clips from their brackets as shown here. The whole cover can now be removed from the frame. It's a good idea at this stage to check over the frame and weld any cracked or broken joints. A lick of paint adds a finishing touch.

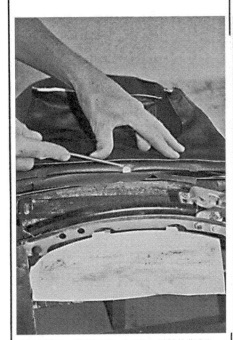

SSC6. Attention can now turn to removing the old squab cover, the bottom of which is held to the frame by clips – easily removed with a screwdriver.

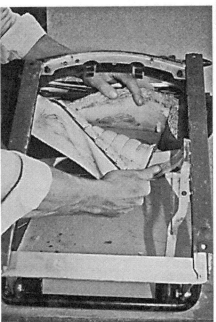

SSC8. As with the seat base, carefully peel back the cover which is glued down onto the supporting foam panel . . .

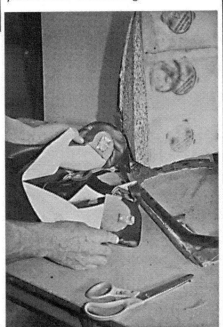

SSC10. Remove the old retaining clips/hardboard pieces from the old cover, insert and glue/staple them into the relevant pockets at the base of the new sidebands.

SSC11. Using the plastic sheet supplied by Newton Commercial, glue a strip around the outer edge of the foam to enable the new cover to slip over and down easily.

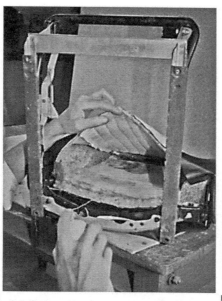

SSC13. As before, apply some glue being careful not to get any on the outer cover surface, wait for it to go tacky . . .

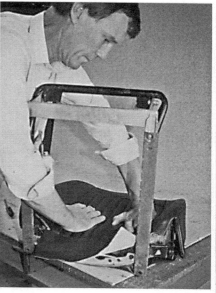

SSC15. . . . then carefully align and press down firmly.

SSC12. The cover should then be centralised on the frame, the side bands pulled down and the retaining clips engaged.

SSC14. . . . keeping the two surfaces apart . . .

SSC16. The front flap . . .

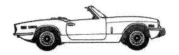

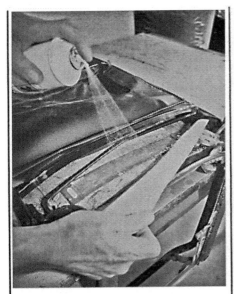

SSC17.▲ . . . and the sides may then be pulled down and glued in place.

SSC18.► The back panel should then be tensioned . . .

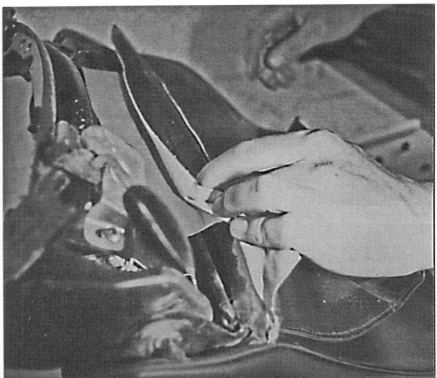

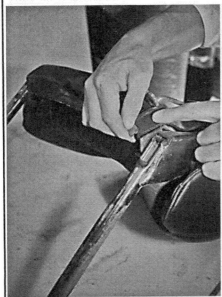

SSC19.▲ . . . and clipped in place.

SSC20.► Complete and as good or better than new. Full details of the range of trim offered, including original specification seat covers as supplied for this section, may be obtained from Newton Commercial the address for whom can be found in the Clubs and Specialists section at the rear of this book.

Fitting a soft-top – Spitfire

The work in this section is again shown being carried out to Richard Swinfield's Mk IV 1500 at Classic Car Restorations in the West Midlands. The trimmer is CCR's 'tame' trim expert, the renowned Steve Simmonds.

SHF1. Assuming the car is a Mk 3 or later, remove the old soft-top from the frame by first prising . . .

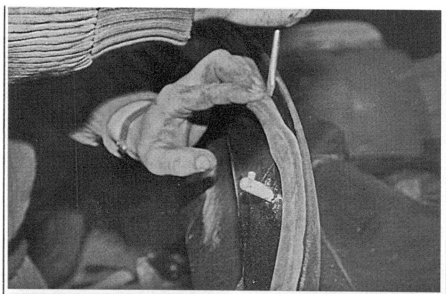

SHF2. . . . and then pulling the rubber strip out of the front rail metal channels.

Toolbox

Impact adhesive, sharp knife, drill, screwdriver, hammer, centre punch (or blunt nail) and a small drift (or bolt).
   Fitting a soft-top is best carried out in warm conditions whether outside or in the garage. If fitting a soft-top on a really hot day, avoid overstretching the material as this could lead to problems in raising the soft-top in cooler weather due to the material being overtight. Don't, however, work in cold conditions as the hood material will be relatively stiff and difficult to work with.
   It's not strictly necessary, but the following sequence has been carried out with the old soft-top and frame off the car to start with.

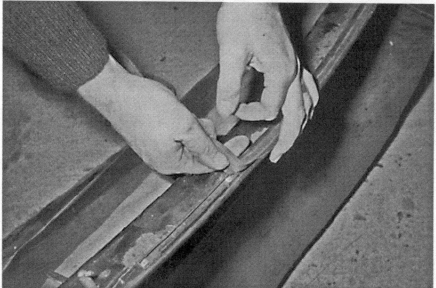

SHF3. These channels should then be removed by carefully drilling out the heads of the pop-rivets which hold them in place. Try to avoid drilling into the top rail itself which might necessitate fitting larger rivets later.

SHF4. The channels, one long and two short curved sections, then simply lift off . . .

SHF5. ▲ . . . allowing the front edge of the material to be pulled back and off. Referring back to the buying guide clearly shows that Spitfire 4 and Mk 2 models don't have this front rail. In these models, the top's front edge simply clips beneath a channel in the top of the windscreen frame with each corner then being secured with poppers.

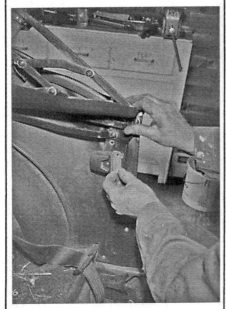

SHF6. ▲ Although this photo actually shows the soft-top frame being removed, it does illustrate the next step which is to refit the frame. As applicable, fix any seat belt fastenings back in place at the same time.

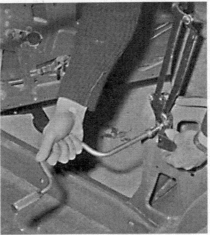

SHF7. ▲ The frame is held by three bolts each side which screw into a caged thread plate held inside the rear wing cavity.

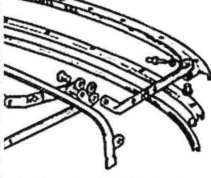

SHF8. With the bolts in place, check all frame joints and irons for wear. Replace any broken rivets and reweld cracked joints before fitting the soft-top. Clamp the front header rail in position as normal.

SHF9. Next, fit the rear deck plate to the rear edge of the soft-top. Ensure that the soft-top is positioned accurately or else a good final result just won't be achieved. Make sure that the three relevant tonneau fastening buttons are also replaced. As with the front rail, Spitfire 4 and Mk 2 models do not use a bolt-down rear rail. Instead, a curved strip of metal about half an inch wide is threaded within the soft-top's rear seam effectively stiffening and reinforcing it. The rear seam is then lodged beneath the two chromed fittings bolted to the

don't throw away the reinforcing bar with the old soft-top. Original tops also have similar strips threaded inside the soft-top seams around the window seal area.

Mk1&2

Mk3

Mk IV & 1500

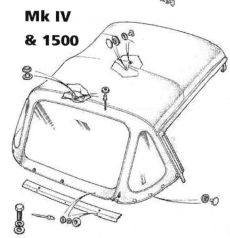

SHF10. These are the OE-quality soft-tops for the various models of Spitfire available from Newton Commercial and a few others. Cheaper hoods tend, among other things, to lack the minor fittings such as button fastenings. Typical button fastenings shown here. These late models use a black plastic finish.

Hood Popper Kit - Set of 8 - Black - RR1280

SHF11. Lay the soft-top over the frame and check everything lines up properly allowing crease free rear and side windows. Mark the inner face of the lower seam exactly opposite the relevant fastenings on the car and then punch a neat hole through the material wide enough to take the outer button stud.

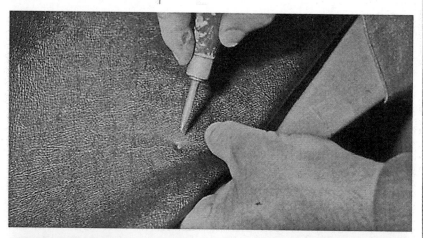

SHF12. The stud can then be pushed through and the cap placed on top. ▶

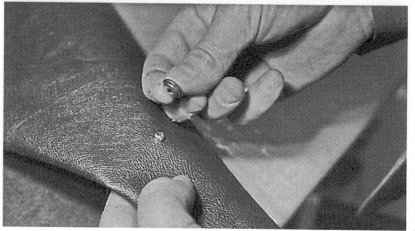

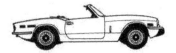

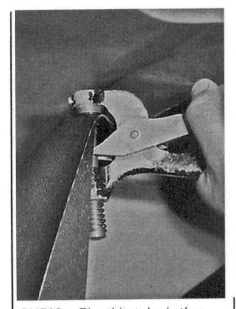

SHF13. The thin tube is then splayed out over the inner face of the cap to hold it in place. Nowadays, the correct tools are widely available quite cheaply on eBay, Amazon and elsewhere.

SHF15. A similar shot but with the more common plastic fitting.

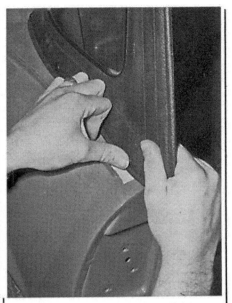

SHF17. . . . and indent it by pushing against the relevant soft-top button. Make sure it's pulled tight into position.

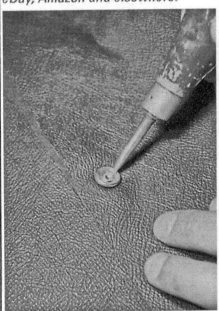

SHF14. This shows the neat finish achieved with the correct tool.

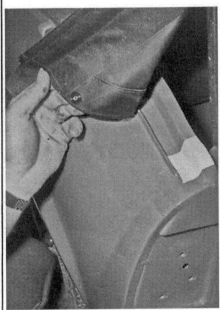

SHF16. If fitting a soft-top to a car which hasn't had a soft-top fitted previously, rear deck fastenings will also have to be fitted. A useful tip for doing this is to place a piece of masking tape over the relevant area . . .

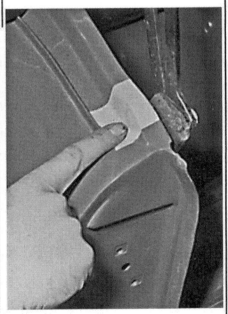

SHF18. A clear mark should result . . .

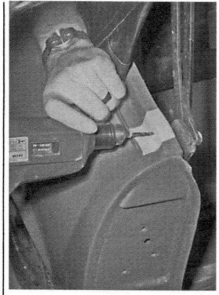

SHF19. . . . which allows accurate drilling. The tape also helps stop the drill bit from slipping off the mark. You may wish to do this part of the work later, when the rest of the hood is in place.

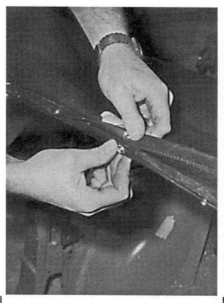

SHF21. With the rear of the soft-top accurately in place, the central bar can be secured with the standard poppers.

SHF23. Fold the soft-top over upon itself and reinforce the line.

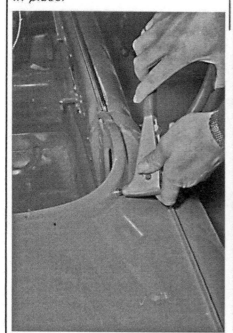

SHF20. As necessary, this technique can be repeated around the rear deck and then new studs pop-riveted in place. Earlier models with metal fastenings used self-tappers instead of rivets.

SHF22. Lay the remaining edge of the soft-top over the front rail and, keeping the material taut, chalk a line to show the innermost edge of the rail.

SHF24. An impact adhesive should be used, rather than one which allows some slide adjustment; the latter type makes it difficult to tension the hood. Use a piece of card between relevant material layers to protect the soft-top from stray glue.

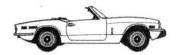

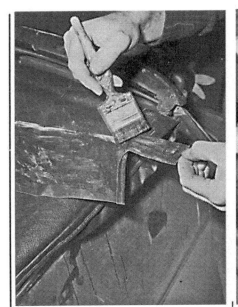

SHF25.   Apply adhesive up to the chalk line . . .

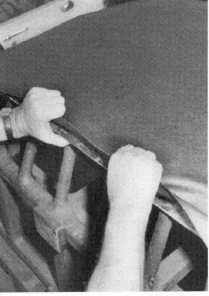

SHF27.   After the glue has gone off for the required time, stretch the material taut over the rail. Start in the centre, then work out to the edges. Check carefully the fit around the (raised) door glasses. Peel back and adjust if necessary.

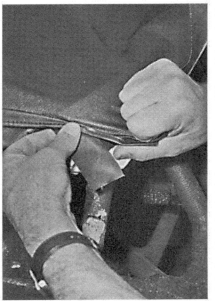

SHF28.   Make sure that the corner tag is left free and not trapped underneath.

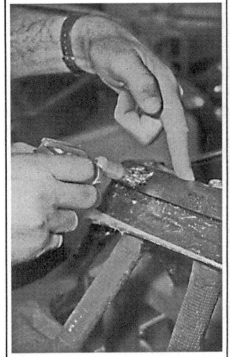

SHF26.   . . . and to the top of the header rail. An old brush is fine for applying the glue but be prepared to wash it in petrol or thinners afterwards – wear suitable gloves and safety glasses. Do not get petrol or other solvents on your skin.

SHF29.   . . . and then firmly smooth the soft-top down into place.

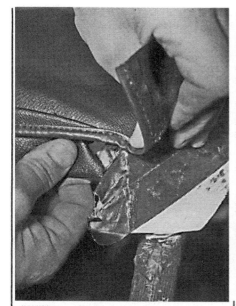

SHF30. Try to ensure any gaps at the corners are as small as possible to prevent leaks.

SHF32. Once the glue has thoroughly dried, paint some more over the corner overlay strip plus another layer on the corresponding area of the inner rail surface.

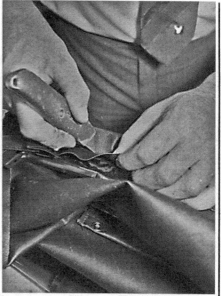

SHF34. Fold over the soft-top material and cut the corner edges in inch wide strips to allow a good crease free finish.

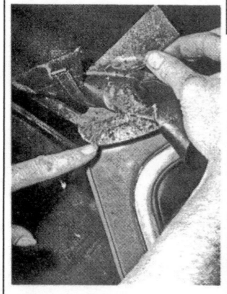

SHF31. If necessary, the corners can be lifted up and glued back down again in a better position.

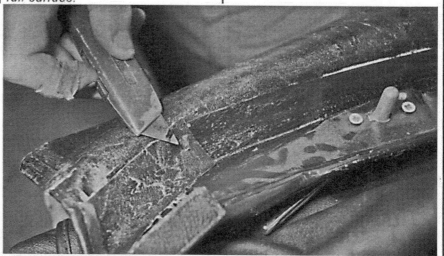

SHF33. After sticking down, any excess can be trimmed off.

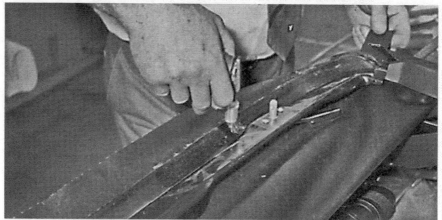

SHF35. Adhesive should then be applied to the remainder of the soft-top material and header rail inner surface . . .

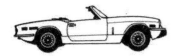
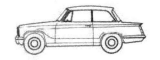

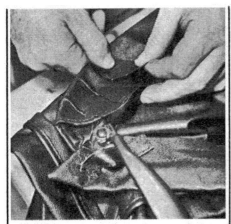

SHF36. . . . left to dry, and then the strips and the rest of the material pressed home.

SHF37. The front rail metal ▶ *channels should now be replaced by first relocating one of the rivet holes . . .*

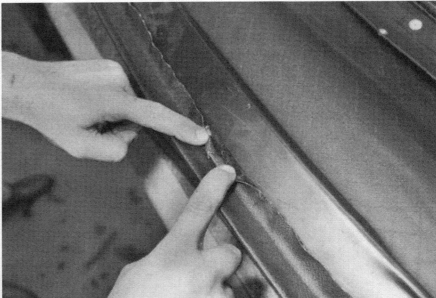

SHF38. . . . punching a hole through the vinyl . . .

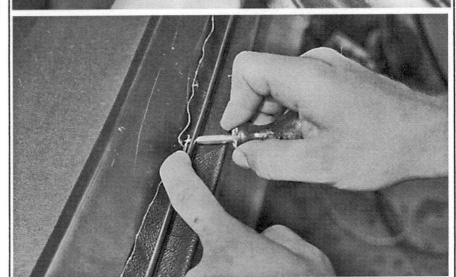

SHF39. . . . and then laying the channels on followed by pop-riveting in place. The location of the first rivet in channel and header rail will ensure that all the other holes line up, too.

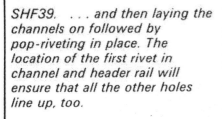

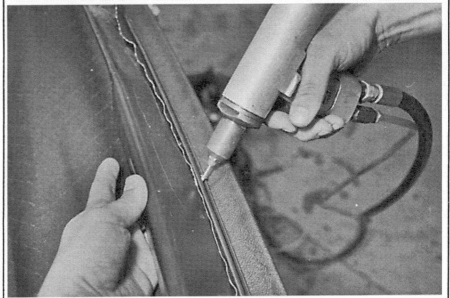

SHF40. Any excess material can then be sliced off (mind your fingers!) . . . ►

SHF41.▲ . . . followed by replacing the front rail seal.

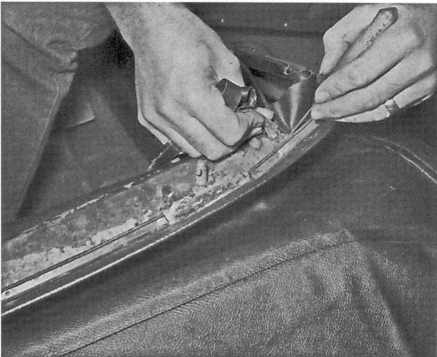

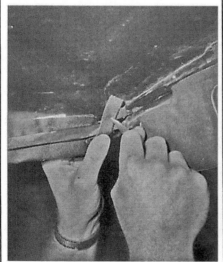

SHF42.▲ Finally, locate the inner pull strip, punch a hole

through . . .

SHF43. . . . and fix in place. ►
This stops the seal strip from blowing away from the glass at the front, when the car is at speed.

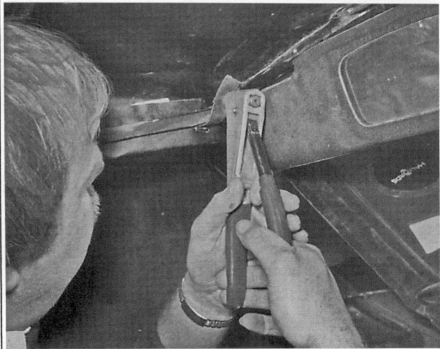

Any small creases can often be removed by carefully warming the inside of the car with an electric heater which softens the vinyl and encourages it to smooth out. Don't go away with the heater on! You must try to get rid of as many wrinkles as you possibly can whilst fitting the soft-top. Some wrinkles will come out over a period of months as the once flat sheets of vinyl 'learn' to accept their new shape.

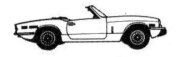

Fitting a Herald/Vitesse soft-top

Many of the principles outlined above are just as applicable for fitting a soft-top to a Herald or Vitesse. However, Herald/Vitesse soft-tops do employ additional design features which are outlined below. The Herald is, again, 'Terry' Johnson's pride and joy.

HVH1. As with a Spitfire soft-top, removal of a Herald/Vitesse soft-top requires the removal of a header rail seal.

HVH2.►However in this case, a row of screws rather than pop rivets need to be removed before the edge of the material can be lifted free. Next, the vertical rubber door glass seals should be pulled out of their metal channels to reveal a further row of screws. Once these have been taken out and the metal channels removed, the return edge of the soft-top material can be peeled off. The lower rear quarters are simply clipped to the deck. A row of 12 thin bolts secures the material at the rear which also serves to retain the bright strip and tonneau cover poppers. Finally, unscrew the two retaining screws holding down the bright strip above the rear window. The strip can then be unclipped. Pop rivets are used to secure these clips and the soft-top material to the rear frame rail so carefully drill them out after which the soft-top should lift off. Store the clips for refitting later.

HVH3. One of the major differences between Herald/Vitesse and Spitfire soft-tops is the use of frame support webbing on the former. As shown here, these can wear but are easily removed by carefully drilling out the securing pop rivets plus, at the rear, removing a couple of screws and a clamp plate each side. As the webbing is removed, support the frame to stop it falling down.

HVH4. Measure off new webbing as required. Note that each strap is made up of two pieces stitched together at an angle so mirror this for each side with the new material. On refitting, clamp the webbing at the rear and work forwards checking the fit against that of the original. Lay the soft-top over the frame and check the length of the rear webbing to the first frame bar matches that of the soft-top. Adjust as necessary.

HVH5. For a nice flush finish flatten off the rivet heads with a hammer.

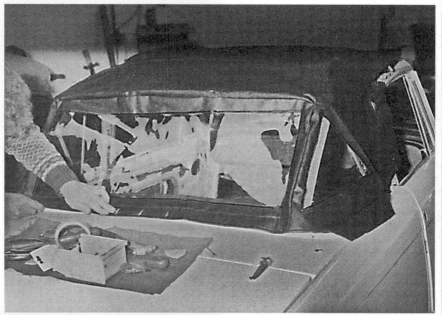

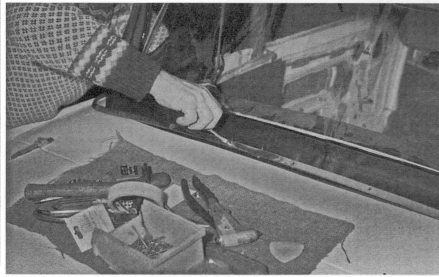

HVH6. ▲ As with a Spitfire soft top, secure the new soft-top at the rear first. Start at the centre and then work outwards. Carefully line up and mark where the retaining screws have to go with some chalk. Holes can then be made with a bradawl . . .

HVH7. . . . and the lower bright strip plus tonneau buttons screwed down on top.

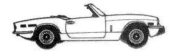

HVH8. Similarly, align and mark the positions for the upper metal finishing strip (it helps to have an assistant inside the car here) and secure the soft-top finisher strip clips to the frame bar with pop rivets.

HVH9. The bright strip can then be clipped and screwed into place. The soft-top can then be secured to the header rail in a similar manner to that shown for the Spitfire though with the obvious differences already pointed out. Latch the soft-top in place and double check everything fits as it should. If not, adjust before finally securing the front rail clamp strip and finishing strip. Don't forget to refit the chromed metal end protectors.

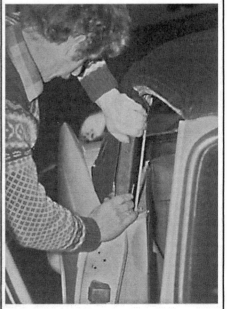

HVH10. ▲ All that's left to do now is to fold over and glue the B-post return strip in position . . .

HVH11.◄ . . . ready for screwing the glass seal channels back into place and slipping in the rubber seals themselves.

Thanks are due to Derek Johnson for photographing this section.

Soft-top folding and stowage

Once you've fitted a new soft-top, you'll want to keep it in good condition. The best thing you can do to keep it that way is to fold and store it properly thus avoiding as much as possible discoloration and scratching.

Spitfire

SHF1. Release the front header rail locking arms as applicable. Some Mk 3 models have buckles similar to the Herald/Vitesse.

SHF2. Unclip the central roof bar and side popper studs. As the soft-top is moved backwards, pull the material out . . .

SHF3. ▶ . . . so it lays flat on the rear deck.

SHF4. With the soft-top mechanism tucked into the well, fold the soft top right over . . .

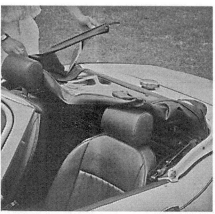

SHF5. ▲ . . . followed by each corner, keeping them and the main window flat and crease free.

SHF6. The whole lot can then be tucked neatly behind the rear seats . . .

SHF7. . . . and a soft-top cover or full tonneau clipped on.

Herald/Vitesse

HF1. Unclasp the screen rail ▶ soft-top buckles and slightly raise the front soft-top rail.

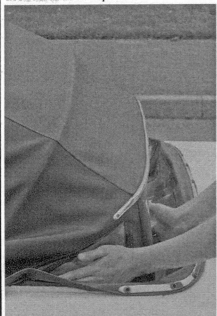

HF2. ▲ Carefully tuck in the rear quarter windows each side and main rear window.

HF3. ▲ Keep tucking the rear screen into the well as you lower the soft-top. Try and keep the chrome strip across the back of the soft-top from rubbing against the window. This is also important on later raising the soft-top.

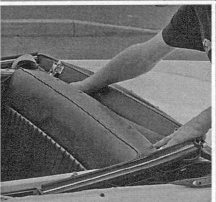

HF4. ◀ As the soft-top disappears into the well, keep the fastening buckles from rubbing the rear seat back and then give a final firm push downwards to set the soft-top beneath the rear deck level.

HF5. ▼ The soft-top well can then be nicely hidden from view with it's cover. Many modern cabriolets with their rather 'add on later' designs aren't nearly as stylish as this.

Door trim removal

The same type of trim fastenings are to be found in all of the cars across the range.

Toolbox

Standard and cross-headed screwdrivers, hammer and a thin nail.

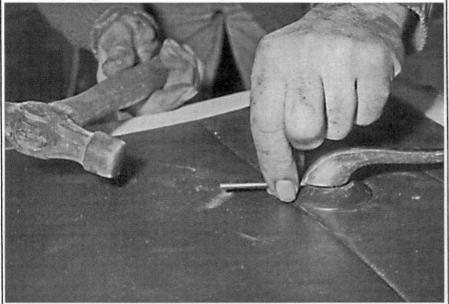

DT1. ▲ Most handles and winder arms are held in place with locking pins which can be tapped through with a nail or similar. It helps to lever and wedge in a screwdriver to create a little clearance between handle base and plastic escutcheon while doing this. This door is lying flat on the work bench.

DT2. Once the pin has been pushed through, the handle may be lifted free.

DT3. ▲ On Heralds and Vitesses fitted with door pockets, remove the screw cap and unscrew a Phillips screw at each end of the pocket top.

DT4. The door trim can then be levered off, being held by push-in compression clips.

DT5. Other panels on all the cars are also held by similar clips, eg., on this GT6 side panel, or Phillips screws and cup washers.

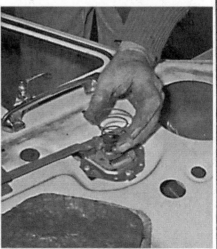

DT6. The door and winder handles are tensioned by springs which simply lift off. Note that the narrow end faces into the door.

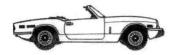

DT7. Inner felt and outer rubber window seals are retained by different clips which can be dislodged with a sharp tap from a screwdriver . . . ▶

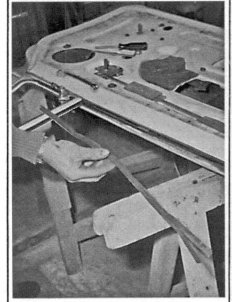

DT8. . . . allowing the seal to be removed . . .

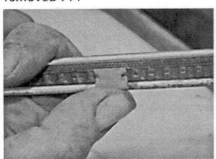

DT9. On replacement, fit new clips to the inner seal . . .

DT10. . . . and outer rubber seal – in the recesses provided.

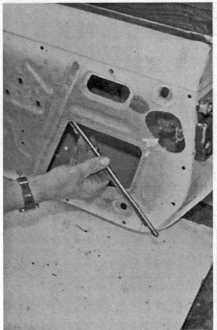

DT11.◀ Feed the seals into the door and secure with clips along the door frame and skin edges. Triumph manuals recommend a pull-up type tool but it's much better, easier and a far less risk to new paintwork if you use a similar action to that shown in DT7. However, in this case have the screwdriver pointing upwards inside the frame. It'll help to have an assistant steadying the seal about each clip as they're being tapped home. Use the palm of your hand to tap up the screwdriver blade.

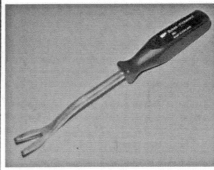

DT12. Sykes-Pickavant make this door trim remover which ensures that pop-off door trim clips don't pull through the hardboard trim backing, something to which older trim panels are particularly prone.

Spitfire IV, 1500 and GT6 Mk 3 door handles

SGH1. Pull-up type handles often fail due to a broken nylon push rod (partly obscured by the spring – bottom left) which means that nothing happens when the handle is lifted. Handles can easily be taken apart and new push rods fitted. They're only a few pence each. When replacing in the door (see SGH6), insert the lug being pointed to first. ▼

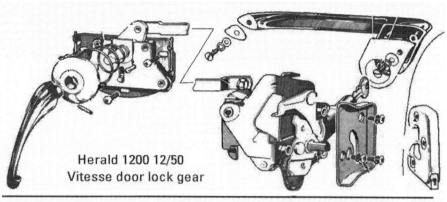

Herald 1200 12/50 Vitesse door lock gear

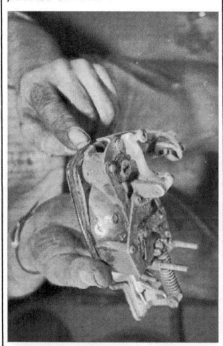

SGH2. With age, door locks become worn and may have to be replaced. Slide off the spring clip . . .

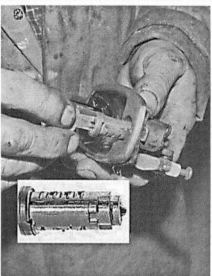

SGH3.▲ . . . and pull out the lock barrel.

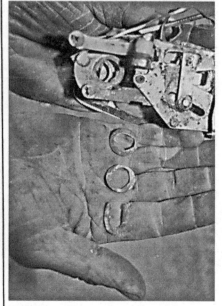

SGH4. The series of washers and clips to be replaced.

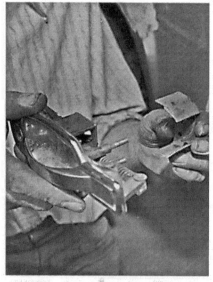

SGH5. Late door handles are held in place with brackets as shown.

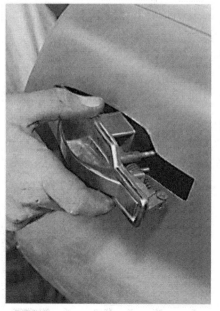

SGH6. Insert the handle and tighten the bracket into place.

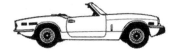

Windscreen frame fitting
Spitfire 4, Mk 2 and Mk 3

On these early models, the windscreen frame can be removed for repair . . .

WF1.► *Before refitting, run sealant around the body . . .*

WF2.► *. . . and windscreen seals. As shown, it's a good idea to cover the lower frame edge with tape. Sealant, as may be expected, spreads out a lot.*

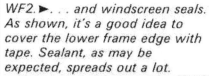

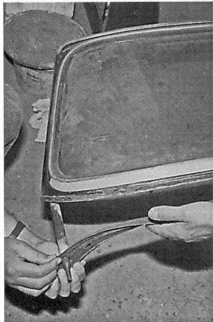

WF3.▲ *Slide the seal over the screen legs . . .*

WF4.► *. . . and fit firmly in place on the car. Retighten the holding bracket.*

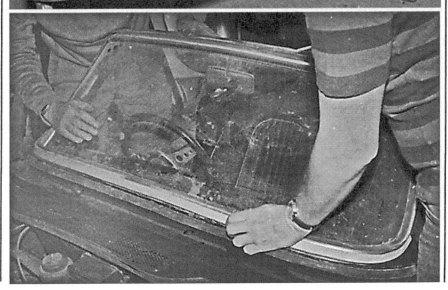

Carpet and interior trim fitting

Carpets bought from a Triumph specialist are usually – though not always; check carefully – better than those bought from 'general' car carpet suppliers, mail order. These were fitted to Richard Swinfield's Spitfire 1500 at Classic Car Restorations.

CF1.► Old and grubby carpets can spoil the overall presentation in even good cars. New carpets can be obtained from many sources, at vastly different prices and varying quality. Shop around.

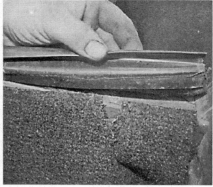

CF3.▲ In this particular case, the top edge is finished off with a push-on rubber strip which is itself glued to the front edge of the rear deck carpet.

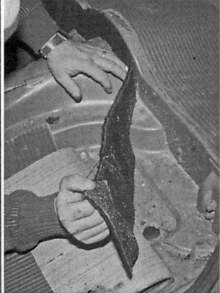

CF2.► Similar techniques are used for fitting carpets in all the Herald family. Extra sound deadening material can be laid beneath the main carpet as desired. Some carpet panels are glued into place with impact type adhesive such as this rear Spitfire panel.

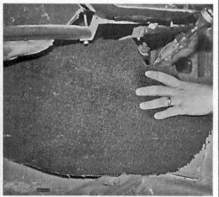

CF4.▲ Often the hardest area to carpet properly is around the gearbox tunnel. Where relevant, try to obtain a correctly heat-moulded carpet section. These enable a much better finish to be achieved than with flat-section carpet panels.

CF5.◄ As with the upright rear panel, side footwell sections are glued in place . . .

CF6.▼ . . . with the top edges tucking under the glove pocket trim.

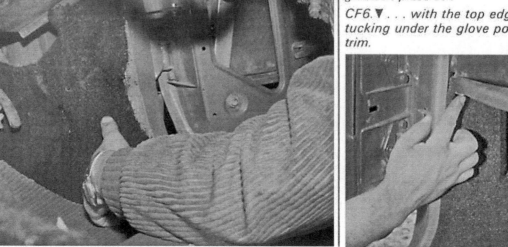

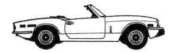

CF7. ▲ On Heralds and Vitesses, the main floor sections continue right up to the door openings. Spitfires and GT6s have separate glued on sill sections. Early Heralds use separate push-over clips to secure the carpet.

CF8. ▲ Later Herald and Vitesses use long strips screwed in position with self-tappers.

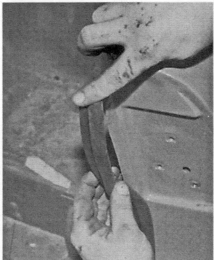

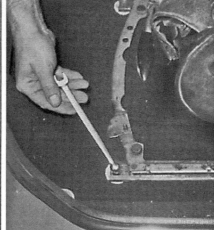

CF9. ▲ With the carpets in place, side vinyl covered panels can be replaced. Fixing is generally by a mixture of self-tappers and push-in compression clips. A wide range of excellent new original spec. panels is available from firms such as Rimmer Bros and Newton Commercial.

CF10. ◄ Though shown with the carpets removed, door trim seals should be replaced after fitting the carpets and side trim. Simply push over the panel seam and where relevant, the carpet/trim edges.

CF11. ◄ With all the carpet and side trim in place, seats are easily replaced by securing four bolts (Spitfires and GT6s) or large self-tappers (Herald and Vitesses); two at each end of the frame.

CF12. Seat belts, too, can now be resecured. Most models were fitted with static types, though later Spitfires were fitted with inertia reel belts.

CF13. If fitting new belts, ensure that they're the correct type and that if they're inertia reel, that they run freely into their holding position without snagging.

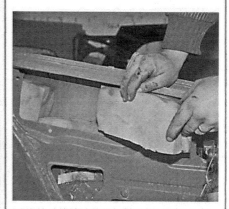

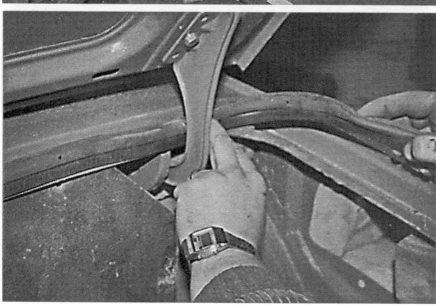

CF14. ▲ Original rear wing sound-deadening foam is absorbent and creates a long term rust problem. Replacements from specialists such as Newton Commercial and Rimmer Bros are non-absorbent.

CF15. ◄ Boot seals too are a simple push over job. Try to position the join behind a hinge. This way it won't be noticed and adds a professional touch.

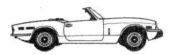

Fitting a new headlining

Fitting a new headlining is perhaps one of the more skilful tasks that the home trim restorer may have to tackle on Herald-based cars. It certainly is possible to carry out a rewarding and professional job using, for instance, one of the excellent replacement headlinings manufactured and supplied by Jim Hawkins Trimming as shown below. However, some patience is required. In order to replace the headlining in a Herald or Vitesse, the roof and rear screen need to be removed first. As shown previously, removing the roof of a Herald or Vitesse should present few problems. Take care when replacing that the new headlining remains undamaged and the roof bolts do not scratch the rear deck. Use plenty of windscreen type sealer on re-assembly to ensure a watertight result. Due to the basic layout, GT6 headlinings can and have to be replaced with the roof in place, though removing the front screen can be helpful. The work was carried out on one of Peter Williams' stable of Triumphs.

Tool box

Modeller's scalpel, heavy duty sharp knife, scissors, screwdriver and headlining adhesive.

HLR1. As the seal was due for replacement, this rear screen was removed by cutting the old seal out. Use a strong, sharp knife but watch those fingers! Early pattern screen rubbers are no longer obtainable, so ensure a suitable replacement is available prior to destroying the old one. Consult your local windscreen fitting centre. Alternatively, the screen should be pushed out before removing the roof in a similar manner as that shown in BR1 under Spitfire body removal. ▶

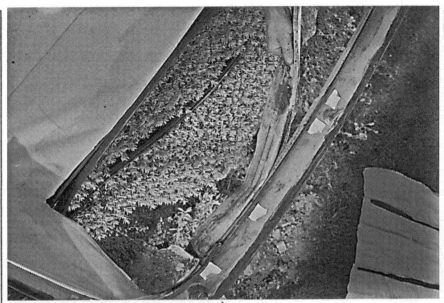

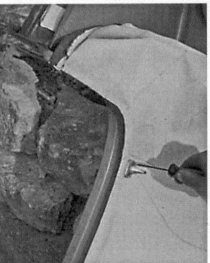

HLR2.▲ With the seal and screen removed, pull off the rear horizontal headlining finisher strip then release the rear quarter panels. Before removing the latter, mark the exact position on the roof edges where the material seams touch – to help with the initial positioning of the new lining.

HLR3.◄ The pair of coat hooks are easily removed.

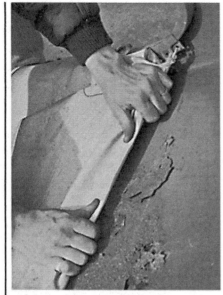

HLR4.   The headlining is tensioned across the roof with a number of wire hangers which engage in brackets fixed alongside the roof edges. Bend them slightly and pull out.

HLR6.   Before fitting the new lining, check out all the roof seams for rust and remedy as required. Fiting the new lining starts with sliding the hanger rods into their correct pockets . . .

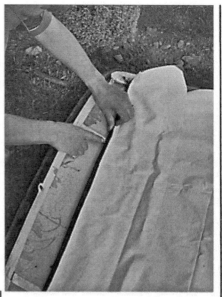

HLR8.   The front rail should also be swivelled around and clipped into two further spring clips as shown to help tension the material.

HLR5.   The wire hangers can then be slid out of their respective pockets in the lining material. Each hanger has a different profile and is colour coded at each end. If the coding is faint, mark each rod as it's withdrawn with a different colour felt tip pen or similar; front, middle, rear etc.

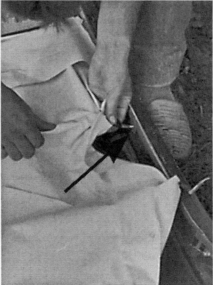

HLR7.   . . . and engaging each end in its bracket.

HLR9.   Using the marks on the roof edges suggested in HLR2, position the rear lining in place with clothes pegs or similar and check for fit.

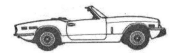

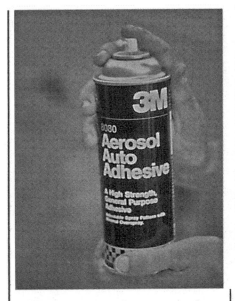

HLR10. Using the correct glue is essential. Some glues can leach through the material ultimately leading to an ugly stain. This one by 3M is ideal. You should be able to buy it through your local 'trade' motor factor – they sell to the public, too, in virtually every case. Age restrictions apply.

HLR11. Adhesive is usually applied to both the headlining and the roof. Use some coarse cutting paper to provide a good key before applying glue to the roof edges. In our headlining fitting sequence, ably carried out by the TSSC's resident expert Bernard Robinson, we 'drew a line' down the centre of the roof, front to back, and tackled one side of the headlining at a time. This approach works very well in practice. Spray an even coat of adhesive onto the rear roof panel edges, over a length of about 18 inches at a time ...

HLR12. ... followed by a similar thin coat onto the corresponding headlining area. Use a large clean sheet between the headlining folds to protect the main surface from adhesive overspray.

HLR13. The edges can then be smoothed over and secured in place. As shown later, it may well be necessary to relift the material and tease into a slightly different position to obtain better tension. The adhesive allows this as it remains tacky for a useful length of time though on odd occasions, you may have to apply a little more.

HLR14. With the lining secured along the rear windscreen top and side edges, Bernard has now applied adhesive to the outer flanges of the roof base and window frame vertical edges ...

HLR15. ... followed by another layer on the material itself. Although the protective sheet looks rather dirty, it was actually totally dry and didn't leave any marks on the new lining.

HLR16. Offer the quarter panel in place.

HLR18. Clothes pegs are very useful in clipping the lining in place as the adhesive sets though not strictly essential as the adhesive used has very good holding properties from initial contact but not severe enough to prevent the material being lifted and repositioned as desired. A small amount of cutting may be required to achieve a nice finish around the corners before glueing and fixing in place.

HLR20. When the rear section has been successfully secured, folding over and glueing along the side flanges simply follows. Adhesive can then be applied at the front edge, the tension firmly taken up . . .

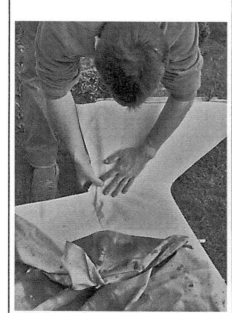

HLR17. Smooth down along the flanges, teasing any creases out as you go. Patience in achieving an exact fit is essential.

HLR19. Keep checking for fit. Here Bernard is adjusting the tension just that little bit more.

HLR21. . . . and the lining secured. Early and late roofs differ at the corners. As shown on this later, ribbed Coupé roof, corner brackets are in evidence. Earlier panels don't have these. All this means in practice is that on later examples, a little more trimming and care is required around these areas.

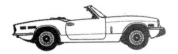

HLR22. With the corners complete, follow on towards the centre.

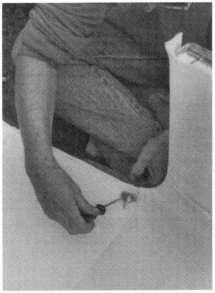

HLR24. With one side complete, the exercise should be repeated on the other. After this, carefully relocate where the coat hanger holes are and screw them back into position.

HLR26. . . . which when glued into place ensures a very neat job.

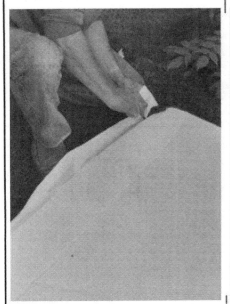

HLR23. Any excess material should be trimmed off with a scalpel.

HLR25. In addition to the main headlining, a separate strip is supplied to finish off the lower edge. For a professional finish turn over each end on itself, as a hem . . .

HLR27. The finished job. Allow yourself a whole day to carry it out. Any tiny wrinkles should drop out after a day or so.

Wing finishers and badges

WFB1. Spitfires and GT6s employ similar external wing flange finishers although the GT6 Mk 1 finishers are wider sectioned than the others. Early ones are stainless steel and are used on the bonnet and rear wings and later ones are finished in black and are used on the rear wings only. To remove, gradually lever up, applying a screwdriver tip at different places along the length. ►

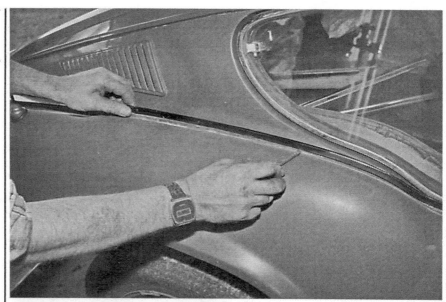

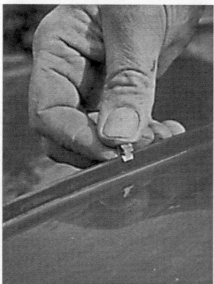

WFB3. ◄ Simply push over the wing flange. About half a dozen for each strip should be sufficient . . .

WFB4. ▼ . . . and then push home the finisher taking a little care to ensure an accurate fit along the length. Spray Corroless along the flange top and inside the finisher before fitting into place.

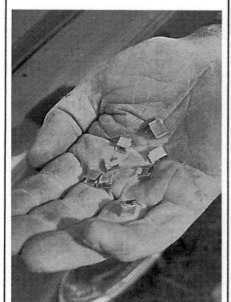

WFB2. ▲ New clips are easily available at a few pence each.

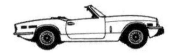

WFB5. Most Heralds and Vitesses use side wing finishers which are again simply levered off to reveal riveted on claw (early) or button-like (late) fastenings.

NOTE FROM ANOTHER ERA: Metal tools run a severe risk of scratching paintwork. It only costs a few quid to buy a set of plastic trim levers, such as these.

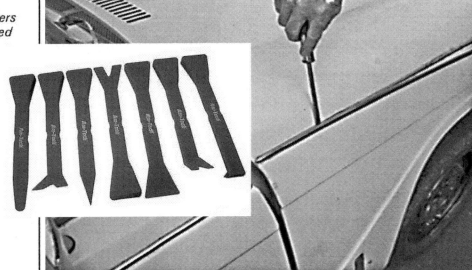

WFB6. Badges on all the cars are generally fixed with clips which push over the badge fixing pins on the inside of the relevant panel. Some badges are held on with flat metal clips as shown here whilst others use a more tube-shaped plastic clip. Normally, both types fit on the inside and not through the panel and are simply pulled off for removal.

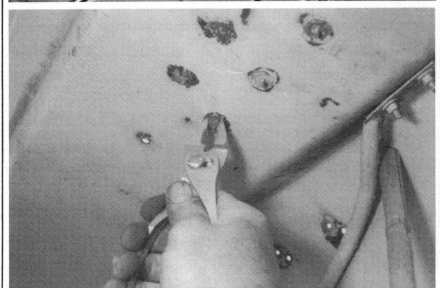

WFB7. A close up view of a Herald badge and the flat-type metal clip.

7 Home Modifications

Introduction

Every car enthusiast likes to think that his or her car is something special and so, may often be interested in refining particular aspects to suit. There's an awful lot than can be done and in the end, it's down to a case of personal preference about whether the car is kept as original or revised to improve things like roadholding, performance, refinement or simply just to create a slightly different style within the overall theme. Much of today's technology just wasn't around when the cars were designed and many simple improvements and refinements can be carried out even by the non-technologically minded: for instance fitting radial tyres to older models, adding improved lighting or even replacing old spark plugs with modern equivalents. The list is endless but to show the sort of things that can be done, we've included a few ideas below.

HM1. By far the most popular modifications concern engines. Whether fitting Weber carburettors . . .

HM2. . . . or fuel injection systems to Spitfires . . .

HM3. . . . or even to Vitesses (or Heralds or GT6s) you really should know a little about what you want before you start. What happens to fuel consumption, insurance ratings etc? Will the fast road or even race cam be tractable in the local supermarket car park or 'nose to tail' into work. All these things need thinking out carefully before going ahead as at this level, mistakes can be expensive. However, if it's for you, there's no reason why not to go ahead and enjoy the car as you want it.

HM4. ◄ Early GT6s obtained a poor roadholding reputation from the British press from their launch which has never been forgotten and which has simply been repeated verbatim in all subsequent motoring reviews, The so-called 'Boulevard Ride' imposed by export considerations can be improved upon by fitting modern uprated shock absorbers all round. SPAX GAS adjustable units are an excellent example.

HM5. Another way of improving GT6 Mk 1 roadholding is to fit a new or reconditioned late GT6 pivoting rear spring in conjunction with a thicker anti-roll bar as fitted to later Spitfires —but fit new bushes. The drive shafts don't need to be changed. Don't fit the similar Spitfire spring as the GT6 item is stiffer. Swing springs are attached to the differential by four rather than six studs so two of the threaded holes in the differential should be blanked off. Alternatively, new manifold 'conventional' type springs are available to tighten up the rear end.

HM6. On a different front, roll over bars of many different makes and styles are a popular addition to all convertibles. The Daimler seats are definitely non-standard.

HM7. In addition to the fuel injection shown earlier, Carl Heinlein's attractive Spitfire 4 has a twin box exhaust system, roll over bar, alloy wheels and chromed bolt through boot rack. No prizes for also spotting the late Spitfire number plate/reversing lamp assembly. For modifications like these to be a success, they need to complement each other, as they certainly do here.

HM8. This Spitfire with GT6 engine and bonnet (plus 'chassis' mods) conversion is very popular especially on the Continent.

HM9. Going even further is this recycled(?) Herald. As you can see, anything's possible and FUN!

Electronic ignition

More reliable starting, better fuel economy, improved performance and reduced servicing are the main advantages expected from fitting electronic ignition systems.

EI1.►A total fit and forget system is promised by the Lumenition Optronic Ignition set-up illustrated here as the original points are replaced with an optical switching unit. Included in the kit as well as full and clear instructions are electronic ignition control box, optical switch with vanes for either four or six cylinder models and all necessary wiring.

EI2.▲ First, disconnect the battery. To fit the optical switching unit to the GT6 Delco Remy D202 unit shown here, the distributor top plate should first be removed by simply undoing the three screws around the outside and lifting it out.

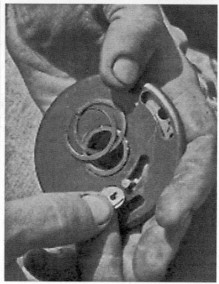

EI3.▲ There's no need to remove the distributor itself but it helps to show the main relevant parts here; distributor, vacuum advance, top plate and contact breakers.

EI4.◄ Different distributors have different fixing kits. When fitting the Lumenition kit onto a D202, the top plate needs to be dismantled – achieved by removing the two central thin spring clips followed by the outer slider spring clip.

EI5.   The two halves can then be separated. As shown, sandwiched between is a felt oil retaining pad.

EI6.   The next step for any distributor is to reduce the height of the original contact breaker pivot pin to allow the free rotation of the optical switching vane. In our example a second hand distributor bought for all of £2 supplied a spare top plate and so the pin was sawn totally off. Lumenition supply full instructions and the maximum allowed length of the pin is given in the kit. An excellent back up service for any technical enquiries is also available.

EI7.   Also on the D202, the breaker gap adjusting cam should be removed by filing the head off underneath — about 10 seconds work.

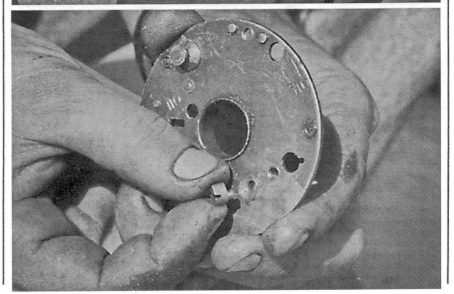

E18. ▲ The optical switching unit should then be screwed in place using the original contact breaker securing screw. A small nut and bolt (not supplied) should also be used to secure the foot end of the switch plate to stop any possible rotation. This makes use of the hole where the contact gap adjusting cam used to be. Other models are simpler with the tail of the bracket being secured underneath a pip on the distributor top plate. Once complete, join the two halves of the top plate back together. As shown, arrange the wires neatly (no capacitor is used) and secure with the grommet supplied. The switching vane is simply pushed over the distributor shaft during the process. 4-cylinder models have four vanes, 6-cylinder models six.

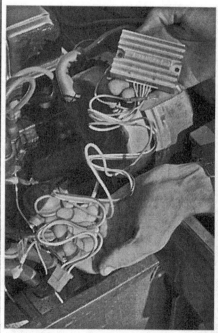

E19. ▲ Once everything is bolted back in place the ignition control box should be wired up and bolted to a suitable place on the bulkhead. Keep the battery leads undone until the wiring route has been thoroughly checked over then reconnect. As necessary, reset the timing, and away you go. No more point replacements and everything remaining in tune.

Oil cooler fitting

OCF1. Many different oil cooler systems are available. This one's by Serck. Every one of the 1500-engined Spitfires should be fitted with an oil cooler; their bottom-ends are prone to failure and such failure can destroy the engine.

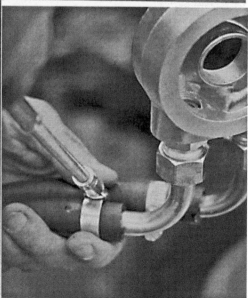

OCF2. This particular version retains the original oil filter; some use a different design and fitting. The first stage is to decide where the oil cooling radiator is to be fitted. Cut hose to length and clamp filter plate conversion in place as applicable. Some units may be supplied with fixed length hose and screw fittings.

OCF3.   The adaptor is then bolted and sealed to the block.

OCF4. ▲ Make sure it's secure but not overtight.

OCF5.   Fit a new filter.

OCF6.   Connect up the radiator and ensure that there are no kinks. If the hose rubs against any metal surface, however slightly, protect it by clipping a length of split larger diameter rubber pipe around the vulnerable area, or alternatively use armoured pipes.

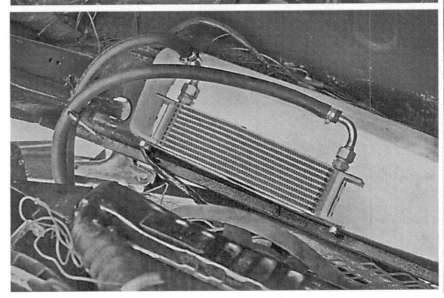

OCF7. The cooler was fitted in the nose cone of this particular car.

OCF8. A more conventional place is in front of the radiator. The gap doesn't have to be anywhere near as large as shown here.

OCF9. The installation of a different kit on a GT6. This system uses screw fittings with an alloy housing adaptor employing a different spin-on oil filter. Note the protecting rubber sleeves on the hose close to the suspension turrets and even the oil dip stick housing. Very effective, simple and cheap.

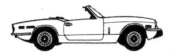

Kenlowe fan fitting

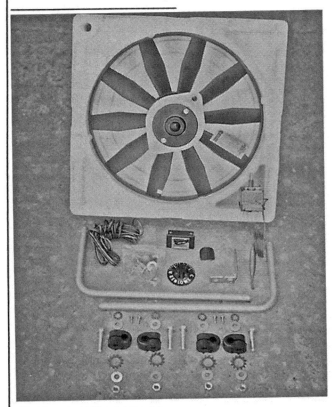

KFF1. Another popular modification aimed at increased refinement, improving useful power available and/or fuel economy is to fit a Kenlowe electric fan.

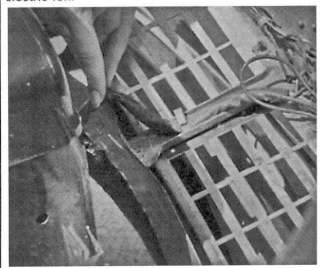

KFF2.▲ Depending on the car (and fan model) decide where the best mounting points are. A GT6 is provided with some very convenient unused chassis holes already, just in the right place!

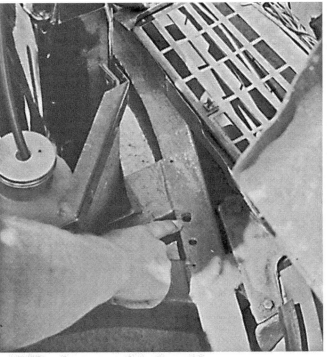

KFF3. As appropriate, the wiring loom can be redirected slightly and reclipped to the fan mounting bars.

KFF4. Check which way round the mounting brackets and unions should go and slide roughly in place.

232

KFF5. Attach the fan in place. Ensure that the fan is attached as described in the instruction manual.

KFF6. Offer the bracket bolts into the chassis holes but leave the nuts off. Adjust each of the four unions along the bracket members so that the motor and fan sit snuggly against the radiator and that the bonnet shuts without catching. The bonnet's inside return lip may need bending slightly. When satisfied, tighten up the locking screw near each chassis mounting point . . .

KFF7. . . . and the motor/bracket fixing bolts.

KFF8. ▲ Lift the unit out of the car and tighten the locking screws at the motor support plate. Fix the whole assembly into the car with bolts at each chassis mounting point. Check that the bonnet still shuts easily. Make adjustments as required.

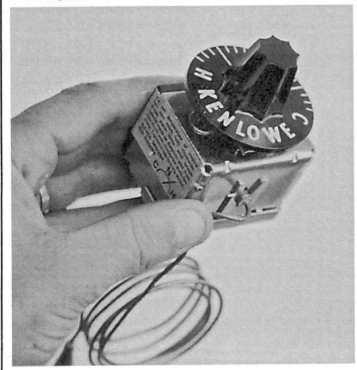

KFF9. ▲ The cut-in temperature is set on a thermostat . . .

KFF10. . . . controlled by a sender unit which fits inside the radiator. Use the special seal provided between radiator pipe and hose. Sender units which fit against the radiator are also available on some models.

KFF11. Refit the hose and reclamp. Once in use, check for leaks. A second clamp may help. As shown, on GT6s, place the clip's worm drive below the radiator pipe as the bonnet is a very tight fit here. A lot of GT6s have little bonnet dents in this region simply because of a lack of knowledge or attention to this detail.

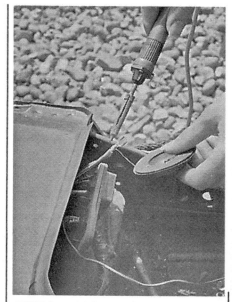

KFF12. Wire the unit in accordance to the fitting instructions. Rather than just crimping the connections, use soldered joints. They make for a much better job.

KFF13. ▼ The manual over-ride switch can be located in any convenient place eg. underneath the dashboard – shown bottom left.

KFF14. The thermostat can be fitted in a number of convenient positions but must be earthed. Once all is complete, idle the engine, ensure that the fan rotates in the correct direction, if not swap over the power leads. Set the thermostat control as detailed in the kit. Check the leaks and road test. Adjust thermostat etc., as necessary.

KFF15. Kenlowe fans are also available to fit in more confined spaces, as found in Vitesses.

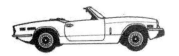

Remote oil filter fitting – Vitesse/GT6

Nearly all of the Triumph engines used in the Herald family suffer from start up rattle due mainly to the layout of the oil filters (worn engines excepted). The filter is either positioned upside down (Heralds and Spitfires) or horizontally (Vitesses and GT6s) and hence while the engine is stationary, oil can drain out. On restarting and while the filter is filling up again the oil pressure in the engine is low and hence for the first couple of seconds whilst this process is happening, bearings run dry the effect of which then causes the annoying rattle. OK as far as it goes as long as the engine isn't revved hard at this stage.

Herald and Spitfire owners learned a long time ago that fitting the correct Unipart oil filter (or EXACT equivalent) with an anti-drain valve, and not just a look alike, cures the problem. Not so easy with the paper elements in Vitesses and GT6s. Below is shown how to fit a very simple but effective remote filter housing which allows an anti-drain type of filter to be fitted to the six-cylinder cars.

Further details may be obtained from Dave Bradley, care of the Triumph Sports Six Club, who designed the kit.

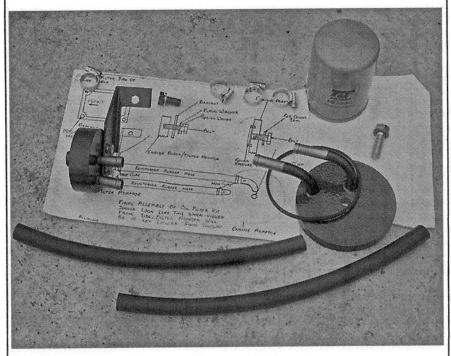

ROF1. The kit of parts with filter adaptor to the left and engine plate to the right.

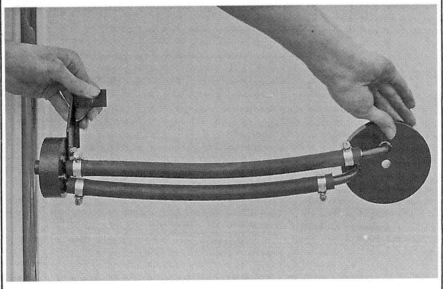

ROF2. Temporarily assembling the kit lets you know where everything goes . . .

ROF3. The remote housing attaches behind this engine mounting securing bolt. A longer bolt is supplied with the kit plus full instructions.

ROF4. Drain the engine oil and remove the old filter bowl assembly. ▶

ROF5.▲ The new engine plate is fitted with a rubber O-ring. Make sure that it seats properly. The outer edge is sealed to the block in the normal way.

ROF6. Push on the rubber hoses which are pre-cut to length and tighten on the engine plate. Don't forget to fit the bolt sealing washer.

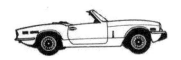

ROF7. Next, do the same thing at the other end.

ROF8. Tighten all the hose clips . . .

ROF9. . . . and fit the correct filter. A list of equivalent filters is also supplied with the kit. There's obviously no point at all in fitting a filter without an anti-drain valve.

ROF10. As with fitting an oil cooler, fit protective sleeves of wider bore rubber tube wherever the oil hoses come in contact with metal surfaces. Simply cut off the required length, slit along one edge and clip on. No extra clamps or clips required.

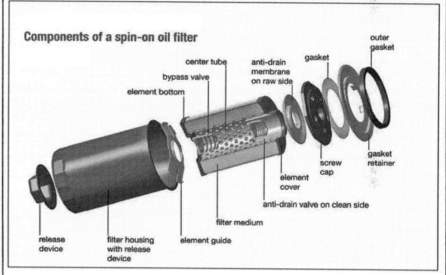

Components of a spin-on oil filter

element bottom — bypass valve — center tube — anti-drain membrane on raw side — gasket — outer gasket — screw cap — gasket retainer — element cover — anti-drain valve on clean side — filter medium — element guide — filter housing with release device — release device

For example, a Mann filter with anti-drain valve.

Grateful acknowledgement is given to *The Courier,* the magazine of the Triumph Sports Six Club in which the original articles of fitting both the oil cooler and remote oil filter first appeared.

APPENDIX 1

Workshop Procedures and Safety First

Professional motor mechanics are trained in safe working procedures, whereas the onus is on you, the home mechanic, to find them out for yourself and act upon them. However enthusiastic you may be about getting on with the job in hand, do take the time to ensure that your safety is not put at risk. A moment's lack of attention can result in an accident, as can failure to observe certain elementary precautions.

There will always be new ways of having accidents, and the following points do not pretend to be a comprehensive list of all dangers; they are intended rather to make you aware of the risks and to encourage a safety-conscious approach to all work you carry out on your vehicle.

Be sure to consult the suppliers of any materials and equipment you may use, and to obtain and read carefully operating and health and safety instructions that they may supply.

Essential DOs and DON'Ts

DON'T rely on a single jack when working underneath the vehicle. Always use reliable additional means of support, such as axle stands, securely placed under a part of the vehicle that you know will not give way.

DON'T attempt to loosen or tighten high-torque nuts (e.g. wheel hub nuts) while the vehicle is on a jack; it may be pulled off.

DON'T start the engine without first ascertaining that the transmission is in neutral (or 'Park' where applicable) and the parking brake applied.

DON'T suddenly remove the filler cap from a hot cooling system – cover it with a cloth and release the pressure gradually first, or you may get scalded by escaping coolant.

DON'T attempt to drain oil, automatic transmission fluid, or coolant until you are sure it has cooled sufficiently to avoid scalding you.

DON'T grasp any part of the engine, exhaust or catalytic converter without first ascertaining that it is sufficiently cool to avoid burning you.

DON'T allow brake fluid or antifreeze to contact vehicle paintwork.

DON'T syphon toxic liquids such as fuel, brake fluid or antifreeze by mouth, or allow them to remain on your skin.

DON'T inhale dust – it may be injurious to health (see Asbestos below).

DON'T allow any spilt oil or grease to remain on the floor – wipe it up straight away, before someone slips on it.

DON'T use ill-fitting spanners or other tools which may slip and cause injury.

DON'T attempt to lift a heavy component which may be beyond your capability – get assistance.

DON'T rush to finish a job, or take unverified short cuts.

DON'T allow children or animals in or around an unattended vehicle.

DON'T park vehicles with catalytic converters over combustible materials such as dry grass, oily rags, etc., if the engine has recently been run. As catalytic converters reach extremely high temperatures, any such materials in close proximity may ignite.

DON'T run vehicles equipped with catalytic converters without the exhaust system heat shields fitted.

DO wear eye protection when using power tools such as an electric drill, sander, bench grinder, etc., and when working under the vehicle.

DO use a barrier cream on your hands prior to undertaking dirty jobs – it will protect your skin from infection as well as making the dirt easier to remove afterwards; but make sure your hands aren't left slippery. Note that long term contact with used engine oil can be a health hazard.

DO keep loose clothing (cuffs, tie, etc.) and long hair well out of the way of moving mechanical parts.

DO remove rings, wrist watch, etc., before working on the vehicle – especially the electrical system.

DO ensure that any lifting tackle used has a safe working load rating adequate for the job, and is used precisely as recommended by the manufacturer.

DO keep your work area tidy – it is only too easy to fall over articles left lying around.

DO get someone to check periodically that all is well, when working alone on the vehicle.

DO carry out work in a logical sequence and check that everything is correctly assembled and tightened afterwards.

DO remember that your vehicle's safety affects that of yourself and others. If in doubt on any point, get specialist advice.

IF, in spite of following these precautions, you are unfortunate enough to injure yourself, seek medical attention as soon as possible.

Fire

Remember at all times that petrol (gasoline) is highly flammable. Never smoke, or have any kind of naked flame around, when working on the vehicle. But the risk does not end there – a spark caused by an electrical short-circuit, by two metal surfaces contacting each other, by a central heating boiler in the garage 'firing up', or even by static electricity built up in your body under certain conditions, can ignite petrol vapour,

which in a confined space is highly explosive.

Always disconnect the battery earth (ground) terminal before working on any part of the fuel system, and never risk spilling fuel on to a hot engine or exhaust.

It is recommended that a fire extinguisher of a type suitable for fuel and electrical fires is kept handy in the garage or workplace at all times. Never try to extinguish a fuel or electrical fire with water.

Fumes

Certain fumes are highly toxic and can quickly cause unconsciousness and even death if inhaled to any extent. Petrol (gasoline) vapour comes into this category, as do the vapours from certain solvents such as trichloroethylene and those from many adhesives. Any draining or pouring of such volatile fluids should be done in a well-ventilated area.

When using cleaning fluids and solvents, read the instructions carefully. Never use any materials from unmarked containers – they may give off poisonous vapours.

Never run the engine of a motor vehicle in an enclosed space such as a garage. Exhaust fumes contain carbon monoxide which is extremely poisonous. If you need to run the engine, always do so in the open air or at least have the rear of the vehicle outside the workplace.

If you are fortunate enough to have the use of an inspection pit, never drain or pour petrol, and never run the engine, while the vehicle is standing over it; the fumes, being heavier than air, will concentrate in the pit with possibly lethal results.

The battery

Never cause a spark, or allow a naked light, near the vehicle battery. It will normally be giving off a certain amount of hydrogen gas, which is highly explosive.

Always disconnect the battery earth (ground) terminal before working on the fuel or electrical systems.

If possible, loosen the filler plugs or cover when charging the battery from an external source. Do not charge at an excessive rate or the battery may burst.

Take care when topping up and when carrying the battery. The acid electrolyte, even when diluted, is very corrosive and should not be allowed to contact the eyes or skin.

If you ever need to prepare electrolyte yourself, always add the acid slowly to the water, and never the other way round. Protect against splashes by wearing rubber gloves and goggles.

Mains electricity

When using an electric power tool, inspection light, etc., which works from the mains, always ensure that the appliance is correctly connected to its plug and that, where necessary, it is properly earthed (grounded). Do not use such appliances in damp conditions and, again, beware of creating a spark or applying excessive heat in the vicinity of fuel or fuel vapour.

Also, before using any mains powered electrical equipment, take one more simple precaution – use an RCD (Residual Current Device) circuit breaker. Then, if there is a short, the RCD circuit breaker minimises the risk of electrocution by instantly cutting the power supply. Buy from any electrical store or DIY centre. RCDs fit simply into your electrical socket before plugging in your electrical equipment.

Ignition HT voltage

A severe electric shock can result from touching certain parts of the ignition system, such as the HT leads, when the engine is running or being cranked, particularly if components are damp or the insulation is defective. Where an electronic ignition system is fitted, the HT voltage is much higher and could prove fatal. Consult your handbook or main dealer if in any doubt. Risk of injury while working on running engines, e.g. adjusting the timing, can arise if the operator touches a high voltage lead and pulls his hand away on to a projection or revolving part.

Welding and bodywork repairs

It is so useful to be able to weld

when carrying out restoration work, and yet there is a good deal that could go dangerously wrong for the uninformed – in fact more than could be covered here. **For safety's sake** you are strongly recommended to seek tuition, in whatever branch of welding you wish to use, from your local evening institute or adult education classes. In addition, all of the information and instructional material produced by the suppliers of materials and equipment you will be using must be studied carefully. You may have to ask your stockist for some of this printed material if it is not made available at the time of purchase.

In addition, it is strongly recommended that *The Car Bodywork Repair Manual*, published by Haynes, is purchased and studied before carrying out any welding or bodywork repairs. Consisting of 292 pages, around 1,000 illustrations and written by Lindsay Porter, the author of this book, *The Car Bodywork Repair Manual* picks the brains of specialists from a variety of fields, and covers arc, MIG and 'gas' welding, panel beating and accident repair, rust repair and treatment, paint spraying, glass-fibre work, filler, lead loading, interiors and much more besides. Alongside a number of projects, the book describes in detail how to carry out each of the techniques involved in car bodywork repair with safety notes where necessary. As such, it is the ideal complement to this book.

Compressed gas cylinders

There are serious hazards associated with the storage and handling of gas cylinders and fittings, and standard precautions should be strictly observed in dealing with them. Ensure that cylinders are stored in safe conditions, properly maintained and always handled with special care and make constant efforts to eliminate the possibilities of leakage, fire and explosion.

The cylinder gases that are commonly used are oxygen, acetylene and liquid petroleum gas (LPG). Safety requirements for all three gases are: Cylinders must be stored in a fire resistant, dry and

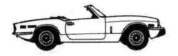

well-ventilated space, away from any source of heat or ignition and protected from ice, snow or direct sunlight. Valves of cylinders in store must always be kept uppermost and closed, even when the cylinder is empty. Cylinders should be handled with care and only by personnel who are reliable, adequately informed and fully aware of all associated hazards. Damaged or leaking cylinders should be immediately taken outside into the open air, and the supplier and fire authorities should be notified immediately. No one should approach a gas cylinder store with a naked light or cigarette. Care should be taken to avoid striking or dropping cylinders, or knocking them together. Cylinders should never be used as rollers. One cylinder should never be filled from another. Every care must be taken to avoid accidental damage to cylinder valves. Valves must be operated without haste, never fully opened hard back against the back stop (so that other users know the valve is open) and never wrenched shut but turned just securely enough to stop the gas. Before removing or loosening any outlet connections, caps or plugs, a check should be made that the valves are closed. When changing cylinders, close all valves and appliance taps, and extinguish naked flames, including pilot jets, before disconnecting them. When reconnecting ensure that all connections and washers are clean and in good condition and do not overtighten them. Immediately a cylinder becomes empty, close its valve.

Safety requirements for acetylene: Cylinders must always be stored and used in the upright position. If a cylinder becomes heated accidentally or becomes hot because of excessive backfiring, immediately shut the valve, detach the regulator, take the cylinder out of doors well away from the building, immerse it in or continuously spray it with water, open the valve and allow the gas to escape until the cylinder is empty. If necessary, notify the emergency fire service without delay.

Safety requirements for oxygen are: No oil or grease should be used on valves or fittings. Cylinders with convex bases should be used in a stand or held securely to a wall.

Safety requirements for LPG are: The store must be kept free of combustible material, corrosive

material and cylinders of oxygen.

Cylinders should only ever be carried upright, securely strapped down, preferably in an open vehicle or with windows open. Carry the suppliers safety data with you. In the event of an accident, notify the Police and Fire Services and hand the safety data to them.

Dangerous liquids and gases

Because of flammable gas given off by batteries when on charge, care should be taken to avoid sparking by switching off the power supply before charger leads are connected or disconnected. Battery terminals should be shielded, since a battery contains energy and a spark can be caused by any conductor which touches its terminals or exposed connecting straps.

When internal combustion engines are operated inside buildings the exhaust fumes must be properly discharged to the open air. Petroleum spirit or mixture must be contained in metal cans which should be kept in a store. In any area where battery charging or the testing of fuel injection systems is carried out there must be good ventilation, and no sources of ignition. Inspection pits often present serious hazards. They should be of adequate length to allow safe access and exit while a car is in position. If there is an inspection pit, petrol may enter it. Since petrol vapour is heavier than air it will remain there and be a hazard if there is any source of ignition. All sources of ignition must therefore be excluded.

Lifting equipment

Special care should be taken when any type of lifting equipment is used. Lifting jacks are for raising vehicles; they should never be used as supports while work is in progress. Jacks must be replaced by adequate rigid supports before any work is begun on the vehicle. Risk of injury while working on running engines, e.g. adjusting the timing, can arise if the operator touches a high voltage lead and pulls his hand away on to a projection or revolving part. On some vehicles the voltage used in the ignition system is so high as to cause injury or death by electrocution.

Consult your handbook or main dealer if in any doubt.

Work with plastics

Work with plastic materials brings additional hazards into workshops. Many of the materials used (polymers, resins, adhesives and materials acting as catalysts and accelerators) readily produce very dangerous situations in the form of poisonous fumes, skin irritants, risk of fire and explosions. Do not allow resin or 2-pack adhesive hardener, or that supplied with filler or 2-pack stopper to come into contact with skin or eyes. Read carefully the safety notes supplied on the tin, tube or packaging.

Jacks and axle stands

Special care should be taken when any type of lifting equipment is used. Any jack is made for lifting the car, not for supporting it. NEVER even consider working under your car using only a jack to support the weight of it. Jacks are only for raising vehicles, and must be replaced by adequate supports before any work is begun on the vehicle; axle stands are available from many discount stores, and all auto parts stores. These stands are absolutely essential if you plan to work under your car. Simple triangular stands (fixed or adjustable) will suit almost all of your working situations. Drive-on ramps are very limiting because of their design and size.

When jacking the car from the front, leave the gearbox in neutral and the brake off until you have placed the axle stands under the frame. Make sure that the car is on level ground first! Then put the car into gear and/or engage the handbrake and lower the jack. Obviously DO NOT put the car in gear if you plan to turn over the engine! Leaving the brake on, or leaving the car in gear while jacking the front of the car will necessarily cause the jack to tip (unless a good quality trolley jack with wheels is being used). This is unavoidable when jacking the car on one side, and the use of the handbrake in this case is recommended.

If the car is older and if it shows signs of weakening at the jack tubes while using the factory jack, it is best

to purchase a good scissors jack or hydraulic jack – preferably trolley-type (depending on your budget).

Workshop safety – summary

1 Always have a fire extinguisher at arm's length whenever welding or when working on the fuel system – under the car, or under the bonnet.
2 NEVER use a naked flame near the petrol tank.
3 Keep your inspection lamp FAR AWAY from any source of dripping petrol (gasoline); for example, while removing the fuel pump.
4 NEVER use petrol (gasoline) to clean parts. Use paraffin (kerosene) or white (mineral) spirits.
5 NO SMOKING!

If you do have a fire, DON'T PANIC. Use the extinguisher effectively by directing it at the base of the fire.

Paint spraying

NEVER use 2-pack, isocyanate-based paints in the home environment or home workshop. Ask your supplier if you are not sure which is which. If you have use of a professional booth, wear an air-fed mask. Wear a charcoal face mask when spraying other paints and maintain ventilation to the spray area. Concentrated fumes are dangerous!

Spray fumes, thinners and paint are highly flammable. Keep away from naked flames or sparks.

Paint spraying safety is too large a subject for this book. See Lindsay Porter's *The Car Bodywork Repair Manual* (Haynes) for further information.

Fuel tank removal

Safety
Never drain a fuel tank indoors or where the highly flammable petrol vapours can gather, such as over a pit. Store petrol drained from the tank in safe, closed, approved containers. If the empty tank is to be stored, have it steam cleaned to remove the petrol vapours. Place a damp rag into any openings and keep tank out of doors for very short term storage. Keep all sparks and flames away from the fuel system whilst working on it.

Before carrying out any major body repairs, it makes good common sense to drain and remove the fuel tank to a place of safety. The remaining fume filled tank is especially dangerous so consider having it properly cleaned out during any extended restoration.

APPENDIX 2

Tools and Working Facilities

Introduction

A selection of good tools is a fundamental requirement for anyone contemplating the maintenance and repair of a motor vehicle. For the owner who does not possess any, their purchase will prove a considerable expense, offsetting some of the savings made by doing-it-yourself. However, provided that the tools purchased are of good quality, they will last for many years and prove an extremely worthwhile investment.

To help the average owner to decide which tools are needed to carry out the various tasks detailed in this manual, we have compiled three lists of tools under the following headings: *Maintenance and minor repair tool kit, Repair and overhaul tool kit,* and *Special tools.* The newcomer to practical mechanics should start off with the *Maintenance and minor repair tool kit* and confine himself to the simpler jobs around the vehicle. Then, as his confidence and experience grows, he can undertake more difficult tasks, buying extra tools as, and when, they are needed. In this way, a *Maintenance and minor repair tool kit* can be built up into a *Repair and overhaul tool kit* over a considerable period of time

without any major cash outlays. The experienced do-it-yourselfer will have a tool kit good enough for most repairs and overhaul procedures and will add tools from the *Special tools* category when he feels the expense is justified by the amount of use these tools will be put to.

Maintenance and minor repair tool kit

The tools given in this list should be considered as a minimum requirement if routine maintenance, servicing and minor repair operations are to be undertaken.

Ideally, purchase sets of open-ended and ring spanners, covering similar size ranges. That way, you will have the correct tools for loosening nuts from bolts having the same head size, for example, since you will have at least two spanners of the same size.

Alternatively, a set of combination spanners (ring one end, open-ended the other), give the advantages of both types of spanner. Although more expensive than open-ended spanners, combination spanners can often help you out in tight

situations, by gripping the nut better than an open-ender.

Combination spanners – 3/8, 7/16, 1/2, 9/16, 5/8, 11/16, 3/4, 13/16, 7/8, 15/16 in. AF.

Combination spanners – 8, 9, 10, 11, 12, 13, 14, 15, 17, 19 mm.

Adjustable spanner – 9 inch
Engine sump/gearbox/rear axle drain plug key (where applicable)
Spark plug spanner (with rubber insert)
Spark plug gap adjustment tool
Set of feeler gauges
Brake adjuster spanner (where applicable)
Brake bleed nipple spanner
Screwdriver – 4 in long x 1/4 in. dia. (plain)
Screwdriver – 4 in long x 1/4 in. dia. (crosshead)
Combination pliers – 6 inch
Hacksaw, junior
Tyre pump
Tyre pressure gauge
Grease gun (where applicable)
Oil can
Fine emery cloth (1 sheet)
Wire brush (small)
Funnel (medium size)

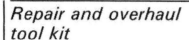

Repair and overhaul tool kit

These tools are virtually essential for anyone undertaking any major repairs to a motor vehicle, and are additional to those given in the Basic list. Included in this list is a comprehensive set of sockets. Although these are expensive they will be found invaluable as they are so versatile – particularly if various drives are included in the set. We recommend the $1/2$ in. square-drive type, as this can be used with most proprietry torque wrenches. On the other hand, $3/8$ in. drive are better for working in confined spaces and, if of good quality will be amply strong enough for work inside the engine bay. If you cannot afford a socket set, even bought piecemeal, then inexpensive tubular box spanners are a useful alternative.

The tools in this list will occasionally need to be supplemented by tools from the Special list.

Sockets (or box spanners) to cover range in previous list
Reversible ratchet drive (for use with sockets)
Extension piece, 10 inch (for use with sockets)
Universal joint (for use with sockets)
Torque wrench (for use with sockets)
'Mole' wrench – 8 inch
Ball pein hammer
Soft-faced hammer, plastic or rubber
Screwdriver – 6 in long x $5/16$ in. dia. (plain)
Screwdriver – 2 in long x $5/16$ in. square (plain)
Screwdriver – $1^1/2$ in. long x $1/4$ in. dia. (crosshead)
Screwdriver – 3 in. long x $1/8$ in. dia. (electrician's)
Pliers – electrician's side cutters
Pliers – needle noses
Pliers – circlip (internal and external)
Cold chisel – $1/2$ inch

Scriber (this can be made by grinding the end of a broken hacksaw blade)
Scriber (this can be made by flattening and sharpening one end of a piece of copper pipe)
Centre punch
Pin punch
Hacksaw
Valve grinding tool
Steel rule/straight-edge
Allen keys
Selection of files
Wire brush (large)
Axle stands
Jack (strong scissor or hydraulic type)

Special tools

The tools in this list are those which are not used regularly, are expensive to buy, or which need to be used in accordance with their manufacturers' instructions. Unless relatively difficult mechanical jobs are undertaken frequently, it will not be economic to buy many of these tools. Where this is the case, you could consider clubbing together with friends (or a motorists' club) to make a joint purchase, or borrowing the tools against a deposit from a local garage or tool hire specialist.

The following list contains only those tools and instruments freely available to the public, and not those special tools produced by the vehicle manufacturer specifically for its dealer network.

Valve spring compressor
Piston ring compressor
Ball joint separator
Universal hub/bearing puller
Impact screwdriver
Micrometer and/or vernier gauge
Carburettor flow balancing device (where applicable)
Dial gauge
Stroboscopic timing light
Dwell angle meter/tachometer

Universal electrical multi-meter
Cylinder compression gauge
Lifting tackle
Trolley jack
Light with extension lead
Rivet gun

Buying tools

Tool factors can be a good source of implements, due to the extensive ranges which they normally stock. On the other hand, accessory shops usually offer excellent quality goods, often at discount prices, so it pays to shop around.

The old maxim "Buy the best tools you can afford" is a good general rule to go by, since cheap tools are seldom good value, especially in the long run. Conversely, it isn't always true that the MOST expensive tools are best. There are plenty of good tools available at reasonable prices, and the shop manager or proprietor will usually be very helpful in giving advice on the best tools for particular jobs.

Care and maintenance of tools

Having purchased a reasonable tool kit, it is necessary to keep the tools in a clean serviceable condition. After use, always wipe off any dirt, grease and metal particles using a clean, dry cloth, before putting the tools away. Never leave them lying around after they have been used. A simple tool rack on the garage or workshop wall, for items such as screwdrivers and pliers is a good idea. Store all normal spanners and sockets in a metal box. Any measuring instruments, gauges, meters, etc. must be carefully stored where they cannot be damaged or become rusty.

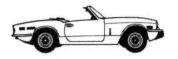

Take a little care when the tools are used. Hammer heads inevitably become marked and screwdrivers lose the keen edge on their blades from time to time. A little timely attention with emery cloth or a file will soon restore items like this to a good serviceable finish.

Another item which may be required, and which has a much more general usage, is an electric drill with a chuck capacity of at least 5/16 in. (8mm). This, together with a good range of twist drills, is virtually essential for fitting accessories such as wing mirrors and reversing lights.

Cordless drills are far more convenient to use and don't carry any electrical risks in use.

Last, but not least, always keep a supply of old newspapers and clean, lint-free rags available, and try to keep any working areas as clean as possible.

Working facilities

Not to be forgotten when discussing tools, is the workshop itself. If anything more than routine maintenance is to be carried out, some form of suitable working area becomes essential.

It is appreciated that many an owner mechanic is forced by circumstance to remove an engine or similar item, without the benefit of a garage or workshop. Having done this, any repairs should always be done under the cover of a roof, if feasible.

Wherever possible, any dismantling should be done on a clean, flat workbench or table at a suitable working height, although engine dismantling is safer carried out on an engine stand (they can be hired sometimes) or on a large card box opened out to give a clean surface on the workshop floor.

Any workbench needs a vice: the larger the better, one with a jaw opening of 4 in. (100 mm) is suitable for most jobs. As mentioned previously, some clean dry storage space is also required for tools, as well as for lubricants, cleaning fluids, touch-up paints and so on, which soon become necessary.

Spanner jaw gap comparison table

AF size	Actual size	Nearest Metric size	Metric size in ins.
4BA	0.248in.	7mm.	0.276in.
2BA	0.320in.	8mm.	0.315in.
7/16.in.	0.440in.	11mm.	0.413in.
1/2in.	0.500in.	13mm.	0.510in.
9/16in.	0.560in.	14mm.	0.550in.
5/8in.	0.630in.	16mm.	0.630in.
11/16in.	0.690in.	18mm.	0.710in.
3/4in.	0.760in.	19mm.	0.750in.
13/16in.	0.820in.	21mm.	0.830in.
7/8in.	0.880in.	22mm.	0.870in.
15/16in.	0.940in.	24mm.	0.945in.
1in.	1.000in.	26mm.	1.020in.

Whitworth size	Actual size	Nearest AF size	AF Actual size
3/16in.	0.450in.	7/16in.	0.440in.
1/4in.	0.530in.	1/2in.	0.500in.
5/16in.	0.604in.	9/16in.	0.560in.
3/8in.	0.720in.	11/16in.	0.690in.
7/16in.	0.830in.	13/16in.	0.820in.
1/2in.	0.930in.	7/8in.	0.880in.
9/16in.	1.020in.	1in.	1.010in.

Whitworth size	Actual size	Nearest Metric size	Metric size in ins.
3/16in.	0.450in.	12mm.	0.470in.
1/4in.	0.530in.	14mm.	0.500in.
5/16in.	0.604in.	15mm.	0.590in.
3/8in.	0.720in.	18mm.	0.710in.
7/16in.	0.830in.	21mm.	0.830in.
1/2in.	0.930in.	24mm.	0.945in.
9/16in.	1.020in.	26mm.	1.020in.

APPENDIX 3

Specifications

Please note that within this section, specifications are given for each model as it was introduced. Although a number of significant modifications which occurred during the production run are given, the majority are to be found in the later section under 'Production Modifications'. Also, specifications which remain unchanged from one model to another are not shown under details for later models.

Triumph Herald Saloon

Built

March 1959 to March (single carb), June (twin carb) 1961
Total number of saloons built (includes Herald 'S'): 76,860
Chassis numbers: G1DL to G73751DL (single carb)
GY1DL to GY11392DL (twin carb)

Engine

Cast iron block and head. Four cylinders in line. Three main bearing crankshaft.
Capacity: 948 cc
Bore and stroke: 63x76 mm
Compression: 8.0:1 single carb.
8.5:1 twin carb.
Single downdraft solex or twin SU H1 carburettors
Single carb Max. power: 34.5 bhp (nett) at 4500 rpm
Max. torque: 48 lbf ft at 2750 rpm
Twin carb Max. power: 42.5 bhp (nett) at 6000 rpm
Max. torque: 49 lbf ft at 3000 rpm

Transmission

Rear wheel drive from front-mounted engine. 4-speed gearbox bolted to rear engine plate.
Clutch: 6^1/$_4$ in coil spring type.
Direct gear change. Synchromesh on 2nd, 3rd and top gears, none on first.
Final drive single carb saloons: 4.875:1. Overall gear ratios 4.875:1 top, 7.09:1 third, 11.99:1 second, 20.82:1 first. Reverse 20.82:1.
Final drive twin carb saloons: 4.55:1. Overall gear ratios 4.55:1 top, 6.62:1 third, 11.20:1 second, 19.45:1 first. Reverse 19.45:1.

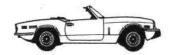 

Gearbox ratios: 1.00:1 top, 1.454:1 third, 2.46:1 second, 4.271:1 first and reverse.
13.25mph/1000rpm single carb.
14.2mph/1000rpm twin carb.

Wheelbase and track

Wheelbase all models: 7 ft 7 $^1/_2$ in
Front track: 4 ft 0 in
Rear track 4 in 0 in

Suspension

Front: independent double wishbone type with coil springs. Telescopic shock absorbers with anti-roll bar.
Rear: Independent swing axle with transverse leaf spring, trailing radius arms and telescopic shock absorbers.

Steering

Rack and pinion telescopic steering column.
$3^3/_4$ turns lock to lock.
Turning circle 25 ft

Brakes

Hydraulic: front 8x1 $^1/_4$ in drums, rear 7x1 $^1/_4$ in drums

Wheels and tyres

5.20-13 in tyres on 3.5 in pressed steel wheels.

Bodywork

4 seater saloon. Separate steel girder backbone chassis.

Dimension and weight

Length: 12 ft 9 in
Width: 5 ft 0 in
Height: 4 ft 4 in
Unladen weight: 1792 lb

Electrical system

12 volt, 43 amp-hr (20 hr rate) battery positive earth.
Dynamo charging system.

Performance

Single carb.
0 – 60 mph: 30.4 sec.
Top speed: 70.1 mph.

Twin carb.
0 – 60 mph: 23.2 sec.
Top speed: 78.8 mph.

Triumph Herald Coupé and Convertible

Specification as for Herald saloon but different body styles:
Built

Coupé: March 1959 to June 1961
Convertible: March 1960 to June 1961
Total number: Coupés 15,153
               Convertibles 8262
Chassis numbers: Y1 to Y23428 (Convertible from Y5632)
('CP-Coupé, 'CV-Convertible)

Engine and transmission

As twin carb saloon

Dimensions

Height Convertible: 4 ft 3 in
Unladen weight: 1764 lb-Coupé, 1770 lb-Convertible

Performance

As per twin carb saloon

Triumph Herald 'S' Saloon

Built

February 1961 to January 1964
Chassis numbers: G60471SP to G73571SP
Engine and transmission as Herald saloon though with
reduced level of trim.

Triumph Herald 1200 Saloon

Built

February 1961 to June 1962 (Mk 1)
July 1962 to December 1970 (Mk 2)
Total number: 201,142
Chassis numbers: GA1DL to GA249873DL not continuous
(Mk 2 – stiffer chassis from chassis number GA80001DL)

Engine

As Herald 948 single carb with:
Capacity increased to 1147 cc
Bore and stroke: 69.3x76 mm
Max. power: 39 bhp at 4500 rpm (48 bhp at 5200 rpm from
November 1964)
Max. torque: 61 lb ft at 2250 rpm (62 lbf ft at 2500 rpm
from November 1964)

Transmission

Final drive ratio 4.11:1. Overall ratios 4.11:1 top, 5.74:1
third, 8.88:1 second, 15.42:1 first. Reverse 15.42:1.
Gearbox ratios 1.00:1 top, 1.40:1 third, 2.16:1 second,
3.75:1 first and reverse.
15.7 mph/1000 rpm top
Clutch: $6^{1/2}$ in. diaphragm type from engine number:
GA204020 and GD 44446

Suspension and tyres

Optional front discs from October 1961 – front track 4 ft
1 in

Dimensions and weight

Unladen weight 1792 lb

Electrical

System changed to negative earth from March 1968 –
Chassis number GA238107

Performance

0-50 mph: 17 sec.
Top speed: 78 mph.

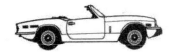

Herald 1200 Coupé

Coupé body style:
Built February 1961 to October 1964
Total number: 5,319
Chassis numbers: GA609CP to GA162103CP

Herald 1200 Convertible

Convertible body style:
Built: February 1961 to September 1967
Total number: 43,295
Chassis numbers: GA266CV to GA234868CV

Herald 1200 Estate

Estate body style

Built

March 1961 to September 1967
Total number: 39,819
Chassis numbers: GA4414SC to GA234990SC

Wheels and tyres

5.60-13 in on 3.5 in rims.

Dimensions and weight

Unladen weight: 1890 lb.

Courier Van

Specification as Herald Estate with reduced trim, steel rear side panels, 5.60-13 in tyres on wider 4.5 in wheels and no front anti-roll bar. Rear suspension uprated.

Built

February 1962 to October 1964
Total number: 4600 approx
Chassis numbers: GA44651V to
GA163205V (not
continuous)
Unladen weight: 1820 lb

Herald 12/50 Saloon

Specification as per Herald 1200. Skylight folding fabric roof fitted as standard

Built

December 1962 to September 1967
Total number: 53,267
Chassis numbers: GD1RS to GD55689RS

Engine

Revised camshaft (taken from current Spitfire model)
Compression ratio: 8.5:1
Max. power: 51 bhp at 5200 rpm
Max. torque: 63 lb ft at 2600 rpm

Suspension and brakes

9.0 in front discs fitted as standard.
Front track: 4 ft 1 in

Performance

0-50 mph: 14.5 sec.
Top speed: 82 mph.

Herald 13/60 Saloon

General specification as Herald 1200 with Mk 2 chassis:

Built

August 1967 to December 1970
Total number: 40,433
Chassis numbers: GE1DL to GE78335DL

Engine

Capacity 1296 cc
Bore and stroke: 73.7x76 mm
Max. power: 61 bhp at 5000 rpm
Max. torque: 73 lb ft at 3000 rpm

Suspension and brakes

As Herald 12/50
Unladen weight: 1876 lb

Performance

0 – 50 mph: 12 sec.
0 – 60 mph: 17.7 sec.
Top speed: 85 mph.

Herald 13/60 Convertible

Specification as 13/60 saloon with convertible body style

Built

August 1967 to September 1971
Total number: 15,467
Chassis numbers: GE5CV to GE83432CV
Unladen weight: 1820 lb

Herald 13/60 Estate

Specification as per 13/60 saloon with estate body style and wider 5.60-13 in tyres on 4.5 in rims.
Built: August 1967 to September 1971
Total number: 11,172
Chassis numbers: GE4SC to GE83433SC
Unladen weight: 1988 lb

Triumph Vitesse 6 – Saloon and Convertible models

Built

May 1962 to September 1966
Total number: saloons 22,814
                   convertibles 8,447
Chassis numbers: HB4DL (saloon), HB47CV (convertible) to
HB34053

Engine

Cast iron block and head. Straight 6-cylinder engine with four
main bearing crankshaft.
Capacity: 1596 cc
Bore and stroke: 66.75x76 mm
Compression ratio 8.75:1
Twin semi-downdraught solex carburettors
Max power: 70 bhp at 5000 rpm
Max. torque: 92 lb ft at 2800 rpm

Transmission

Rear wheel drive from front-mounted engine. 4-speed
gearbox bolted to rear engine plate. Direct gear change.
Synchromesh on second, third and top gears. None on first.
Final drive 4.11:1.
Overall gear ratios: 4.11:1 (3.30:1 overdrive) top, 5.16:1
(4.14:1 overdrive) third, 7.31:1 second, 12.06:1 first and
reverse.
Gearbox ratios: 1.00:1 top, 1.25:1 third, 1.78:1 second, 2.93:1
first and reverse.
Optional D-Type Laycock de Normanville overdrive geared at
0.8:1.
16.14 mph/1000 rpm top
20.4 mph/1000 rpm overdrive top
Clutch 8 in diameter, coil spring type

Wheelbase and track

Wheelbase: 7 ft 7 1/2 in
Front track: 4 ft 1 in
Rear track: 4 ft 0 in

Suspension

Front: Independent double wishbone type with coil springs.
Telescopic shock absorbers with anti-roll bar.
Rear: Independent swing axle with transverse leaf spring,
trailing radius arms and telescopic shock absorbers.

Steering

Rack and pinion with impact absorbing steering column.
3 3/4 turns lock to lock
Turning circle 25 ft

Brakes

Hydraulic:
9 in diameter front discs
8x1 1/4 in rear drums

Wheels and tyres

5.60-13 in tyres on 3.5 in pressed steel rims

Bodywork

4 seater saloon. Separate steel girder backbone chassis.

Dimensions and weight

Length: 12 ft 9 in
Width: 5 ft 0 in
Height: 4 ft 4 in
Unladen weight: 2044 lb

Electrical system

43 amp-hr positive earth with dynamo charging system

Performance

Solex carbs	Stromberg carbs
0 – 60 mph: 17.6 sec	0 – 60 mph: 15.5 sec
Top speed: 89 mph	Top speed: 91 mph

Vitesse 2 litre – Saloon and Convertible models

Specification as Vitesse 6 but:

Built

September 1966 to September 1968
Total number: saloon: 7,328
                    convertible: 3,502
Chassis numbers: HC6 to HC12079

Engine

Capacity: 1998 cc
Bore and stroke: 74.7x76 mm
Compression ratio 9.5:1
Twin Zenith Stromberg CD150 carburettors
Max. power: 95 bhp at 5000 rpm
Max. torque: 117 lbf ft at 3000 rpm

Transmission

Final drive: 3.89:1. Synchromesh on all forward gears.
Overall ratios: 3.89 top (3.11 overdrive), 4.86:1 (3.93:1 overdrive) third, 6.92:1 second, 10.30:1 first. Reverse 12.06:1.
Gearbox ratios: 1.00:1 top, 1.25:1 third, 1.78:1 second, 2.65:1 first, 3.10:1 reverse.
17.3 mph/1000 rpm top
21.6 mph/1000 rpm overdrive top
Clutch: 8$^{1}/_{2}$ in. diameter diaphragm type.

Suspension and brakes

9.7 in diameter front discs

Steering

Turning circle 25 ft 3 in
4 $^{3}/_{8}$ turns lock to lock

Wheels and tyres

5.60-13 in tyres on 4.5J pressed steel rims

Dimensions and weight

Height: 4 ft 5 $^{3}/_{4}$ in

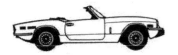

Electrical system

56 amp-hr battery negative earth.

Performance

0 – 60 mph: 12.6 sec
Top speed: 95 mph

Vitesse 2-Litre Mk. 2 – Saloon and Convertible models

Specification as Vitesse 2 Litre but:

Built

July 1968 to July 1971
Total number: saloon: 5,649
                 convertible: 3,472
Chassis numbers – saloon: HC50001DL0 to HC57996DL
     –   convertible: HC50006CV   to
       HC58109CV

Engine

Compression ratio: 9.25:1
Max. power 104 bhp at 5300 rpm

Suspension

Independent rear suspension with bottom wishbone and transverse leaf spring featuring rubber 'rotoflex' coupled driveshafts and lever arm shock absorbers

Wheels and tyres

155x13 in radial tyres on 4.5 in pressed steel rims

Performance

0 – 60 mph: 11.9 sec
Top speed: 101 mph

Triumph Spitfire 4

Built

October 1962 to December 1964.
Total number: 45,573.
Chassis numbers: FC1 to FC44656

Engine

Cast iron block and head.
Four cylinders set in-line. Three-bearing crankshaft.
Capacity 1147 cc.
Bore and Stroke: 69.3 76 mm
Compression: 9.0:1
Twin 1 1/2 in. SU HS2 carburettors
Max power: 63 bhp at 5750 rpm
Max power: 67 lbf ft at 3500 rpm

Transmission

Rear wheel drive from front mounted engine. 4-speed gearbox mounted on rear engine plate.
Clutch: 6 1/4 in coil springs
Direct gear change. Synchromesh on second, third and top

gears – none on first. Final drive 4.11:1.
Overall gear ratios 4.11:1 top, 5.74:1 third, 8.88:1 second,
15.42:1 first. Reverse 15.42:1
Gearbox ratios: 1.00:1 top, 1.40:1 third, 2.16:1 second,
3.75:1 first and reverse.
15.7 mph/1000 rpm top gear non-overdrive
19.1 mph/1000 rpm top gear optional D-type overdrive
(from September 1963)

Wheelbase and track

Wheelbase all models: 6 ft 11 in
Track: front 4 ft 1 in, rear 4 ft 0 in

Suspension

Front: Independent double wishbone type with coil springs.
Telescopic shock absorbers with anti-roll bar.
Rear: Independent swing axle with transverse leaf spring,
trailing radius arms and telescopic shock absorbers.

Steering

Rack and pinion with impact absorbing steering column.
3.75 turns lock to lock.
Turning circle: 24 ft.

Brakes

Hydraulic: 9 in diameter front discs
7x1 $1/4$ in rear drums

Wheels and tyres

5.20-13 in tyres on 3.5 in rim pressed steel wheels
Optional 4.5 in centre lock wire wheels.

Bodywork

2 seater sports convertible built on separate steel backbone
chassis

Dimensions and weight

Length: 12 ft 1 in
Width: 4 ft 9 in
Height: 3 ft 1$1/2$ in
Unladen weight: 1568 lb

Electrical system

12 volt positive earth.
43 amp-hr battery and dynamo charging system.

Performance

0 – 50 mph 11 sec
0 – 60 mph 17 sec
Top speed 92 mph
Touring fuel consumption 38 mpg

Triumph Spitfire 4 Mk.2

General specifications as Spitfire 4 but:

Built

December 1964 to January 1967.

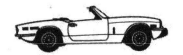

Total number: 37,409
Chassis numbers FC50001 to FC88904

Engine

Revised camshaft. Four branch tubular exhaust manifold.
Max. power: 67 bhp at 6000 rpm
Max. torque: 67 lbf ft at 3750 rpm

Performance

0 – 50 mph: 11 sec
0 – 60 mph: 15.5 sec
Top speed 92 mph

Triumph Spitfire Mk.3

General specifications as Spitfire 4, but:
Built

January 1967 to December 1970
Total number: 635,320
Chassis numbers: FD1 to FD15306
          FD20000 to FD51967
  (Oct 1969-) FD75000 to FD92803

Engine

Capacity: 1296 cc
Bore and stroke: 73.7x76 mm
Max. power: 75 bhp at 6000 rpm
Max. torque: 75 lbf ft at 4000 rpm

Transmission

$6^{1}/_{2}$ in diaphragm clutch

Wheels and tyres

$4^{1}/_{2}$J pressed steel wheels from October 1969
Optional 145 – 13 in radial tyres

Dimensions

Length: 12 ft 3 in

Electrical system

Negative earth

Performance

0 – 50 mph: 10 sec.
0 – 60 mph: 14 sec.
Top speed: 95 mph

Triumph Spitfire Mk.IV

General specifications as Spitfire Mk.3 but:
Built

November 1970 to December 1974
Total number: 70,021
Chassis numbers: FH3 to FH64995

Engine

Max power: 63 bhp (DIN) at 6000 rpm
Max torque: 69 lbf ft at 3500 rpm

Transmission

All synchromesh gearbox
7$^{1}/_{4}$ in diaphragm clutch
Final drive 3.89:1
Overall gear ratios: 3.89:1 top (3.12:1 optional overdrive),
5.41:1 third (4.33:1 overdrive), 8.41:1 second, 13.65:1 first.
Reverse 15.0:1.
Gearbox ratios: 1.00:1 top, 1.39:1 third, 2.16:1 second,
3.50:1 first, 3.99:1 reverse.
16.7 mph/1000 rpm top gear non-overdrive.
20.8 mph/1000 rpm with overdrive.

Wheelbase and track

Track: rear 4 ft 1 in.
Increased further to 4 ft 2 in from chassis number FH50001

Wheels and tyres

145-13 in radial tyres on 4.5 in pressed steel rims.
Optional bolt-on wire wheels (option later dropped)

Suspension

Front: Stiffer anti-roll bar fitted
Rear: Independent as per Spitfire 4 but with pivoting rear
transverse leaf spring.

Dimensions and weight

Length: 12 ft 5 in
Width: 4 ft 10$^{1}/_{2}$ in
Unladen weight: 1717 lb

Electrical system

Alternator charging system fitted

Performance

0 – 50 mph: 11 sec
0 – 60 mph: 16.2 sec
Top speed: 90 mph

Triumph Spitfire 1500

General specifications as Spitfire Mk.IV but:
Built

December 1974 to August 1980
Total number: 95,829
Chassis numbers: FH 75001 to FH130001 then to
TFADW5AT 009898

Engine

Capacity: 1493 cc
Bore and stroke 73.7x87.5 mm
Twin HS4 carburettors
Max. power: 71 bhp (DIN) at 5500 rpm
Max. torque: 82 lbf ft at 3000 rpm

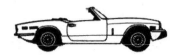

Transmission

Final drive 3.63:1
Revised single rail gearbox with same gearing as Mk.IV.
Overall ratios 3.63:1 top (2.90:1 with optional overdrive),
5.05:1 third (4.04:1 overdrive), 7.84:1 second, 12.70:1 first.
Reverse 13.99:1
Gearbox ratios:
18 mph/1000 rpm top non-overdrive
22.6 mph/1000 rpm top overdrive
Optional J-Type overdrive.

Wheels and tyres

155SR – 13 in tyres on 4.5 in pressed steel wheels. (Final
cars had 5 in wheels).

Unladen weight

1750 lb.

Performance

0 – 50 mph: 8.8 sec.
0 – 60 mph: 11.8 sec
Top speed: 100 mph

Triumph GT6

Built

July 1966 to September 1968
Total number: 15,818

Chassis numbers

KC1 to KC13752

Engine

Cast iron block and head.
Straight 6-cylinder engine with 4 main crankshaft bearings.
Capacity: 1998 cc
Bore and stroke: 74.7x76 mm
Compression ratio: 9.5:1
Twin Zenith Stromberg CD150 carburettors
Max. power: 95 bhp at 5000 rpm
Max. torque 117 lb ft at 3000 rpm

Transmission

Rear wheel drive from front-mounted engine. 4-speed
gearbox bolted to rear engine plate. Direct gear change.
Clutch: $8^1/2$ in diaphragm type
All synchromesh gearbox. Final drive 3.27:1 (3.89:1 with
optional overdrive).
Overall ratios – non-overdrive: 3.27:1 top, 4.11:1 third,
5.82:1 second, 8.66:1 first. Reverse 10.13:1.
Overall ratios with overdrive: 3.89:1 top (3.11:1 overdrive),
4.86:1 third (3.89 overdrive), 6.92:1 second, 10.30 first.
Reverse 12.06:1

Gearbox ratios

1.00:1 top, 1.25:1 third, 1.78:1 second, 2.65:1 first, 3.10:1
reverse

20.1 mph/1000 rpm top non-overdrive
21.2 mph top overdrive (3.89:1 final drive)

Wheelbase and track

Wheelbase 6 ft 11 in
Track: front 4 ft 1 in, rear 4 ft 0 in

Suspension

Front: Independent double wishbone type with coil springs.
Telescopic shock absorbers with anti-roll bar.
Rear: Independent swing axle with transverse leaf spring,
trailing radius arm and telescopic shock absorbers.

Steering

Rack and pinion with impact absorbing steering column.
4 1/4 turns lock to lock
Turning circle 25 ft 3 in

Brakes

9.7 in diameter front discs
8x1 1/4 in rear drums

Wheels and tyres

155 – 13 in radial tyres on 4.5 pressed steel or optional
centre lock wire wheels.

Bodywork

2-seater sports Coupe. Opening rear tailgate. Optional 2+2
rear seats.

Dimensions and weight

Length 12 ft 1 in
Width: 4 ft 9 in
Height: 3 ft 11 in
Unladen weight: 1904 lb

Electrical system

12 volt negative earth. 56 amp-hr battery with dynamo

Performance

0 – 50 mph: 7.8 sec
0 – 60 mph: 11.1 sec
Top speed: 108 mph
Touring fuel consumption: 31 mph

Triumph GT6 Mk. 2

General specifications as GT6 but:
Built

July 1968 to December 1970
Total number: 12,066
Chassis numbers: KC50001 to KC58046

Engine

Compression ratio: 9.25:1
Max. power: 104 bhp at 5300 rpm

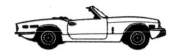

Transmission
As GT6 but overdrive now available with either 3.89:1 or 3.27:1 final drive.

Overall ratio revisions with 3.27:1 final drive: 3.27:1 top (2.62:1 with overdrive), 4.11:1 third (3.29:1 overdrive).

20.1 mph/1000 rpm top gear (3.27:1 final drive)
25.2 mph/1000 rpm top gear (3.27:1 final drive) with overdrive

Wheelbase and track

Rear track: increased to 4 ft 1 in

Suspension

Independent rear suspension with bottom wishbone and transverse rear leaf spring featuring rubber 'rotoflex' coupled drive shafts.

Length

12 ft 3 in

Electrical system

Alternator charging system

Performance

0 – 50 mph: 7.2 sec
0 – 60 mph: 10.0 sec
Top speed: 111 mph

Triumph GT6 Mk.3

Specifications as per GT6 Mk.2 but:

Built

October 1970 to December 1973
Total number: 13,042
Chassis numbers: KE1 to KE24218 (not continuous)

Transmission

3.89 final drive standard with optional overdrive.
Overall reverse gear ratio 9.85:1 non-overdrive, 11.71:1 (overdrive).

Suspension

Rear suspension changed to swing spring type from chassis number KE20001-February 1973. (Rear track increased to 4 ft 2 in)
Larger rear brake drums – 8x1$\frac{1}{2}$ in from 1973

Wheels and tyres

Optional wire wheels no longer offered.

Dimensions and weight

Length: 12 ft 5 in
Width: 4 ft 10 $\frac{1}{2}$ in
Weight: 2030 lb

Performance

0 – 50 mph: 7.7 sec. 0 – 60 mph: 10.1 sec
Top speed: 112 mph.

APPENDIX 4

Production Modifications

Triumph Herald

The first Heralds, 948 Coupés and Saloons were produced from March 1959. Both models used the same 'Mark 1' chassis (a stiffer chassis being introduced from chassis number GA80001) and featured similar two-door body styles though with different roof sections. Very early cars (to G15449, Y3565 and GY431) up to August 1959 featured wider dog-leg inner wheel arches fitted with rubber splash curtains, replaced with narrower panels with the introduction of separate metal side engine valances. Bonnet location inner fixtures also varied on early cars with either flat or 'V' shaped fabric lined plates being used. (Later, all Herald based models used the now familiar rubber cones). All 948 Coupés were fitted with twin H1 SU carbs.

Other differences included rear badge variations, early models having a continuous chromed TRIUMPH letters strip just underneath the recessed number plate lamp whilst on later cars this was omitted but a larger lamp was fitted. Early rear lamp units had smooth orange indicator lenses with a separate internal lens. Later units omitted the internal lens and employed an inner ribbed design. Likewise, early Coupés were given a scripted Coupé badge on the rear of the boot lid which was omitted on later cars. Continuing this theme, early Coupés were given a 'Herald' badge on the rear wing which was later replaced with crossed 'SV' flags – also fitted on convertibles.

Door handles on 948s included key-operated locks for both driver and passenger sides, the lock being part of the internal door mechanism and the button push not being part of the handle as on later cars.

Internally, saloons featured a fold down rear seat squab which gave additional access to the rear boot space. Although the equivalent in the Coupé also folded (a rear seat was an optional extra in Coupé models), a fixed trim panel remained in place behind. Door trims were two-tone with a white strip along the top plus in twin-carb. models elasticated map pockets. Very early models were given vinyl door pull loops whereas bolt-on chrome handles featured on later cars.

Some instruments were supplied with pink wisteria faces though more than likely these have now faded to white. Twin-carb. models featured separate fuel and temperature gauges. The two spoke steering wheel, control knobs and switches were grey with white lettering. The dashboard switch layout changed from side-by-side to semi-circular on later models which later still, included a bright metal strip 'finger board'. Early models (grey switchgear) weren't provided with a headlamp flasher in the main lighting stalk as were later, black switchgear, models, other detailed differences on very early models included an amber, rather than the later green dashboard indicator repeat lamp. 948 and early 1200 model's headlamp main beam warning lamps were red rather than blue.

Both Coupés and Saloons featured chromed central bonnet handles. In addition, twin-carb. models were fitted with a bright strip running from the front edge of the handle to the front of the bonnet. Twin-carb. saloons, prefixed GY rather than G, were available from January 1960 from GY1158DL.

March 1960. 948 Convertible introduced. Chassis number Y5632CV onwards – the well designed fully folding hood retracting into a stowage space behind the rear seats. Rear passenger space reduced as a consequence.

June 1960. Previously smooth sided Coupé roof replaced with ribbed design and extra rain guttering introduced – a notorious rust trap.

February 1961. Herald 'S' introduced from G60471SP. This more basic Herald saloon featured HERALD letters above the flat grid pattern radiator grille which also lost its central vertical division bar. Other models featured TRIUMPH letters. Front sidelights were also of a smaller single bulb type rather than the larger twin-bulb units generally found on other models. (Some 'S' type bonnets did appear on standard deluxe (DL) models). Also on 'S' variants, the central bonnet handle was replaced by a full length chrome strip. The screen washers and heater were optional extras.

February 1961. First 1200 models built in Saloon (GA1DL), Coupé (GA609CP) and convertible (GA266CV) forms. Generally, though not exclusively, recognised by HERALD letters above grille, small sidelights plus 1200 badge on boot lid. White rubber bumpers now fitted with revised front valance incorporating ventilation slot, standard heater and improved seating. The rear seat squab now became fixed. Instrument and switch gear changed colour to black/white rather than grey. As opposed to 948s, all 1200 models were fitted with a single solex carburettor as standard. Twin SUs were still available but as an optional extra. Differential now 4.11:1 on all 1200 models rather than 4.55:1 on twin carb or 4.875:1 single carb 948 models. Lower gearbox ratios were also revised. Top gear remained 1:1.

March 1961. First 1200 estate versions built from GA4414SC. 948 single-carb. saloons discontinued. Final chassis number G64435DL.

June 1961. 948 twin-carb Saloon and Coupé discontinued. Final chassis numbers GY11392DL and Y23428CP respectively.

October 1961. Front disc brakes offered as an optional extra on all models – front track increased to 4 ft 1 in as a consequence.

February 1962. Courier Van introduced from GA4465IV. Similar to the estate but with the basic interior's early style thinly padded seats, grey switches and steering wheel as per 948s, Herald 'S' front grille and steel panels rather than side rear quarter windows. COURIER letters on rear door.

July 1962. Stiffer chassis introduced from chassis number GA80001DL. (This date is probably correct, but not certainly so).

March 1963. Herald 12/50 introduced from GD1RS. Similar to the saloon range but with fabric sun roof as standard and increased power. Heater and disc front brakes were both fitted as standard. Revised trim included 12/50 badges on the boot lid and rear wing. Roof 'h' badge on rear quarter differed from other models in that it was red and not blue.

January 1964. Herald 'S' discontinued. Final chassis number G73571SP

October 1964. 1200 Coupé and Courier Van discontinued. Final chassis number GA162103CP and GA163205V

November 1964. 1200 engine given more power by the use of an uprated camshaft taken from the 12/50.
Max. power: 48 bhp at 5200 rpm
Max. torque: 62 lbf ft at 2500 rpm

February 1966. Herald 1200 – $6^1/2$ in diaphragm clutch fitted.

September 1966. 12/50 rear wing badges removed.

August 1967. Herald 12/50 discontinued. Final chassis number GD55689RS.
    Herald 13/60 introduced in Saloon (GE1DL), Convertible (GE5CV) and Estate (GE4SC) versions. Revised bonnet with slanted single 7 inch headlamps either side of full width grille of 9 horizontal alloy bars in 3 sections. Smaller full chrome over-riders plus slightly revised valance. Single Stromberg CD150 carb. fitted. Increased power and revised interior facia with 2 large dials and control switches in

recessed panel. Seating trim also revised to allow more rear passenger space. Negative earth electrical system fitted.

September 1967. 1200 Convertible and Estate discontinued. Final chassis numbers GA234868CV and GA234990SC.

March 1968. 1200 models fitted with negative earth electrical system from chassis numbers GA238107 and GB57263.

December 1970. 1200 and 13/60 Saloons discontinued. Final chassis numbers GA249873DL and GE78335DL respectively.

September 1971. 13/60 Convertible and Estate versions discontinued. Final chassis numbers GE83432CV and GE83433SC.

Triumph Vitesse

Sharing many Herald body panels, the 'Vitesse 6' or 1600 was launched in May 1962 in Saloon and Convertible models. As standard it featured a 6-cylinder in line 1596cc engine fed by twin Solex carbs. producing 70 bhp. Though still no synchromesh on first gear, internal gearing was revised (the back axle remained at 4.11:1 as for the Herald 1200) and a D-Type Laycock overdrive was offered as an optional extra. Externally, the Vitesse could be distinguished from its Herald 948 and 1200 stablemates by a revised bonnet design with slanted four-headlamp installation. This same design was later modified to provide the styling mood of the Herald 13/60 as given above. Other major external differences included smaller front chrome over-riders, again copied on the 13/60, aluminium bumpers and an oblong full-width mesh grille. Front disc brakes and larger rear drums than the Herald were fitted as standard. Hidden from view was the introduction of the much more robust 'Mk.2' chassis mentioned above with a wider box section, an extra bridge section across the rear to help stiffen the shock absorber and differential mounting areas and revised front end and waist sections, the latter to allow the fitting of overdrive.

May 1962. Vitesse 6 introduced in saloon (HB 4DL) and Convertible (HB 47CV) forms. 'h' roof badge on the Herald changed to 'Triumph' on the Vitesse 6.

March 1963. Fabric skylight sun roof available as an optional extra on Saloon models.

September 1963: Facia redesigned to include separate round fuel and temperature gauges (the latter not previously included) and a large rev. counter. Other minor controls were also repositioned at this stage. A map pocket appeared in the passenger footwell. Elasticated door pockets were always available as standard.

July 1965: Twin Stromberg CD150 carbs. fitted from chassis number HB28061 (engine number HB27986E) with revised air filters to match. Power increased by approximately 12 bhp.

September 1966: Vitesse 1600 discontinued. Final chassis number HB34053. A larger bore (same stroke) 2-Litre engine now used in both Saloon and Convertible models of the new Vitesse 2 litre from chassis number HC6 onwards. All synchromesh gearbox and 3.89:1 back axle. The car also featured more powerful brakes and a larger diaphragm clutch and was switched from a positive to a negative earth system.

External differences included '2-Litre' emblems on the front grille, wing and rear boot lid. A reversing light incorporating the number plate lamp was now included within the boot lid alloy strip/number plate lamp scroud as standard. Internally a 3-spoke leather trimmed steering wheel was fitted.

July 1968. Saloon and Convertible Mk2 2-Litre Vitesse introduced from chassis numbers HC50001DLO (the 'O' signifying the fitment of overdrive on this particular car) and HC50006CV respectively. Increased power from revised 2 litre engine featuring the TR 'full width head'. Modified rear

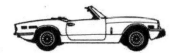

suspension with rotoflex coupled driveshafts, additional lower wishbones and lever arm shock absorbers. Externally distinguished from earlier models by 'Rostyle' like trims on wheels with 5 dummy nuts, a revised radiator grille similar to the Herald 13/60, different badging front and rear and a grey metal plate filling in rear boot lid recess behind number plate. Later Mk.2 models also featured front sidelight units with smooth glass fronts rather than those having a pronounced point as described above for earlier cars (Heralds and Vitesses). Interior revisions included a restyled facia with control knobs housed in a recessed rectangular panel and on the very last cars a knee high ignition/steering lock was fitted – hence no ignition key hole on dashboard.

September 1968. Mk.1 Vitesse 2-Litre discontinued. Final chassis number HC12079.

July 1971. Mk.2 2-Litre Vitesse discontinued. Final chassis numbers HC57996DL Saloon, HC58109CV Convertible.

Triumph Spitfire

October 1962. Introduced from chassis number FC1L, the Triumph Spitfire 4 featured twin-carbs, 2-seater soft top sports bodywork and fully independent front and rear suspension. Front disc brakes were standard. Like the Herald, the Spitfire featured a fully hinged front end but employed raised external flanges along the wing top bonnet line, these being covered by a stainless steel trim strip.

September 1963. D-Type Laycock de Normanville overdrive and stylish hardtop made available as optional extras.

December 1964. Spitfire 4, retrospectively known as Mk.1 discontinued from chassis number FC44656. Spitfire 4 Mk.2 introduced from chassis number FC 50001. Similar in style to the Mk.1 but featuring increased power due to a revised camshaft, the use of a tubular 4 branch exhaust manifold and a water-cooled inlet manifold. Interior improvements included improved seat cushioning and moulded carpets (rather than rubber). The body coloured paint finish to door cappings and dashboard in the Spitfire 4 were now covered in black leather cloth trim. Externally, the later model Spitfires may be distinguished by the Mk.2 emblem below the boot lid 'Spitfire' script and the use of a 5 horizontal bars radiator grille as opposed to the 8 bars unit on the Mk.1.

January 1967. Mk.2 Spitfire discontinued. Final chassis number FC88904.
Spitfire Mk.3 produced from chassis number FD1 onwards. Featuring increased power from its 1296 cc, as opposed to 1147 cc, engine with revised alloy inlet and cast iron exhaust manifolds, integral folding hood and raised front bumper with rubber insert over-riders. Facia instrument panel veneered with black surround. Fly-off handbrake replaced with conventional type.
Other external differences included separate driver and passenger door locks and revised handles. (Spitfire 4 Mk.1 and Mk.2 passenger doors were locked using a tab mounted on the inside of the door). Front sidelights and indicators were now housed in a single oblong unit below the bumper line set in revised bonnet corner sections. The radiator grille was now made wider and excluded the central vertical division bar. The bonnet badge shield was omitted on the later model. At the rear the quarter bumpers lost their over-riders and a 'Mk.3' badge replaced the 'Mk.2'. The '4' in the 'Spitfire 4' script was also dropped. Twin reversing lamps inboard of the indicators were made standard fittings.
Within the Spitfire Mk.3 production period, two types of hood/header rail fastenings were used. One, the most common, employing swivelling locking arms and the second, pull over catches similar in action to those used on Herald and Vitesse convertibles.

October 1969. From chassis number FD75000 the original body coloured windscreen surround changed to matt black. Radiator grille – also black. Flat spoked 15 in steering wheel. Badging revised from script to rectangular SPITFIRE plates on bonnet and rear wings plus similar TRIUMPH plate on boot lid, scripted 'Overdrive' remaining where applicable. Reversing and number plate lamps now incorporated in a single central housing. Claimed top speed 100 mph (depending on conditions – advertising brochure of the day). Wider 4½J wheels fitted and soft top provided with a zip out rear window. Extra padding provided around console.

November 1970. Spitfire Mk.IV announced from chassis number FH3. Featured on all new body style with deseamed smoother bonnet, squared off tail, to fit in with Triumph's current corporate image, with

revised lights and full width rear bumper. Different Mk.IV badges to front and rear. Matt black grille and revised interior with new seats and trim panels with recessed door handles inside and out. Black surround facia with main instruments moved from centre to in front of driver. All synchromesh gearbox fitted with 3.89:1 differential. Swing-spring rear suspension introduced giving improved road holding. Bolt-on rather than centre lock wire wheels offered as an optional extra. Windscreen surround now welded to main body as opposed to bolted. Improved hood fitted with zip out rear window. Change to more angular optional hardtop featuring opening rear quarter windows. D-Type overdrive still optional extra but operating switch now integral with gear lever knob.

December 1970. Mk.3 discontinued. Final chassis number FD92803.

February 1973. Mk.IV revised from chassis number FH50001 to include restyled instruments with veneer rather than black surround. Reclining seats introduced with provision for headrests. Longer rear driveshafts fitted to give an increase of 2 in (to 4 ft 2 in) to the rear track.

August 1973. J-Type overdrive replaces D-Type. Bolt-on wire wheel option dropped.

December 1973. Spoiler fitted beneath front bumper from chassis number FH60001.

December 1974. Spitfire Mk.IV discontinued at chassis number FH64995.
   Spitfire 1500 introduced from FH75001 with larger 1493cc engine. Gearbox revised to single rail type with longer geared 3.63:1 back axle. Badge plates front and rear replaced with transfers. Hazard and seat belt warning lamps fitted. Additional 'De Luxe' pack including door mirror, headrests, central armrest and map reading lamp offered as optional extras. Rear panel flange trim black rather than bright metal to match rear wing top.

January 1976. De Luxe pack and laminated windscreen fitted as standard from chassis number FH81880.

March 1977. Revisions from chassis number FH100001 include the fitting of black plastic rather than chrome door handle recesses and a smaller solid spoked steering wheel. TR7 stalk switchgear fitted to steering column. Seats improved to include brushed nylon 'houndstooth' centre panels.

August 1980. Spitfire 1500 discontinued from chassis number TFADW5AT009898.

Triumph GT6

Continuing Triumph's theme for fitting large, lazy engines into small bodies came the introduction of the GT6 in October 1966. The GT6 featured a 2-seater fixed head Coupe style built on the Spitfire chassis (with some minor modifications) and mirrored the appearance of the Spitfire 4 Mk.2 of the day with low front bumpers, separate side and indicator lamps at the front and quarter rear bumpers with over-riders at the rear.
   As standard, the car was fitted with the Mk.1 variant of the smooth straight-six 2 litre engine distinguished from its more powerful successor by external alloy push-rod tubes and chromed rocker box cover. (Vitesse 1600 engines also featured these alloy tubes which in time may be the cause of oil seepage around the cylinder head – usually not a great problem). Externally, the bonnet varied from that of the Spitfire in the pronounced bulge required to take the longer engine and additional bonnet-top cooling louvres. Badging was restricted to TRIUMPH letters and shield on the bonnet accompanied by more letters and chromed GT6 shield at the rear below the top hinged opening rear window. An occasional 2+2 rear seat was available as an optional extra.
   Overdrive was an optional extra which was accompanied with a change in the differential ratio from 3.27:1 to 3.89:1. The gearbox was an all synchromesh design.

October 1966. Triumph GT6 introduced from chassis number KC1. Early models featured a fly-off handbrake, replaced with a conventional type during the model run. At the same time, a wider rimmed leather trimmed steering wheel was fitted of the same basic size and design as the original. Slight changes to seat design also occurred during model run. Centre lock wire wheels were another optional extra, as was the heater!

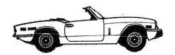

September 1968. GT6 Mk.1 discontinued. Final chassis number KC13752.

October 1968. GT6 Mk.2 introduced from chassis number KC50001. Main feature differences included the fitting of a more powerful version of the 2 litre engine (as per the Vitesse Mk.2) and a modified rear suspension with rotoflex rubber couplings and lower wishbones. Rear shock absorbers now mounted on the inner wheel arch, not on the chassis. Rear track increased by 1 in. to 4 ft.1 in. At the front the bumper was raised and included rubber insert over-riders. Similar to the Mk.3 Spitfire revisions, the chrome rear over-riders were omitted from the GT6 Mk.2 specification. Also usefully at the rear, a heated rear window was fitted as standard. (The large rear glass area was prone to misting in the original GT6). Wire elements were arranged vertically.

Due to some overheating problems experienced in early cars, extra side louvers were added to the front bonnet wings. Cream enamel and chrome GT6 Mk.2 badges fitted front and rear (some domestic cars were also fitted with US spec 'GT6 Plus' badges)

Inside, black headlinings were fitted together with new inner door handles and a new facia design incorporating slider heater controls (heater now standard), rocker switches and face air vents (others were also provided at knee height). The rear deck loading platform was shorter than that in the Mk1.

External rear three-quarter vents were also added which were given chromed external grilles. Wheels featured 'Rostyle' – like nave plates. For the overdrive option, both 3.27:1 and 3.89:1 back axle ratios could be specified.

October 1969. From chassis number KC75031: Matt black windscreen surround introduced and reversing lamp and number plate lamps combined into a single central unit. Interior changes included restyled reclining seats, off-white headlining and the fitting of a flat spoked steering wheel.

October 1970. GT6 Mk.3 introduced from chassis number KE1. Featured revised smooth bonnet which lacked the previous cooling louvers and chopped off tail end with horizontal light units. The front bumper was also changed and the rear quarter bumpers replaced by a single full width design. At the front a black radiator grille was fitted and Mk.3 badge plates replaced those of the Mk.3. Further external changes included revised profile rear quarter windows and painted ventilation grilles. Although keeping the same frame, the rear window featured horizontal wire elements and a different push button operated lock.

Internal revisions included different seats and steering wheel, a knee high ignition/steering lock and the shifting of the overdrive switch from the steering column to the top of the gear lever. Optional overdrive was accompanied by a 3.89 differential as standard.

December 1970. GT6 Mk.2 discontinued. Final chassis number KC83298.

February 1973: Lower wishbone type rear suspension replaced with swing axle type from chassis number KE20001. Rear track increased 1 in. to 4 ft 2 in. Interior revisions made included brush-nylon covered seats, restyled instruments and the fitting of Sundym tinted glass. A brake servo was now fitted as standard.

December 1973. GT6 Mk.3 production discontinued. Final chassis number KE24218.

Facing page: top
PM1. As shown here, 948 saloons featured smooth bumpers/valances and a chromed central bonnet handle. Twin-carb. models may be distinguished by an additional stainless steel strip running from the front edge of the bonnet to the front of the handle. Non-standard on this attractive example is the front valance which should have a different lower profile without a ventilation slot.

Facing page: bottom
PM2. Although rebuilt with some non-original revisions, this shot of Bill Sunderland's Courier Van clearly shows the revised grille fitted to Vans and 948 'S' models. (Peter Williams and Bill Sunderland were responsible, in the main, for this vehicle's restoration).

PM3. In contrast, this 1200 saloon is fitted with white rubber bumper inserts and a full length stainless steel central strip and does not have a bonnet handle (though some early 1200 models did). Note also the HERALD letters and small sidelights which were fitted to some 1200s (and 948 Ss – on these models, the Triumph shield was fitted on top of the bonnet). Some models were fitted with black wheels.

PM4. Continuing the same theme is this 1200 Herald estate on which the front corner rubber inserts are missing.

PM5. A later 1200 – back to TRIUMPH and large sidelights.

PM6. The radiator grille of the Herald 12/50 was without a central metal bar but featured a thin stainless steel strip instead. The roof was fitted with a fabric 'skylight' sunroof as standard.

PM7. Instantly recognisable by its angled-up bonnet corners, 9 bar full-width radiator grille and smaller chrome over-riders is the 13/60.

PM8. Underneath, very early 948 bonnets featured 'dog-leg' inner wheel arches fitted with large rubber curtains instead of the separate engine bay valance plates fitted on later models.

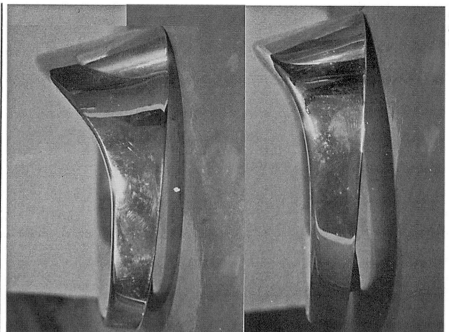

PM9. 948 and early 1200 models featured slightly longer chrome headlamp surrounds.

PM10. Also, earlier models featured a distinctive spot welded top bonnet intake panel . . .

PM11. . . . which on later bonnets was of a different design and part of the bonnet pressing.

PM12.► Early 948 Coupés sported a 'herald' badge on the top of the rear wings . . .

PM13.▼ . . . plus a scripted 'Coupé' badge at the rear. Note also the early fitment TRIUMPH badge and recessed number plate lamp.

PM14.▼ Later models had separate TRIUMPH letters on top of the boot lid and a different number plate lamp. The Coupé badge was dropped on both later 948 and 1200 models. The 'herald' rear wing badge was replaced with crossed flags on later Coupés which also featured on Convertibles. On 948 and 1200 saloons, the wing badging was omitted, leaving a space . . . .

PM15. . . . on all except early 12/50s which featured a 12/50 badge though this too was dropped on later models. The Vitesse alloy valance trims shown here are non-original.

PM16. The rear badging was changed yet again for the 13/60 with a different number plate lamp assembly and revised badge details.

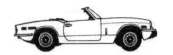 

PM17.   The easiest way to tell a Mk.1 from a Mk.2 chassis is to look at the rear chassis cross-member. Mk.1 chassis alone were made with a hole through which the exhaust system passed.

PM18.   In contrast to the fibreboard dashes of the Herald 948 shown in BG32, later models featured wood-fronted dashboards. Late 13/60s (possibly only convertibles) and late Vitesses were also fitted with steering column lock/ignition switches.

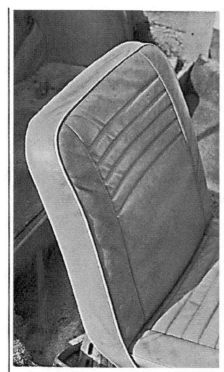

PM19. Thinly padded seats were only fitted to early Heralds and Courier Vans.

PM20. Later models were fitted with more comfortable, heavily padded seat covers.

PM21. The rear light lenses on earlier models also differed from later cars. Close inspection shows these early units to have separate inner lenses with smooth outer coloured covers.

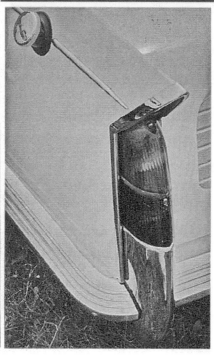

PM22. Later models featured ribbing on the inner surfaces of the outer covers, forming a lens, which allowed the separate inner lenses to be omitted.

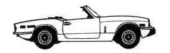

PM23. Other differences in this area included the fitting of three piece chrome trims to later models rather than the single piece unit fitted on earlier cars.

PM24. 948s were also fitted with different door handle/lock units. On 948s, each door had its own key operated lock, the barrel of which was part of the internal lock mechanism. On later models (beneath), the lock barrel (provided on the driver's side only unless specified otherwise) and push buttons are part of the handle.

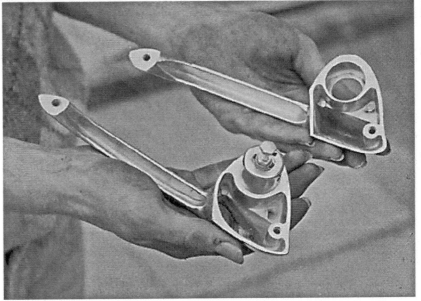

PM25.   Single carb. 948s and 1200s were fitted with down-draught Solex units compared with . . .

PM26.   . . . single side draught Stromberg carburettors fitted to 13/60 models. Twin carb 948 and 1200 models used SUs as shown under 'Buying Guide'.

PM27.   The Vitesse 6. Similar in front-end styling to the Herald 13/60 but with twin-5in. headlamps, fine grille and alloy overbumpers.

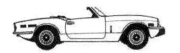

PM28. At the rear, the number plate lamp assembly of the 13/60 was widened for the Vitesse 6 and distinctive script badging was fitted. The lights below the rear valance are non-standard.

PM29. The front end styling of the Vitesse 2-Litre remained faithful to the '6' but was given additional '2-L' badges on the front, sides and rear. Notice the slots in the headlamp surrounds on the Vitesse 6 and 2-Litre (Mk.1) models.

PM30.   On the 2-Litre model,
badges changed again and a
separate reversing light/number
plate lamp was fitted.

PM31.   A close up view of the
slotted headlamp surround. The
surrounds on Mk.2 Vitesse
2-Litre cars didn't have any slots.
Most Vitesses and all Heralds
(where fitted with larger
sidelights) had front sidelight
glasses with a pronounced
point . . . ◄

PM32. ►. . . these were changed
to smooth fronted units during
the latter part of the Vitesse
2-Litre Mk.2 production run
(around 1970). As with the
Herald 13/60, the Vitesse 2-Litre
Mk.2 was fitted with a similar,
though shorter 9 bar front
radiator grille. Details of the rear
end styling of the Mk.2 with its
grey boot plate insert and
badging is shown in BG46.

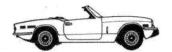

PM33. Early Vitesse 6 models were fitted with twin Solex carburettors, separate radiator expansion tank and distinctive air filter housing assembly.

PM34. Later 1600, 2-Litre and Mk.2 models all looked much the same. This is a Mk.2. The 1600 and 2-Litre Mk.1 engines both had separate, easily seen aluminium push rod tubes within the cylinder head.

PM35. This shot shows the basic detailing expected on a Spitfire 4 with 8 bar fine mesh grille, bonnet top Triumph shield and low bumpers.

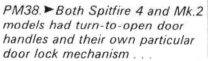

PM36.   Comparing a Spitfire 4 with the Mk.2 shows the later model (on the left) to have a 5 bar grille but otherwise externally remaining much the same.

PM37.◄ Original Spitfire 4s had a painted dashboard surround and a Herald-type 2-spoke steering wheel. Mk.2 versions were given an extra 'Mk.2' boot badge beneath the scripted 'Spitfire 4' which was fitted to both models. Models with overdrive were fitted with a scripted 'Overdrive' badge on the left-hand side of the boot lid.

PM38.► Both Spitfire 4 and Mk.2 models had turn-to-open door handles and their own particular door lock mechanism . . .

PM39.▲ . . . the passenger door being locked by turning this little knob on the inside.

PM41.▼ Major changes at the front for the Spitfire Mk.3 were the raised front bumpers, oblong sidelights and different grille. New rubber insert over-riders were fitted at the front and the rear chrome over-riders fitted on earlier models were dropped. The top of bonnet Triumph emblem was also omitted.

PM40. With the hood sticks being secured, when not in use, in the boot, the hood was stored behind the quick release rear cockpit panel.

PM42. Inside, instruments were given a wood surround and a new steering wheel was fitted. Proper carpets rather than rubber mats were fitted from the Mk.2. A nice touch here is the original type single speaker fitted in the passenger glove pocket.

PM43. The last of the Mk.3s were given matt black windscreen surrounds, black grille and an oblong SPITFIRE badge rather than TRIUMPH letters.

PM44. Styling changes at the rear also included different badges and revised reversing and number plate lamp arrangements as per later Mk.2 GT6s. The exhaust system and badge to the left of the boot lid are non-original.

PM45. Spitfire Mk.IV and 1500 versions shared similar front end styling though a spoiler was only fitted as standard on later models.

PM46. On the latest 1500 models, the thin column switches of earlier models were replaced with those from the TR7. Early Mk.IV models were also fitted with black dashboards. Clearly shown here is the gear lever mounted overdrive switch found on Mk.IV and 1500 Spitfires. Earlier models had column-mounted switches.

PM47. This Mk.3 engine bay shares most of its basic features with all of the earlier models though the Spitfire 4 like the Vitesse 6 was given a separate radiator expansion tank. Some air filter boxes were black as shown, others silver-grey.

PM48. In comparison, this later Spitfire 1500 shows a few more revisions with different HS4 carbs, air filter trunking and a revised braking and cooling system. The windscreen wiper motor is also different and the throttle is now cable rather than rod operated.

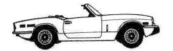

PM49. With the different body style came a revised hood. Hoods from late Mk.3 onwards came with zip out rear windows. This car is recognisable as a late Spitfire 1500 by the black surround door handle assembly. Fuel filler caps on Mk.IV and 1500 models were more angular than on earlier models.

PM50. More angular too was the Mk.IV/1500 hardtop which also included opening rear side windows. Notice the black tail panel surrounds. Although the rear wing trim was black on both models, the rear trim was bright metal on the Mk.IV. Wheels are non-standard.

PM51. Alternators were fitted to both Mk.IV and 1500 Spitfires.

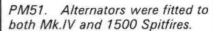

PM52. The GT6. Similar in style to the Spitfire 4 though with bonnet bulge and the same full width grille as fitted to the Mk.3 Spitfire.

PM53. At the rear, again similar styling to the early Spitfires but with a top hinged clear glass tailgate plus 'GT6' shield. Original exhaust systems were two-box in-line single-pipe units.

PM54.   Early Mk.2 GT6s looked rather bare in comparison with revised badges. Revisions included the fitting of rear quarter vents, different exhaust and a heated rear window with vertically arranged wires. Later Mk.2 GT6s had a similar rear end treatment to that of late Mk.3 Spitfires as shown in figure PM44.

PM55.   At the front, the Mk.2 shared many styling similarities with the Mk.3 Spitfire. Extra front wing bonnet louvers were fitted compared with the Mk.1 GT6 2-Litre. Wheels, like the Vitesse 2 litre Mk.2, sported Rostyle-like wheel trims with dummy 5-stud effect. A fabric sunroof was an optional extra.

PM56. Like the Spitfire Mk.IV and 1500, the Mk.3 GT6 was restyled with de-seamed bonnet. Additionally, the bonnet bulge was reprofiled and a 2 inch deeper windscreen was fitted . . .

PM57. . . . as were different badges.

PM58. The corporate restyling was continued at the rear also. The tailgate was fitted with a different handle and also a different heated rear screen glass with horizontally arranged wires. The main tailgate section was the same for every GT6. Hence a Mk.3 heated window tailgate may be fitted to a Mk.1. Just change the handle over to complete. On final models, green tinted 'Sundym' glass was fitted.

PM59. Wheels were also revised.

PM60. ▼ The end of the GT6 line – Mk.3 engine bay.

PM61. ◄ All GT6s featured lots of wood veneer on the dashboard plus lots of different style knobs on the retrospectively named 'Mk.1'. This model also has the earlier fly-off hand brake – dropped for a conventional type on later Mk.1s, though some early Mk2 GT6s also had the fly-off handbrake.

PM62. Mk.2 and Mk.3 GT6s had similar instrument layouts and air ball ventilation systems. Later cars were given consecutively different steering wheels, and on Mk.3s different inner door handles plus cloth seats on later models.

APPENDIX 5

Chassis and Mechanical Identification

The following is an incomplete guide to chassis and mechanical identification. It covers the main types, though not all 'export' models, and will be a useful guide when purchasing a car or components.

Herald

	Commission No.	Engine	Gearbox	Differential	Ratio
948 Saloon	G	G	G	G	4.875:1
948 Twin-Carb Saloon	GY	Y	G	Y	4.55:1
948 Coupé/Conv.	Y	Y	G	Y	4.55:1
1200	GA	GA/GD	GA	GA	4.11:1
1200 Export	GB	GD	GA	GA/GE	4.11:1
Courier	GA	GA	GA	GA	4.11:1
12/50	GD	GD	GA	GA	4.11:1
13/60	GE	GE/GK	GA	GE	4.11:1

Vitesse

	Commission No.	Engine	Gearbox	Differential	Ratio
'6'	HB	HB	HB	HB	4.11:1
2 Litre Mk.1	HC	HC	HC	FD	3.89:1
2 Litre Mk.2	HC50001-	HC50001-	HC	HC50001-	3.89:1

Spitfire

	Commission No.	Engine	Gearbox	Differential	Ratio
'4'	FC	FC	FC	FC	4.11:1
'4' Mk.2	FC50001-	FC50001-	FC	FC	4.11:1
Mk. 3	FD	FD	FD	FC	4.11:1
Mk.IV	FH	FH	FH	FH	3.89:1
1500	FH75001-	FM	FR	FR	3.63:1
1500 post-October 1979	TFADW1AT –	Non-Overdrive			
	TFADW5AT	Overdrive			

GT6

Mk.1	KC	KC (KD5001-) (anti smog)	KC	KC	3.27:1
Mk.2	KC50001-	KC50001- (KD50001-) (GT6 + anti smog)	KC	KC50001- KD50001-	3.27:1 3.89:1
Mk.3	KE	KE	KE	KC KD (as GT6 Mk.2)	3.27:1 3.89:1

Mk.3 Export
Commission numbers KF- USA, KG- Sweden
Engine numbers KF UE (late)- USA, KG- Sweden

Chassis suffix letters
DL	Saloon
CP	Coupé
CV	Convertible
SC	Estate
V	Courier Van
RS	Sunshine roof
O	Overdrive
L	Left-hand steering
U	USA spec.
UC	California spec.

Engine suffix letters
E	Engine
L	Low compression
H	High compression

Paint prefix letters
A	Acrylic paint

Trim prefix letters
L	Leather
C	Cloth

APPENDIX 6

Production Figures

Herald

1959 – 64	948 Saloon and S	76,860
1959 – 61	948 Coupé	15,153
1960 – 61	948 Convertible	8,262
1961 – 70	1200 Saloon	201,142
1961 – 64	1200 Coupé	5,319
1961 – 67	1200 Convertible	43,295
1961 – 67	1200 Estate	39,819
1961 – 64	Courier Van	4,600
1962 – 67	12/50 Saloon	53,267
1967 – 71	13/60 Saloon	40,433
1967 – 71	13/60 Convertible	15,467
1967 – 71	13/60 Estate	11,172

Vitesse

1962 – 66	6 Saloon	22,814
1962 – 66	6 Convertible	8,447
1966 – 68	2L Mk1 Saloon	7,328
1966 – 68	2L Mk1 Convertible	3,502
1968 – 71	2L Mk2 Saloon	5,649
1968 – 71	2L Mk2 Convertible	3,472

Spitfire

1962 – 64	4	45,573
1964 – 67	4 Mk2	37,409
1967 – 70	Mk3	65,320
1970 – 74	MkIV	70,021
1974 – 80	1500	95,829

GT6

1966 – 68	Mk1	15,818
1968 – 70	Mk2	12,066
1970 – 73	Mk3	13,042

APPENDIX 7

Paint/trim Options

Paint/Trim options

Paint and Trim combinations are notoriously difficult to establish, as even factory records are sometimes economical with the truth! This guide is as close as anyone is likely to get and 'grey' areas (no pun intended!) are clearly indicated – where they are known about . . .

Before purchasing paint for your car, have your supplier check with a paint sample (or 'colour chip') against the original colour to ensure that you are purchasing the colour that you require.

Specified body colour/trim combinations September 1960

Herald 948 Saloon – monotone body colours standard, duo-tone available at extra cost.
Herald 948 Coupe – duo-tone only.
Herald 948 Convertible – Monotone only. Hoods black or Sebring White.
Trim material – Vynide, leather optional extra. On export models, Imperial Grey Cloth seat facings were available at no extra cost.

Monotone body colour schemes

Paint	Trim
Coffee	Coffee
Signal Red	Black or Phantom Grey
Sebring White	Black or Matador Red
Monaco Blue	Phantom Grey
Powder Blue	Phantom Grey or Black
Lichfield Green	Phantom Grey or Matador Red
Black	Black or Matador Red
Phantom Grey	Phantom Grey or Matador Red
Pale Yellow	Black

Earlier colour schemes also included:

Alpine Mauve	Phantom Grey or Alpine Mauve
Targo Purple	Targo Purple
Monaco Blue	Alpine Mauve

Duo-tone body colours schemes

Paint / **Trim**
Upper and lower body colour/centre colour

Paint	Trim
Phantom Grey/ Sebring White	Phantom Grey or Matador Red
Coffee/Sebring White	Coffee
Monaco Blue/ Sebring White	Phantom Grey
Lichfield Green/ Sebring White	Phantom Grey or Matador Red
Black/Sebring White	Black or Matador Red
Powder Blue/ Sebring White	Phantom Grey or Black
Signal Red/ Sebring White	Phantom Grey or Black
Pale Yellow/ Sebring White	Black

Earlier colour schemes also included

Paint	Trim
Alpine Mauve/ Sebring White	Alpine Mauve
Black/Alpine Mauve	Alpine Mauve
Targo Purple/ Sebring White	Targo Purple

Specified body colour/trim combinations December 1961

Herald 1200 Saloon – Monotone body colour standard, duo-tone available at extra cost.
Herald 1200 Coupe – as 1200 Saloon.
Herald 1200 Convertible – monotone body colour only. Hoods available in Black or Sebring White.
Herald 1200 Estate – monotone body colour only.
Herald 'S' Saloon (948) – Monotone body colour only.

Monotone body colour schemes

Paint	Trim
Sebring White	Matador Red or Black
Black	Matador Red
Lichfield Green	Phantom Grey or Matador Red
Powder Blue	Phantom Grey
Signal Red	Black
Phantom Grey	Phantom Grey or Matador Red
Pale Yellow	Black
Renoir Blue	Phantom Grey – (not available for the Herald 'S')
Coffee	Coffee – (Herald 'S' only)

Duo-tone body colour schemes

Paint	Trim
Upper and lower body colour/centre body colour	
Black/Sebring White	Black or Matador Red
Lichfield Green/ Sebring White	Phantom Grey or Matador Red
Powder Blue/ Sebring White	Phantom Grey or Black
Signal Red/ Sebring White	Black
Phantom Grey/ Sebring White	Phantom Grey or Matador Red
Pale Yellow/ Sebring White	Black
Renoir Blue/ Sebring White	Phantom Grey

Specified body colour/trim combinations September 1962

Herald 1200 Saloon and Coupe as above: standard mono-tone, optional duo-tone. (Save Black trim not listed with Powder Blue body)
Herald 1200 and Vitesse 6 Convertibles, standard mono-tone colours as per Herald 1200 Saloon.
Duo-tone body colours available on Vitesse Convertibles only. Hoods in black or white.
Herald 1200 Estate – mono-tone body colours only as listed above for standard Herald 1200 Saloon.
Herald 'S' Saloon – mono-tone body colours only as listed above. Coffee option dropped.
Vitesse 6 Saloon – standard mono-tone, optional duo-tone as per Herald 1200 Saloon.
Both Vitesse Saloons and Convertibles were also available in an additional duo-tone body scheme with white as the upper and lower body colour plus a centre black flash – trim colours Black or Matador Red.

Courier Van – monotone body colours only.

No optional leather trim

Paint	Trim
Renoir Blue	
Lichfield Green	
Phantom Grey	Phantom Grey
Spa White	

Spitfire 4 – monotone body colours

Hoods available in black or white.

Paint	Trim
White	Red, Black or Blue.
Black	Red, Black or Blue
Lichfield Green	Red
Powder Blue	Black or Blue
Signal Red	Red or Black
Phantom Grey	Red
Pale Yellow	Black

Herald 1200 Saloon and Coupé, Herald 12/50 Saloon – mono-tone body colours standard, duo tone available at extra cost.
Herald Convertible, Estate and Courier – mono-tone body colours only.
Vitesse Saloon and Convertible – mono-tone body colours standard, duo-tone available at extra cost. Convertible hoods available in black or white.
Spitfire 4 – mono-tone body colours only. Hoods available in black or white.

Herald/Vitesse mono-tone body colour schemes

Paint	Trim
Black	Matador Red
White	Matador Red
Wedgwood	Midnight Blue
Cactus	Matador Red
Olive	Cactus
Gunmetal	Midnight Blue
Conifer	Cactus
Jonquil	Black
Cherry	Cactus

Herald duo-tone colour schemes (where applicable)

Paint	Trim
Upper and lower body colour/centre body colour	
Black/White	Matador Red
Black/Cactus	Cactus
Olive/Cactus	Cactus
Gunmetal/Wedgwood	Midnight Blue
Conifer/Cactus	Cactus
Jonquil/White	Black
Cherry/White	Matador Red

Vitesse duo-tone colour schemes (where applicable)

Paint	Trim
White/Black	Matador Red
Wedgwood/Black	Midnight Blue
Black/Cactus	Matador Red
Cactus/Black	Matador Red
Olive/Cactus	Cactus
Gunmetal/White	Midnight Blue
Conifer/White	Cactus
Jonquil/White	Black
Cherry/Cactus	Cactus

Courier van mono-tone body colour schemes

Paint	Trim
White	
Wedgwood	Matador Red
Gunmetal	

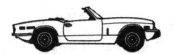

Spitfire 4

Paint	Trim
Black	Red
White	Red
Wedgwood	Midnight Blue
Conifer	Black
Jonquil	Black
Cherry	Black

Revisions October 1963

Added to range

Herald/Vitesse mono-tone body colour schemes

Paint	Trim
White	Matador Red or Black
Conifer	Matador Red or Cactus
Signal Red	Black

Herald/Vitesse duo-tone body colour schemes

Paint	Trim
Conifer/White	Matador Red or Cactus
Signal Red/White	Black

Spitfire 4

Paint	Trim
White	Red or Black

Revisions April 1965

Herald/Vitesse mono-tones

Added to range

Paint	Trim
Royal Blue	Black or Midnight Blue

Discontinued
Jonquil

Herald duo-tone body colours

Discontinued body colour options
Black/Cactus
Jonquil/White

Vitesse duo-tones

Added to range

Paint	Trim
White/Black	Matador Red or Black
Royal Blue/White	Black or Midnight Blue
Black/White	Matador Red
Cherry/White	Matador Red

Discontinued
Black/Cactus
Cherry/Cactus

Spitfire 4 Mk.2

Added options to previous Spitfire 4

Paint	Trim
Signal Red	Black
Royal Blue	Black or Midnight Blue

Discontinued
Jonquil
Cherry

Revisions October 1965

Herald/Vitesse mono-tones

Added to range

Paint	Trim
Dolphin Grey	Matador Red

Discontinued
Black

Herald duo-tones

Discontinued
Black/White

Vitesse duo-tones

Discontinued
White/Black
Wedgwood/Black
Black/White
Cactus/Black
Royal Blue/White

Spitfire Mk.2

Discontinued
Black

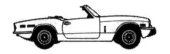

Specified body colour/trim combinations October 1966

Herald 1200 Saloon, Convertible and Estate, Herald 12/50 Saloon, Vitesse 2-Litre

All Monotone Colours
Convertible hoods available in black or white

Paint	Trim
Dolphin Grey	Matador Red or Midnight Blue
White	Matador Red, Black or Midnight Blue
Royal Blue	Black or Midnight Blue
Wedgwood	Black or Midnight Blue
Cactus	Matador Red
Olive	Cactus
Gunmetal	Midnight Blue
Conifer	Matador Red or Cactus
Signal Red	Black
Cherry	Black, Cactus or Matador Red

Spitfire 4 Mk.2, GT6 Mk.1

Paint	Trim
White	Black or Red
Wedgwood	Midnight Blue
Conifer	Black
Signal Red	Black
Royal Blue	Black or Midnight Blue

Specified body colour/trim combinations September 1969

Herald 13/60 Saloon, Convertible and Estate, Vitesse 2 litre Mk.2 Saloon and Convertible

Paint	Trim
White	Matador Red, Tan or Black
Royal Blue	Shadow Blue or Black
Wedgwood	Shadow Blue or Black
Sienna	Tan or Black
Laurel	Matador Red, Tan or Black
Damson	Tan or Black
Signal Red	Tan or Black
Valencia Blue	Tan or Black
Jasmine	Tan or Black
Slate Grey	Matador Red or Shadow Blue

Spitfire Mk.3, GT6 Mk.2

Paint	Trim
White	Matador Red, Tan or Black
Wedgwood	Shadow Blue or Black
Laurel	Matador Red or Black
Royal Blue	Shadow Blue or Black
Signal Red	Tan or Black
Valencia Blue	Tan or Black
Jasmine	Tan or Black
Damson	Tan or Black
Sienna	Tan or Black

Specified body colour trim combinations 1971

Herald 13/60 Saloon, Convertible and Estate, Vitesse 2-Litre Mk.2

Paint	Trim
White	Matador Red, Tan or Black
Wedgwood	Shadow Blue or Black
Sienna	Tan or Black
Laurel	Tan or Black
Damson	Tan or Black
Signal Red	Tan or Black
Valencia Blue	Tan or Black
Saffron	Tan or Black
Slate Grey	Matador Red or Shadow Blue

Spitfire and GT6 but probably only Spitfire Mk.IV and early GT6 Mk.3

Paint	Trim
White	Shadow Blue, Tan or Black
Wedgwood	Shadow Blue or Black
Laurel	Tan or Black
Sapphire Blue	Silver Grey or Shadow Blue
Signal Red	Tan or Black
Valencia Blue	Tan or Black
Saffron	Tan or Black
Damson	Silver Grey, Tan or Black
Sienna	Tan or Black

It has not been possible to be definitive about the later GT6, although it has been (frustratingly!) established that some are definitely different. Body colours listed for later GT6 Mk.3s included Pimento, Carmine and Magenta reds, Sienna Brown, Saffron and Mimosa Yellows, Laurel and Emerald greens, Wedgwood, Sapphire, Mallard and French blues, Grey and White. However, it *could* be that final GT6 colours were the same as listed below for 1974 Spitfire 1500s. Late GT6 Mk.3 interiors were Tan, Chocolate, Black.

Spitfire 1500

Hoods available in black only

Paint	Trim (Vinyl)
Carmine	Black or Beige
White	Black or Beige
Pimento	Black
Mimosa	Black or Beige
Maple	Black or Beige
Java	Black or Beige
British Racing Green	Black or Beige
French Blue	Black
Delft	Black or Beige
Topaz	Black or Beige

There may well be changes for later 1500s that are not indicated here. For instance, it is possible that Inca Yellow comes in on late cars.

APPENDIX 8

Clubs and Specialists

The following addresses and telephone numbers were believed to be correct at the time of going to press. However, as these are subject to change, particularly telephone area codes, no guarantee can be given for their continued accuracy.

Car clubs

With the rise of the classic car movement over the last ten years, ownership of any of the wide range of cars based on the Herald chassis has never been as easy or as enjoyable. The leader amongst Clubs devoted to these often (in the past) underrated cars is undoubtedly the Triumph Sports Six Club.

Triumph Sports Six Club

Established in 1977 by Paul Swanson, the Club was formed with the aim of promoting and preserving all cars based on the Herald chassis including Heralds, Vitesses, Spitfires, GT6s and the Bond Equipe. Though so named, the TSSC is not an exclusive sports car owners club (though there is a very active competitions section which competes in sprints, circuit racing and hillclimbs) and many members are equally enthusiastic about GT6s as they are about the original 948 Coupé, or even the Herald derivitive van, the Courier.

The Club's name was derived from that given to the US export Vitesse which was aptly called the 'Sports Six'. The number six is also relevant as the TSSC caters for six distinct vehicle types, including the five given above with the sixth being 'Specials'. These include any cars based on the Herald chassis, or components including models such as Moss, Burlington, Vincent, etc. The Club also has a Amphicar register for the German built amphibious convertible which shares the Herald 1200's engine – mounted in the rear in this rather special car.

Having celebrated its tenth birthday in 1987, the TSSC has grown to become the largest Triumph Car Club in the world with a membership of over 10,000 from over 30 countries. Although large, the Club has retained a small club atmosphere by the method of actively promoting over 80 local areas covering the whole country who organise their own social events and meetings with monthly 'Noggin and Natters' and other more widely based get-togethers many of which have risen to National status offering a broad range of social events throughout the year. The central organising body also organises an annual International Concours Weekend which attracts thousands of enthusiastic members from right across the country and abroad.

The Club's services include a high quality 68 page monthly magazine, *The Courier*, issued to all members which includes topics of general interest and those with a high technical content, special offers for tools and accessories, RAC scheme details and classified sections for buying and selling spares and cars. Register secretaries for each model type are on hand to sort out any problem members may have. Also included is a separate 16 page pull out magazine totally devoted to local area news. In addition, a third magazine, *The Turning Circle*, is issued bi-annually. Each issue reviews a different model, covering owners' views and experiences plus restorations and road tests, etc. The Triumph Sports Six Club was also one of the first Clubs to pioneer and run a 'Self Help' breakdown service, now included in a TSSC members' handbook and to establish a members' comprehensive, exclusive and fully agreed value insurance scheme.

Triumph Sports Six Club Ltd
Sunderland Court, Main Street, Lubenham,
Market Harborough,
Leicestershire LE16 9TF
Tel: 01858 434424
www.tssc.org.uk
Email: info@tssc.org.uk

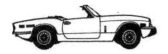

Club Triumph

'The friendly Motor Club for Standard and Triumph Owners and Enthusiasts'. Caters for all models. Recognised by the Royal Automobile Club. Membership gives the opportunity to meet and exhange views with other members who have similar interests. Various discount schemes are periodically available and a calendar of both social and competitive events is organised according to the general interest of the members. Wherever possible help and/or advice is available concerning more technical matters. In addition you will receive a metal car badge, membership card, club rules, and issues of *Torque Triumph* magazine to keep you informed of club activities. Find them at *www.club.triumph.org.uk* Registered Office: Suite A, 10th Floor, Maple House, High Street, Potters Bar, Herts, EN6 5BS. NB Club Triumph is run entirely by its members for its members and does not have paid employees.

Other clubs

There are many area centres in both the UK, USA and other countries. Their contact addresses are varied and prone to change.

In the UK there is a Government list semi-hidden: at the time of writing, search for "*gov.uk list-of-vehicle-owners-clubs.pdf*".

In the USA, a good starting point may be "*www.oldcarsweekly.com/club-directory*".

And no prizes for guessing where "*aussiemotoring.com/vintage-and-veteran/vintage-veteran-car-clubs*" will take you to...

Specialists

Black & Decker produce the full range of electrical power tools. Of most interest to the restorer are: rechargeable (cordless) drills, power screwdrivers (useful for nuts and bolts, too), jigsaw, mini-grinder, random orbit sander, for professional body/paint preparation standards, paint polishing mop-cum-large sander/grinder.

Clarke International, Hemnall Street, Epping, Essex, CM16 4LG. Tel: 01992 565 300. Manufacturers of an impressive range of quality workshop equipment for the amateur and professional: MIG welders, spot and arc welders (plus brazing attachments), spray guns and compressors in all shapes and sizes. Highly recommended.

Classic Car Restorations carried out most of the work featured in this book. The company is no longer in existence.

Inverter Fusion Ltd. Heathpark Way, Heathpark Industrial Estate, Honiton, Devon, EX14 1BB, UK. Tel: +44 (0) 1404 549791 *www,inverterfusion.co.uk* Full range of modern, high-tech welding and plasma cutting equipment.

There are several car insurers specialising in classic cars. Here's one of the most well-established: **Peter James Insurance,** 772 Hagley Road West, Oldbury, West Midlands, B68 0PJ. Tel: 0121 506 6040 www.peterjamesinsurance.co.uk

This is a large car insurance company that also provides essential Agreed Value for classics, enabling you to protect the true value of your car in the event of an accident.

Kenlowe Ltd, Burchetts Green, Maidenhead SL6 6QU. Tel: 01628 823 303. *www.kenlowe.com* Manufacturers of electric cooling fans for all the cars featured here.

Lumenition Ltd. Distributed by **Autocar Electrical Equipment Co. Ltd**, 49/51 Tiverton Street, London SE1 6NZ. Tel: 0171 403 4334. *www.http://autocar-electrical.co.uk* Manufacturers of optically triggered electronic ignition systems with a very friendly and helpful back-up department.

Newton Commercial, Eastlands Industrial Estate, Leiston, Suffolk, IP16 4LL. Tel: 01728 832 880. *www.newtoncomm.co.uk* Manufacturers of the famous and comprehensive range of original-equipment style interior trim for almost all of the vehicles covered in this manual.

Sykes-Pickavant Ltd

Here's what I wrote back in the 1980s:

Sykes-Pickavant's range of hand tools is superb! The angle drive ratchet extensions give a semi-universal joint effect in tight corners, while the surface drive sockets avoid rounding nuts because effort is applied to the flats, not of the points of the nut or bolt. Beautifully finished, made in the UK, they are tools to last a lifetime and to be proud of.

...and today:
Sykes-Pickavant has been manufacturing and distributing tools since 1921. The Sykes-Pickavant brand is well known worldwide as a guarantee of quality products, service and real value for money.

Until recently, the company was owned by Facom Tools and the Stanley Corporation. Now, once again it is an independently owned company, fully responsible for its own development.

Sykes-Pickavant is a UK market leader in the supply of Specialist Automotive Tools and Hand Held Diagnostic Equipment.

Unit 4 Cannel Road
Zone 3 - Burntwood Business Park
Burntwood
Staffordshire
WS7 3FU
UK
Tel: (0)1543 679900
www.sykes-pickavant.com

APPENDIX 9

British and American Technical Terms

As this book has been written in England, it uses the appropriate English component names, phrases, and spelling. Some of these differ from those used in America. Normally, these cause no difficulty, but to make sure, a glossary is printed below. In ordering spare parts remember the parts list may use some of these words:

English	American	English	American
Accelerator	Gas pedal	Leading shoe (of brake)	Primary shoe
Aerial	Antenna	Locks	Latches
Anti-roll bar	Stabiliser or sway bar	Methylated spirit	Denatured alcohol
Big-end bearing	Rod bearing	Motorway	Freeway, turnpike etc
Bonnet (engine cover)	Hood	Number plate	License plate
Boot (luggage compartment)	Trunk	Paraffin	Kerosene
Bulkhead	Firewall	Petrol	Gasoline (gas)
Bush	Bushing	Petrol tank	Gas tank
Cam follower or tappet	Valve lifter or tappet	'Pinking'	'Pinging'
Carburettor	Carburetor	Prise (force apart)	Pry
Catch	Latch	Propeller shaft	Driveshaft
Choke/venturi	Barrel	Quarterlight	Quarter window
Circlip	Snap-ring	Retread	Recap
Clearance	Lash	Reverse	Back-up
Crownwheel	Ring gear (of differential)	Rocker cover	Valve cover
Damper	Shock absorber, shock	Saloon	Sedan
Disc (brake)	Rotor/disk	Seized	Frozen
Distance piece	Spacer	Sidelight	Parking light
Drop arm	Pitman arm	Silencer	Muffler
Drop head coupe	Convertible	Sill panel (beneath doors)	Rocker panel
Dynamo	Generator (DC)	Small end, little end	Piston pin or wrist pin
Earth (electrical)	Ground	Spanner	Wrench
Engineer's blue	Prussian blue	Split cotter (for valve spring cap)	Lock (for valve spring retainer)
Estate car	Station wagon	Split pin	Cotter pin
Exhaust manifold	Header	Steering arm	Spindle arm
Fault finding/diagnosis	Troubleshooting	Sump	Oil pan
Float chamber	Float bowl	Swarf	Metal chips or debris
Free-play	Lash	Tab washer	Tang or lock
Freewheel	Coast	Tappet	Valve lifter
Gearbox	Transmission	Thrust bearing	Throw-out bearing
Gearchange	Shift	Top gear	High
Grub screw	Setscrew, Allen screw	Trackrod (of steering)	Tie-rod (or connecting rod)
Gudgeon pin	Piston pin or wrist pin	Trailing shoe (of brake)	Secondary shoe
Halfshaft	Axleshaft	Transmission	Whole drive line
Handbrake	Parking brake	Tyre	Tire
Hood	Soft top	Van	Panel wagon/van
Hot spot	Heat riser	Vice	Vise
Indicator	Turn signal	Wheel nut	Lug nut
Interior light	Dome lamp	Windscreen	Windshield
Layshaft (of gearbox)	Countershaft	Wing/mudguard	Fender

Miscellaneous points

An oil seal is fitted to components lubricated by grease!

A 'damper' is a shock absorber, it damps out bouncing and absorbs shock of bump impact. Both names are correct, and both are used haphazardly.

Note that British drum brakes are different from the Bendix type that is common in America, so different descriptive names result. The shoe end furthest from the hydraulic wheel cylinder is on a pivot, interconnection between the shoes as on Bendix brakes is most uncommon. Therefore the phrase 'Primary' or 'Secondary' shoe does not apply. A shoe is said to be 'Leading' or 'Trailing'. A 'Leading' shoe is one on which a point on the drum, as it rotates forward, reaches the shoe at the end worked by the hydraulic cylinder before the anchor end. The opposite is a 'Trailing' shoe and this one has no self-servo from the wrapping effect of the rotating drum.

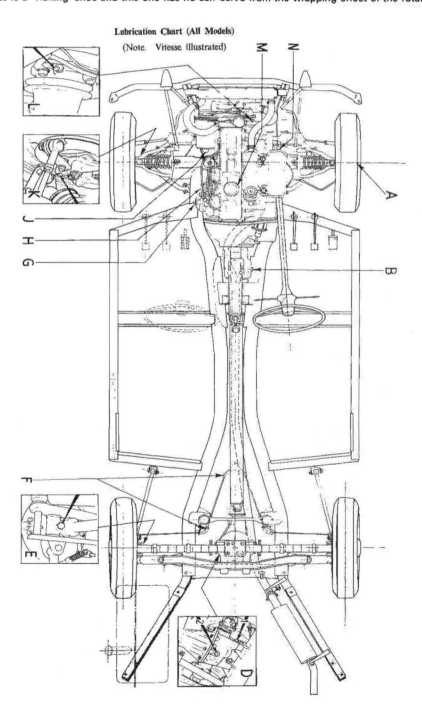

Lubrication Chart (All Models)

(Note. Vitesse illustrated)

This section is a short extract from Lindsay Porter's *"Classic Car Bodywork Manual"* available from Amazon and all good bookshops and classic car component outlets.

MIG WELDING

▲ W1. *Small cylinders like these are convenient, but expensive if there's a lot to do. Full cylinders are far more economical. 'No gas' MIG welders allow you to keep welding when you run out, although weld quality drops away considerably with a large amount of spatter.*

▲ W2. *MIG is a form of arc welding, except that instead of using an electrode in the form of a stick which has to be changed once it is worn out, the machine contains an almost endless reel of wire which passes down the supply pipe shown here and out of the end of the handset. So, there is no stopping to change rods and no continuous re-adjustment of the distance between torch and workpiece.*

▲ W3. *Inside the machine is the spindle (on left) on to which the reel of wire has to be fitted, and the feed mechanism which pushes the wire out and along the supply pipe.*

▲ W4. *The supply pipe also has to provide an electric current and this is simply passed into the welding wire at the handset end of the supply pipe. It is this current which melts the weld pool and the wire at the business end.*

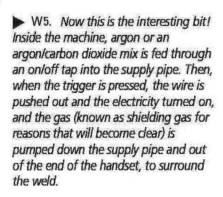

▶ W5. *Now this is the interesting bit! Inside the machine, argon or an argon/carbon dioxide mix is fed through an on/off tap into the supply pipe. Then, when the trigger is pressed, the wire is pushed out and the electricity turned on, and the gas (known as shielding gas for reasons that will become clear) is pumped down the supply pipe and out of the end of the handset, to surround the weld.*

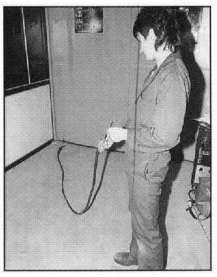

▲ W6. *Aluminium alloy can also be welded with MIG. It just takes argon gas in preference to argon/CO₂, aluminium-compatible welding wire, and a new supply pipe liner, coated with teflon. This prevents the 'sticky' aluminium wire from binding in the supply pipe.*

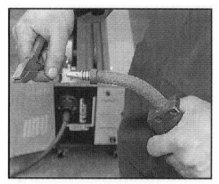

▲ W7. Once the machine has been set up, the wire is fed through the pipe by holding the trigger 'on' until it emerges, then cutting it off to length ...

▲ W10. It is possible to fit and use a CO_2 bottle of the sort that your local publican uses for making all those things fizzy in the cellar. You have to use a special adaptor and in cool weather the whole thing is liable to freeze up as the high-pressure CO_2 is released. (Industrial users of CO_2 use special and expensive heaters to prevent this from happening.) Argon-mix also gives a better result with a smoother weld, better penetration over a wider spread and less spatter, so it is certainly preferable to CO_2.

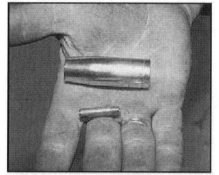

▲ W8. ... before screwing and clipping into place the correct tip for the wire to pass through and the shroud which goes around it and directs the gas.

THE FIRST WELD

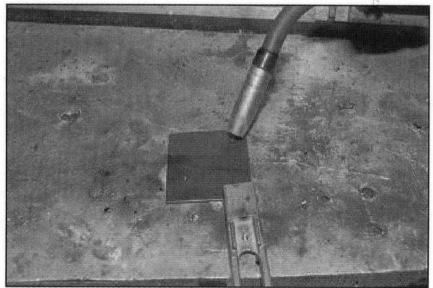

▲ W9. BOC Ltd have become aware of the great demand for these small MIG welders and have brought out a range of small Argon-mix and argon bottles, which are absolutely ideal for the DIY user and small garage. They are changeable at any of the many BOC centres.

▲ W11. Simply set the machine to the settings indicated in the handbook for the thickness of plate being welded and clamp the earth lead into place. Then hold the nozzle at 70° or so, with the nozzle opening pointing in the direction that the weld is to take. The end of the nozzle should be held just a little way from the surface of the workpiece.

▶ *W12. When you're ready, pull the mask in front of your face, press the trigger and move the handset at about the speed of drawing a very slow line with a felt-tipped pen. Note how clean the weld is when the machine is set up correctly and there is no paint or rust to inhibit the weld. The gas, blown around the weld, is an inert gas which does not react in any way with the weld, but keeps it clear of the (oxidising) gases in the air until after the weld has 'frozen'. It also helps to cool the weld and so helps to cut down on distortion.*

▶ *W13.* **Important**: *MIG welding is really very bright, so follow the safety instructions for arc welding. The UV light given off can be very damaging to anyone (even any pet) watching with unshielded eyes. You can tell whether a MIG weld is going well just by the sound. It should give a crisp crackling sound. If the wire speed setting on the machine is too high, the weld will start off burning deep into the metal and then quickly burn through, or the wire may 'bounce' on the workpiece. On the other hand, if the wire speed is too low, the weld will progress with a spluttering sound and may burn back into the wire feed tip.*

▶ *W14. Next try a butt-weld, which is of course much closer to 'real' welding. Select a couple of pieces of scrap of the thickness you intend using, place them close together and hold the handset so that the wire is touching the gap. There is no risk of causing a weld to flash across accidentally because, unlike standard arc welding, no circuit takes place until the trigger is pressed. Hold the mask in front of the face and 'tack' the two pieces together. Run a seam down the joint, zig-zagging very slightly, so that the weld pool feeds equally into both pieces. There is far less risk of burning through with MIG than with any of the other main methods.*

▲ W15.Before carrying out a fillet weld of this type, place sufficient tack welds to hold the material in place while any necessary adjustment is carried out.

▲ W16.Bisect the angle between both pieces with the welding nozzle and be prepared to work the nozzle very slightly from side to side, to ensure that there is sufficient penetration into both pieces.

▲ W17. Here, the more common lap-joint is being tried. Again tack welds have been positioned first.

▲ W18. Note how the first seam weld was stopped and then restarted with no risk of inclusions as with other weld types. This time, it is important to gain sufficient penetration into the lower piece, so it may be necessary to favour it just slightly at the expense of the edge of the top piece.

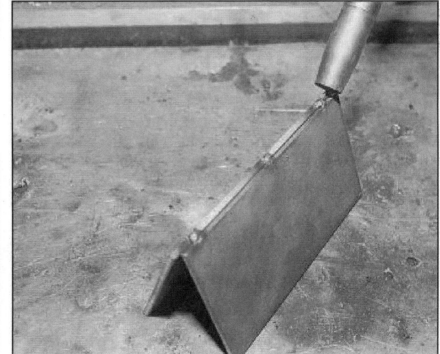

▲ W19. When welding an external angle, try tacking the two pieces together to form a 'vee'. This is much easier to weld and gives a stronger joint than having one piece overlap the other.

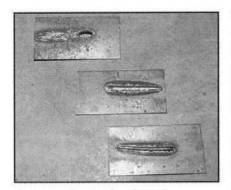

▲ W20. The top plate here shows a weld where the amperage and/or wire speed settings have been too high; the lower plate shows a thin, stringy weld where either the settings were too low or the handset passed too quickly over the plate; while the centre plate shows a weld that is just about right!

Experienced oxy-acetylene welders should beware that the torch should not be 'swirled' as would be an oxy-acetylene torch. You can weld in either direction but right-to-left for a right-handed person gives better visibility whilst the weld is taking place and improves gas flow over the weld.

MIG WELDING IN AWKWARD PLACES

Whenever possible, welds should be carried out flat but sometimes, of course, this is just not possible. Tipping the car over just to run a weld up a split wing is not exactly practical! Vertical welds are best carried out 'downhill', starting from the top, with the smaller sized machines being considered here; butt welds require a straight-on approach while fillets are best tackled with slight zig-zagging. Forehand welding (ie in the direction in which the nozzle opening is pointing) is recommended for all vertical or horizontal welds, so that the best gas shielding is obtained.

MIG welding out of doors is not recommended unless unavoidable because the wind tends to blow the shielding gas off the weld leaving a poor, untidy weld. Try building a localised wind break around the job and turn the gas flow-rate up higher.

▲ W21. Holes, like these superfluous dashboard holes, can be filled up by welding one side of the hole (say, at the 3 o'clock position) then the other (9 o'clock) then the remaining (12 o'clock and 6 o'clock) positions can be welded, and so on until the hole is filled. The tendency will be for the welder to burn through. Get over this by just pulsing the welder for a couple of seconds at a time.

▲ W22. These short-sharp welds can then be cleaned up to a perfect finish with the finisher, proving that no weakening inclusions are found in a MIG weld.

MIG SPOT-WELDING

▲ W23. Here, a repair patch is being MIG welded to the corner of a car tailgate. It is held in place first with a self-tapping screw to ensure a good fit with minimal distortion.

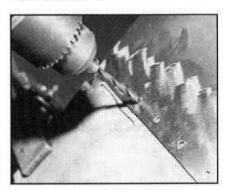

▲ W24. Small holes are drilled through the top plate only.

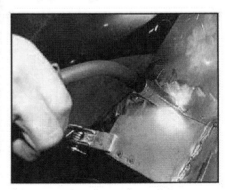

▲ W25. Then, the MIG nozzle is changed for a spot-welding nozzle, which simply holds the wire guide a set distance away from the workpiece. The nozzle is pressed down on to the job rather than held away as in seam welding.

▲ W26. The right-hand edge was seam welded, but the neat button-spot welds can be seen along the top. There is no point in allowing too much build up. Always practise on scrap metal first and try to lever the finished weld apart with a screwdriver. This proves that settings and timing are correct. All SIP machines larger than the 120N have a timer built in so that pulsed welds and spot welds can be programmed automatically.

▲ W27. After welding, clean the 'spots' off flush with a minigrinder.

NB Always disconnect the vehicle alternator before MIG welding because the current will damage it.

SAFETY
In general, follow the safety rules for arc welding (see relevant section and 'Safety' section at the beginning of the book) and remember that newly MIG-welded panels are still hot enough to burn when touched. Care should be taken when flammable materials are near the weld and when a fuel tank is nearby, even though heat spread is less from MIG than any other form of welding except spot welding proper.

SPOT-WELDING

▲ W28. With a spot-welder, two pieces of steel are fuse-welded at the point where the two electrodes on the machine are squeezed together using the handle shown. At the point where they come together, an electric current is passed between them, melting the steel at that point and making the weld.

▲ W29. All modern cars are put together with thousands of spot-welds; factories are dominated by the awe-inspiring efficiency of spot-welding robots dancing and twirling rapidly from one set of welds to another. A spot-welder enables you to carry out quick, clean, original-type welds.

▲ W30. A spot-welder gives the cleanest welds of any system and is probably the easiest to use, but it still has to be set up and used correctly. First, these out-of-alignment electrodes have to be correctly lined up and the electrode tips cut back to the correct profile with the spot-welder.

▲ W31. The arms can be adjusted by slackening them off with an allen key or they can be changed for various shapes and sizes of arm, designed to reach round many of the obstructions found in car bodywork.

▶ W32. The amount of pressure has to be adjusted according to the maker's instructions and on models equipped with a timer, the correct length of weld can be pre-set for the material being used.

▶ W33. Try out the settings on scrap metal before starting to work. Metal **must** be clean and free of rust, paint or any other impurities and it must also be clamped close, without relying on the spot-welder arms to pull the pieces together. The weld on the left looks perfect, but the one on the right looks as though the timer was given too high a setting or, with a 'manual' spot-welder, the lever was held down for too long. Always check weld strength on the practice piece by trying to prise it open with a screwdriver. Weak welds are, quite obviously, a great danger.

◀ W34. The spot-welder in use. In an ideal situation there will be little or no sparking. If there is too much going on, suspect the weld strength. No special protective clothing or eye shields are needed when spot-welding but take all the usual precautions when working with electrical equipment.

SPOT-WELDING – NOTES

• If you are spot-welding thick metal, line the electrodes up with the metal held between the tips.
• If too much pressure is set, the spot weld will be a deep dimple; if too little, the weld will arc and burn.
• If the tips glow red hot, the welder has been left on for too long, or the tips may need cutting back to the correct profile.
• If you burn right through, the reason will be: metal rusty or contaminated; or, too little pressure set on the arms; or, welder left on too long coupled with too much pressure.

Printed in Great Britain
by Amazon